Redefining
FINANCIAL
LITERACY

UNLOCKING THE HIDDEN FORCES
OF YOUR FINANCIAL FUTURE

CINDY COUYOUMJIAN, CFP®

with R.F. GEORGY

GREENLEAF
BOOK GROUP PRESS

Published by Greenleaf Book Group Press
Austin, Texas
www.gbgpress.com

Distributed by Greenleaf Book Group

For ordering information or special discounts for bulk purchases, please contact Greenleaf Book Group at PO Box 91869, Austin, TX 78709, 512.891.6100.

Design and composition by Greenleaf Book Group and Brian Phillips
Cover design by Greenleaf Book Group, Brian Phillips, and Vince Giuseffi
Cover image copyright Chones. Used under license from Shutterstock.com

Publisher's Cataloging-in-Publication data is available.

Print ISBN: 978-1-62634-740-3

eBook ISBN: 978-1-62634-741-0

Part of the Tree Neutral* program, which offsets the number of trees consumed in the production and printing of this book by taking proactive steps, such as planting trees in direct proportion to the number of trees used: www.treeneutral.com

TreeNeutral

Printed in the United States of America on acid-free paper

21 22 23 24 25 26 27   10 9 8 7 6 5 4 3 2 1

First Edition

For my parents, Clara and John Koczkodan

Thank you for instilling in me the virtues of hard work, integrity, and an overarching spiritual impulse toward others.

Thank you for teaching me the timeless lesson that putting the needs of others before my own is the way to live a good life.

CONTENTS

ACKNOWLEDGMENTS

I would like to acknowledge my Cinergy Financial family for their tireless efforts and dedication to this book. The following people have been with me for the past 15 years and I simply could not have completed this book without their help and support. I want to thank Connie Hernandez, Danny Martinez, Prisma Oseguera, and Thess Williams. I would also like to thank Michelle Lopez, who has been with the Cinergy family for nine years, for her unwavering commitment and dedication to me. I also want to thank Joanne Cleaver for helping me through the early draft of this book.

I must give a special thank-you to Leticia Hewko, who has been my business partner, friend, confidant, and support for the past seven years. She worked countless hours holding up my practice so that I could write this book. I am forever grateful for her friendship, business relationship, and the sisterhood we shared during this process. I have five sisters and I count Leticia as my sixth.

I would also like to offer a special thank-you to my high school coach and mentor, Jan Sanders. Coach Sanders epitomized the Aristotelian notion of sustained excellence. She inspired generations of young women to dream the impossible and achieve the improbable. She shaped and directed my own dreams both within and beyond sports. She instilled within me the kind of passion and competitive spirit that transcended both space and time. Her far-reaching influence is imprinted upon my consciousness and echoes through this book.

Finally, I want to thank my husband, Harry, and my two beautiful children, Kobe and Claire, for putting up with me during the writing of this book. I spent endless days and sleepless nights to get this book done, and they have been my rock. They kept me grounded, focused, and centered. Without their love and support, this book would not have seen the light of day.

PREFACE

"Knowing is not enough; we must apply.
Willing is not enough; we must do."

–J.W. VON GOETHE

———

I have spent most of my adult life in the financial sector. I spent eight grueling years studying and preparing for several licenses administered by the Financial Industry Regulatory Authority (FINRA). I earned the prestigious certified financial planner (CFP) designation in 1992. To put this in perspective, women make up only 23% of all certified financial planners. The CFP exam is a rigorous day-long exam that only 60% will pass to become CFPs.[1] I'm not just listing these achievements to brag; it's to show that I've done my homework. I know how investment works, and I know the standard wisdom taught in classes and seminars and practiced in financial planning firms across the country.

However, after spending years applying my knowledge to the real world, I began to see that the standard wisdom doesn't always necessarily work. When the dot-com bubble burst, it led to the stock market crash of 2002. By 2003 many of my clients had lost a significant amount of money due to the crash. My investment strategy at the time was the 60/40 portfolio—60% invested in stocks for a high return potential at high risk, and 40% in bonds for a low return potential at lower risk. Although my clients understood that market crashes occur, I was emotionally devastated. The stock market crash was the result of forces beyond my control, but I internalized the losses as if they were my fault. I felt responsible and became despondent. Setbacks like this, however, define us. Setbacks are punctuated moments that often help us take great leaps forward.

I started to question everything I had learned. I questioned the financial industry and my place in it. I experienced doubt and uncertainty. Doubt is a crippling feeling that freezes you into inaction. Once doubt finds its way into your soul, you become burdened by incessantly questioning everything, including your identity. I was so distraught that I was ready to leave the financial industry.

That's when I went to see my pastor for guidance. I told him what had happened and how I was feeling. The wisdom he imparted was invaluable. First, he asked me a few simple questions. He asked whether I was a truthful person. I immediately answered that yes, of course I was. He then proceeded to ask me other questions in rapid-fire succession. Did I have integrity? Did I care about my clients? Did I have passion for what I did? I answered yes to all of his questions.

He then looked me in the eye and told me that I had a moral obligation not to leave my clients. In fact, he told me, I have a moral obligation not to leave my *future* clients because they will need guidance. His final words to me were powerful in their capacity to jolt me out of my all-consuming doubt. He told me to move forward by embracing the divine spark of ethical engagement in order to help others. He told me to think about all the women that need my help. He was correct, of course, particularly about the women who will need my guidance.

For centuries, I believe that women have been ignored, alienated, sidelined, and marginalized. We have existed on the margins of society and as footnotes in the pages of history. Despite the fact that women have made significant gains, there is a long way to go if we are to bridge the economic gender gap. According to a report issued by the Pew Research Center, 57% of Americans think the United States has not gone far enough when granting women equal rights; 77% said that sexual harassment is a major obstacle to women's equality; 67% pointed to women not having the same legal rights as men; 66% mentioned different societal expectations between men and women as the cause; and 64% said not enough women are in positions of power.[2] I wrote this book to address the glaring problem of what I believe to be poor financial literacy for both men and women. Women, in particular, deserve some attention here, as they often perform worse than men in terms of financial awareness, in my experience.

Although my pastor's counsel gave me plenty to think about, it was the fact he mentioned women that forced me to confront my personal struggles as a woman trying to make it in the financial world, which has been dominated by men. I had to fight and crawl my way up the corporate ladder. I had to constantly knock on a glass ceiling that seemed to remind me, in unmistakable language, that I don't belong. I stood on the shoulders of those who came before me in order to continue to fight for change.

The theme of this book is redefining financial literacy, but within that sphere of financial knowledge, there is a need for women to embrace their role as powerful agents of change. Consider that women, as recently as the 1970s, predominantly worked as secretaries on Wall Street. Most of these women "had to wear hats and gloves. In the bathrooms, they had light bulbs with the partner's [boss] name. The partner would ring you up. If you were in the bathroom, you had to run out immediately."[3] One might think we've moved a long way since the 1970s, but in many ways, we haven't.

Let me go back to my pastor. His words both comforted and reenergized my spirit. I wanted to continue helping my clients, but I didn't want to continue with my current investment strategy; it just wasn't working. Over the next several years I immersed myself in a rigorous study of economics, history, politics, and investment strategies. I suspected there was something wrong with the 60/40 model. I looked for books or articles, but I couldn't find anything. I went to conferences hoping someone would highlight what I felt were problems with the 60/40 strategy. Unfortunately, none of the speakers seemed to question the potential risks of investing 60% of your money in stocks and 40% in bonds. Not to be deterred, I pushed on. I made it my mission to find a better way to help my clients invest their hard-earned money. I devoted years to learning everything I could about the modern portfolio theory, which had given rise to the 60/40 investment strategy.

In one of those moments of reflection, I experienced a powerful epiphany. The problem I see with the 60/40 investment strategy is twofold. First, having a 60% exposure to stocks is potentially risky, particularly when bonds fail to offer sufficient returns to offset the losses from stocks. The other problem is correlation—how two things move together, like risk and reward. The old wisdom was that risk and reward correlated in a predictable way: As risk increases, so does potential reward. However, stocks and bonds aren't independent of one another. They both fluctuate through time, and they affect each other; they also tend to correlate. The movement of stocks will often affect the hedging properties of bonds (their lower risk for a reasonable reward opportunity). Historically, "when stocks crash, money moves into the bond market and other safe haven assets to protect capital."[4] But in recent years, some stocks and bonds have moved in the same direction. That is, as stocks fell, the bond market fell right along with it, taking with it one obvious safe haven for investments that are pulled out of the stock market. This defeats the purpose of the 60/40 strategy.

To learn a new type of investment strategy, I had to distance myself from my once-comfortable, tried-and-true allocation strategy. This mentality had been ingrained in me over 17 years and the endless hours I needed to achieve those coveted securities licenses and certification to become a financial planner.

These days, a world of investment opportunities has become available to individual investors. Some of these asset classes were historically restricted to major institutional endowments like universities. But now, with the help of progressive independent advisors like myself, suitable individual retail investors can harness some of the power and potential for greater stability of the multi-asset investment strategies at the heart of the endowment model. This is a complex strategy that requires a professional and progressive advisor at the wheel. But you must develop your own knowledge as well in order to ask the right questions to direct your investment future.

Many of these asset classes were not available to me back in 2003 when I first started exploring a fundamentally different approach for my clients. I wish I could tell you that some brilliant investor guru handed me a manual on the dynamic strategies of the endowment model, but no such guru existed. Instead, I have spent the past 16 years developing a unique path for the retail investor, which I call the REALM model. Although it shares some features with David Swensen's Yale model of endowment fund management, I developed the REALM model independently, through rigorous education, hard work, trial and error, sweat and tears, and unrelenting determination. I learned a great deal from other experienced advisors as well—specifically, the models used by financial managers. I determined which professionally managed funds I felt are worth the fees, based on the respective and unique strategies used. Finally, I was profoundly influenced to write this book after reading Mebane T. Faber and Eric W. Richardson's *The Ivy Portfolio*.[5]

Along the way, I also realized there was a struggle going on in America: Retail investors needed more knowledge and education to appreciate and understand that investing could be forward thinking and innovative and that certain strategies beyond stocks and bonds could be used to potentially manage risk in a market that could easily shatter a portfolio. By the time you finish reading this book, you will have sufficient knowledge about the REALM model to discuss the possibility of adapting it with your trusted advisor.

Independent advisors are well positioned to adopt the endowment model because they can have the freedom to pick the right assets for each client's strategy. Some of the lesser-known types of asset classes require individual investors to meet suitability standards as well as have enough liquidity to sustain a longer holding period. Although many advisors are reluctant to implement new investment strategies, it is important that you have this conversation with your advisor about different investment options.

What I am saying is that we all have to do our homework. Financial literacy—understanding not only the wisdom of the day but also how the system works—is needed for both advisors and investors, so that we, the advisors, can develop and deliver cutting-edge strategies for our clients, and you, as the investor, can help safeguard your own future. Much of the information in this book, which is well researched, cannot help you unless you change your mindset and biases that have accumulated over a lifetime.

The aim of this book is to redefine financial literacy in such a way as to change your mindset about investing. Knowledge alone is not enough to change our behavior. Consider that we live in an age with a near-infinite supply of information, and yet, for many of us, I believe that our financial literacy is woefully inadequate. Financial information is available to us, but unless we transform that information into knowledge, and knowledge into action, then the information simply becomes background noise. Knowledge needs to be engaged, grappled with, and ultimately applied. It is the application of knowledge that should be of interest to all of us. You see, knowledge alone is hollow and empty. Knowledge needs to be applied and actionable. The knowledge you will gain from this book is designed to both challenge and change your mindset about your financial future, which can lead to a change in actionable habits and behavior. The process of taking a piece of information and making decisions is more complex than you might realize. According to Nobel Prize–winning economist Daniel Kahneman, who is considered one of the founders of behavioral finance, our brain processes the world in two ways.

One way we process information, or what Kahneman calls system 1, is "fast thinking," which is associated with snap decisions or subconscious thoughts. The second way our brain processes information is "slow thinking," or system 2, which involves deeper, conscious analysis. System 2 is associated with agency, choice, and concentration.[6] Let's suppose you suddenly have $1,000 and must decide what to do with it. Immediately, system 1 wants to spend the money on a vacation or to go shopping. The more thoughtful system 2 wants to save the money for retirement. Both systems exist in a state of tension; one is irrational and seeks immediate gratification; the other is more rational and involves a deeper level of thinking. This is why financial literacy is not enough. As noted, knowledge must be both enlightening and actionable. To reconcile the tension between the rational and irrational part of our brain, we need to redefine financial literacy by addressing the problem of how. You may have some knowledge about the financial world, but how do you act on this knowledge?

The first step you need to take in order to change your mindset is to confront your beliefs about money. Our beliefs are shaped by childhood experiences, the people we interact with, social media, what we read, and other forces. The philosopher William Kingdon Clifford, in his essay "The Ethics of Belief," argued, "It is wrong always, everywhere, and for anyone to believe anything on insufficient evidence."[7] Whether it is right or wrong is beside the point; we all have beliefs that are based on insufficient evidence. This is why it is difficult to change our mindset with facts and research. Unless we confront our beliefs, our habits can continue to steer us in the wrong direction.

Here is a practical step you can take to explore your beliefs and biases. Write down your beliefs in response to a few simple questions:

- How did your parents deal with money?

- How do you feel after purchasing something you didn't really need?

- How do you feel about having debt?

- How do you envision your retirement will turn out?

- How challenging is it to save money?

- How do you feel about people who are rich?

- How often do you think about investing?

- How comfortable are you with change?

Your answers will reveal a great deal about your relationship to money. For example, how do your beliefs line up with facts and research? Once you recognize the difference between facts and beliefs, you can then begin to make informed decisions. If your old habits were shaped by beliefs rather than facts, then you need to change your mindset. You need to create new habits based on actionable information.

This leads me to introduce the concept of actionable habits. Let's go back to the problem of what to do with that $1,000 you recently received. Instead of spending it in order to satisfy your emotional need for instant gratification, you may want to pause and consider your knee-jerk reaction. Rather than acting impulsively, sit down and take a breath. Can you derive pleasure and satisfaction from spending a smaller portion of your money? Here is an actionable habit: Spend $300 on whatever you desire and save the remaining $700 for your retirement. Let me define actionable habits as baby steps that you take to form small habits that would yield large results.

You need to understand that our brain operates on a pleasure/pain principle. Our subconscious decision making tends to light up the reward center of the brain. This knowledge can lead to an actionable habit. For example, define a monthly savings goal, and once you achieve your goal, reward yourself with a small indulgence. The point here is that actionable habits will gradually change your mindset about the need to plan and prepare for your retirement. Another way of defining actionable habits is to think about microeconomics versus macroeconomics.

Microeconomics is "the study of economics at the level of individual consumers, groups of consumers, or firms."[8] Economics at the micro level is in essence the study of how we manage our money and resources. The choices you make about how much money to save, invest, and spend represent the micro level of managing your resources. Financial awareness begins at the micro level and expands outward to the macro level.

Macroeconomics is the study of how the overall economy works. Think of macroeconomics as studying the big picture, while microeconomics is the study of how you manage your money and resources. Big-picture economics has an impact on your money-management strategy, which is why it is important to have a basic understanding of the hidden forces that affect your financial decisions.

One of the glaring problems I see in our educational system is the lack of financial education. In the few high schools where finance is taught, it is typically from the microeconomic perspective. What you need to understand is that "financial literacy is also important on the larger 'macro' level. Literacy in general has implications for individual success and failure, but also for the success and failure for the broader society."[9] The absence of financial literacy at the macro level is so glaring, in my opinion, that if you do a simple search on Amazon.com, you will be hard pressed to find a book that incorporates a macro view. The point here is that when you understand how the hidden forces of history, politics, and economics impact your money, you can begin to prepare for your retirement future.

In Chapter 4 you will read a great deal about these hidden forces that impact your financial future. According to David Swensen, who is the manager of Yale's endowment fund, "A rich understanding of human psychology, a reasonable appreciation of financial theory, a deep awareness of history, and a broad exposure to current events all contribute to the development of well-informed portfolio strategies."[10] Swensen became the fund manager for Yale in 1985 when the fund was valued at $1 billion. In 2019 the Yale endowment fund ballooned to $29.4 billion. You might be asking yourself how did he do this? He did it by going against conventional wisdom and by building a multi-asset class strategy. He did it by having an appreciation for the historical, psychological, and economic forces that shape the world of finance.

David Swensen succeeded by going against the collective wisdom of those who lack the necessary knowledge to succeed, and who nevertheless present themselves as the experts. Swensen was a contrarian, which is to say he defied conventional wisdom and in doing so made Yale billions of dollars. Swensen believed that "you have to diversify against the collective ignorance."[11] The point I'm trying to make is that investing demands that you understand the hidden forces that influence your money as well as the actionable habits that you need to change in order to be successful.

Part of Swensen's diversification strategy was to incorporate asset classes that other institutional investors shied away from. In addition to offering several asset classes, including real estate, private equity, and venture capital, Swensen was one of the early adopters of cryptocurrency. In 2018 Swensen's team invested in "Andreessen Horowitz's inaugural $300 million crypto fund."[12] Cryptocurrency is another source of alternative investment, although not one that I currently offer. You may have heard of cryptocurrency and thought to yourself what kind of nonsense is this?

Think about how you purchase goods and services. If you use cash, which is becoming less likely today, the money was given to you by a bank. If you use a credit or debit card, again the bank helped facilitate your transactions because you use your bank account to make credit card payments. Cryptocurrency, simply put, is a type of electronic peer-to-peer transaction without the bank acting as intermediary. Simply because you can't physically hold a cryptocurrency, such as Bitcoin, doesn't mean it is not real. Cryptocurrency was developed in the 1980s but started to take off in 2008, partly in response to the global financial meltdown. As of May 23, 2020, the value of one Bitcoin is $9,200.24. Bitcoin, which is the most popular cryptocurrency, trades on an exchange and has the potential of being a powerful asset class in a multi-asset-class strategy. Yale is not the only endowment to adopt cryptocurrency. In fact, 94% of university endowments have been allocating crypto-related investments since 2018.[13] Before you make a decision on investing in Cryptocurrency, such as Bitcoin, you need to understand the potentially high risk involved when investing in cryptocurrency. There is also a real chance the SEC, and other regulators, won't be able to help you recover your investment, even in cases of fraud.

If there is one takeaway from this book, it is that you need to change your mindset by using actionable habits. Following are several actionable habits that you can begin to implement immediately.

- Pay yourself: Elevate the concept of savings as a priority. Most people have their paycheck deposited into their checking or savings account. Create an account earmarked specifically for your savings. After receiving each paycheck, transfer a fixed amount to that account.

- Spend mindfully: Instead of shutting down the reward system in your brain, change how you reward yourself. Every time you transfer money into your savings, reward yourself with something that you enjoy. This could be something as simple as a special meal you've been craving.

- Track your spending: This is something people try to avoid, since it may confirm their worst fears about their spending habits. Here is something you could do: Use actual cash (not a debit card) for items on which you typically overspend. There is something about debit cards that shields us from fully grasping how much we spend on things we do not need. If you break a hundred dollars into twenties, you will realize how quickly your money is depleted.

- Reduce your debt: Many of us fall into the habit of paying the minimum on our credit cards. This is also connected to the reward center of the brain. If we pay the minimum, we realize we have some extra cash to spend. Here is an actionable habit: Start adding an extra amount to your minimum payment. A good rule of thumb to consider here is to add 20% to your minimum payment. For example, if your minimum payment is $100, pay $120. Do this on your car loans and any other debt you may have. In the long run, you will reduce your debt and save money by not paying unnecessary interest.

- Start investing: Investing for our retirement is one of those things that we often procrastinate about. We all lead busy lives, which is why dealing with something like retirement can seem overwhelming. Remember, we need to confront our beliefs if we are to change our mindset. Here is an actionable step you can take: Schedule an appointment with a financial planner. This one simple step will help you explore your beliefs about money, as well as give you practical decision-making options.

In addition to improving your financial awareness and developing actionable habits, it is imperative that you find a financial advisor to help you navigate the complex terrain of investment strategies. According to Michael Aloi, writing for The Motley Fool, there are several reasons you need a financial advisor in our fast-paced and complex world of today.

- Information overload: This one is obvious. We have an avalanche of information, but we don't always have the time to make sense of it. This is where a qualified advisor can help you separate relevant information from background noise.
- Too many choices: Consider that in the United States there are roughly 10,000 mutual funds and exchange-traded funds (ETFs) to choose from. Most of us are busy with work and family and simply do not have the time to choose which fund is right for us.

- Too little time: Living in the digital age is a fast-moving experience. Even with our multitasking ability, there may not be enough time to determine which investment vehicle is right for us. We need to devote time to improve and expand our knowledge about the financial world, but many of us need help with the actual implementation of our investment goals.

- Lack of expertise: Regardless of how much we learn about basic finance, economics, history, and so on, a qualified advisor has both expertise in this area and years of experience.

- Personal biases (mindset): As I've said earlier, putting your biases in check is critical to changing your habits. A qualified advisor can help you uncover, and ultimately change, your mindset, which could lead you to implement new actionable habits.[14]

In short, this book is about redefining financial literacy in such a way as to broaden our understanding and awareness of the hidden forces that impact how we manage money. Financial literacy is about understanding, and overcoming, our biases and beliefs in order to change our mindset, which can ultimately lead us to change our behavior. The subtitle of this book is "Unlocking the Hidden Forces of Your Financial Future," which has two meanings. The political, historical, and economic forces are often hidden from us, and yet they have a profound impact on our money. By unlocking these forces, we reveal them, analyze them, and can find ways to counteract them. The act of unlocking something is also an act of finding a solution. In other words, by unlocking the hidden forces, I am simultaneously giving you a potentially powerful way to overcome them.

Introduction

FINANCIAL LITERACY

"Financial illiteracy is not an issue unique to any one population.
It affects everyone: men and women, young and old, across all socio-
economic lines. No longer can we stand by and ignore this problem.
The economic future of the United States depends on it."

–PRESIDENT GEORGE W. BUSH'S ADVISORY COUNCIL ON FINANCIAL LITERACY

———

The American Dream has long been a beacon of hope for millions of people who struggled to make a better life for themselves and their children. This idealized version of capitalism, which has long been presented as a kind of economic contract, promised us that if we worked hard and diligently saved, we would enjoy the benefits of homeownership and a comfortable retirement. As you will read in this book, the pursuit of the American Dream has become more elusive today than ever before. When you consider there have been 10 market corrections in the past 20 years and two bear markets, you begin to understand the difficulty in trying to navigate the uncertainty of today's financial landscape.[1]

To exacerbate matters, the economic fallout of COVID-19 is creating a new category of financial vulnerability where millions of Americans, who were once financially secure, "face rapidly dwindling resources and mounting uncertainty about the financial path forward."[2] The full extent of the economic devastation that will result from this pandemic is yet to be written, but we can be sure of one thing: the disruption to our lives will create an ongoing sense of doubt, fear, and uncertainty.

It is this dialectic movement of biology on the one hand and economics on the other that have converged to create a powerful sense of uncertainty about what tomorrow will hold. To gain a perspective, Prudential conducted a survey. The results are quite sobering: "the majority of survey respondents have seen income cut in half (or worse), with one-third having lost all income. Nearly half do not have enough emergency savings to last another six months and 24% will run out of money in less than 30 days, leaving an astounding 90% of the 1,100 households surveyed as financially insecure."[3] For many of us who are retired, or will soon retire, the future does not seem to be smiling upon us at the moment.

There is a pervasive concern that our hard-earned money will no longer be sufficient to sustain us through retirement. The fundamentals of the market have shifted; the traditional definitions of balance and risk management don't always still apply to a globally interconnected and interdependent market. The risk of outliving your money is fast becoming the new normal for many, and for some who have already retired, it is rapidly becoming a stubborn reality.

This concern is both grounded and shaped by some of the same tired investment advice:

- Start saving early, and don't let up.
- Split your portfolio between stocks and bonds, and shift the balance from stocks to bonds as you age.
- Pick funds based on lower fees, follow the advice of financial managers, and rely on ratings to pick winning funds.
- Count on government bonds to carry you through retirement, given their guaranteed principal and consistent returns.
- Stay in it for the long haul, and ignore the inevitable daily swings of the market.

What the past has taught us is that although the markets do have the potential to rise over a distant time horizon, this paradigm is no longer tenable or desirable for many investors in today's complex globalized world.

Current research suggests that our estimated age of retirement doesn't always match the age people actually retire; some tend to retire earlier, and some have to keep working because they don't have the wherewithal to sustain them. That first outcome—retiring early—can significantly affect your likelihood of meeting your retirement income goals, because the time you have to save or for your invested money to grow is reduced, your Social Security benefit (if it is available at that point) might be reduced, and you could be retired for a longer period, which will require more money.

I find that one of the reasons people put off retirement planning is the daunting prospect of trying to anticipate and account for multiple variables. These may include future market returns, future interest rates, risk level, financial needs and desires, the sequence-of-return risk, Social Security's eventual fate, unexpected health events, inflation, spending needs, and a host of other possibilities.

Because of that daunting and seemingly capricious fortune-telling, when it comes to investing, we often find it easier to accept the wisdom of others without question—and without necessarily understanding the options. Given the complexity and esoteric nature of the financial world, many of us would much rather leave our fate to the experts and specialists whose job is to help secure our future. Financial planning is indeed a difficult field, requiring a huge investment of time, study, and knowledge, but I'm not suggesting that you need to become an expert yourself. Instead, hire an expert, but make sure your own knowledge is adequate to determine that you've found the right professional to work with, and to increase your own chances of making reasonable retirement goals—and then meeting those goals.

According to former Federal Reserve chairman Alan Greenspan, "The number one problem in today's generation and economy is lack of financial literacy."[4] The irony, of course, is that America represents the world's most powerful economy, and yet we spend "a whopping two cents on financial literacy for every $100 spent on education."[5] Consider this:

- 40% of adults rate their own knowledge of personal finance as extremely low and state that they need guidance.

- 60% of adults have no budget.

- Less than 50% of Americans live within their means or have saved for an emergency.

- More than 30% of Americans pay only the minimum on their credit card each month.

- The average American family's credit card debt is $15,000, and they owe $33,000 in student loans.

- 85% of Americans are worried they are not ready for retirement.[6]

What we are witnessing today appears to be nothing short of a social crisis, unprecedented in scope and far-reaching in its implications. The "Financial Literacy: Prosperity Begins with Knowledge" study found that 84% of the American public has never participated in a financial literacy program.[7] As a result of poor financial literacy, 43% of student loan borrowers are defaulting on their loans and 33% of American adults have $0 saved for retirement.[8] According to the National Financial Educators Council, which administers an annual 30-question financial literacy test to over 53,000 people in all 50 states, the results have not been promising. In 2019, the average score of 15- to 18-year-olds was an abysmal 65%. While this is an alarmingly low score, it represents an improvement from the 2014 test, where the average score was 60%.[9] When you ask Americans if teaching high school students financial literacy is important, the vast majority agree that it is important. In fact, according to the National Financial Educators Council survey in August of 2020, 84.5% of those surveyed agreed that schools should teach financial literacy in high school.[10] Although there is incremental improvement in financial knowledge and awareness, it is my opinion that more needs to be done.

Financial illiteracy does not, of course, occur in a vacuum. The financial planning industry spends around $17 billion a year to market products and services to consumers, but it spends only $670 million on educating those consumers.[11] Although many financial advisors recognize the problem of financial literacy, "only 4 in 10 advisors are doing anything to address the problem, meaning the majority are ignoring the issue."[12] With a reasonable level of financial literacy, you can advocate for your own future.

The profound irony of our worsening financial literacy is that we live in the information age. Thanks to Google and other search engines, we live in a world with a near-infinite supply of information, yet this digital technology can give the false impression that we are far more enlightened today than in generations past. We are bombarded with trivia and struggle to separate it from crucial or even trustworthy information. This can lead to a sense of overconfidence that could be detrimental to your retirement goals. However, relying on a financial advisor blindly, without a basic understanding—or, arguably worse, *only* a basic understanding—of how the financial world operates, can affect your ability to ask relevant questions and make crucial decisions.

Part of this digitization is the current automated world of algorithm-driven platforms and deep-learning machines, including automated financial advisors that encourage us to surrender our autonomy in exchange for convenience. Many individual investors feel they can go it alone by relying on these automated systems: Around 75% of Americans manage their finances without a professional financial advisor.[13] I wrote this book to give you the necessary financial knowledge and awareness so that you can vet a trustworthy advisor who will put your needs and retirement goals first.

THE SUPPORT SYSTEM IS DISAPPEARING

One of the reasons I believe that financial literacy is disturbingly low is that many of us tend to think of it as not directly related to our lives. Many of us have developed the belief that an education will help us secure a decent-paying job. If we work hard enough, we may put some money aside for our pension, and Social Security will take care of the rest. But this linear and static way of thinking about the future is, in my opinion, outdated. The mechanisms that many of us thought we could rely on for a comfortable retirement are breaking down. Social Security might not be as secure as people think, pensions have mostly gone the way of the dodo, and we're living longer, so our retirement funds have to last even longer.

For the last few decades US corporations have ceased offering pensions; instead, they now offer defined-contribution plans like 401(k)s.[14] This shift has moved the onus for financial decision making from the employer—as it was with pensions—to the employees. We must now determine for ourselves how much to contribute, what to invest in, and how to distribute our funds in retirement.[15] This is why the role of financial advisors and our own financial literacy are more important than ever before. Americans like you and me will have to rely on our own ability to invest in our future. We have to empower ourselves with accurate knowledge and trustworthy professional guidance to invest for the future.

WE'RE LIVING LONGER

The fundamental fact is that people are living longer. We need to plan for as many as 20 to 30 years of retirement now instead of the 10 to 15 years of the 1980s.[16] In fact, according to Daniel Hill, president and CEO of Virginia-based Hill Wealth Strategies, the current retirement investment strategies are "problematic because, as inflation rises, so will expenses."[17] As our expenses increase over a longer period of time, a static portfolio may not offer the necessary returns that will sustain us throughout our retirement. A model that doesn't move with the times may not offer us protection against sudden market movements.[18] Without a more versatile investment strategy, you may not be able to generate enough income to sustain you through retirement.[19]

PENSIONS

Let's suppose you are one of the 20 million public-sector employees relying on a pension to help you through your retirement years.[20] You should be aware that "a traditionally balanced pension portfolio [like a pension fund] lost more than 5 percent for the year [2018]."[21] Think of this for a moment: You work hard all your life, secure in the knowledge that your pension will carry you through your golden years, only to realize that your pension may not be there when you need it.

According to Moody's, "public pension investment losses were nearing $1 trillion during the first quarter [2020]...State and local government had a combined $4.1 trillion in unfunded retirement liabilities before the pandemic hit."[22] Underfunded pensions are partially the result of exaggerated estimates of market returns. In other words, "too-optimistic estimates of market return, which determine how much governments must pay to fund the balance, have left many [pension] plans massively underfunded even as the advisors who managed them received huge fees."[23]

In fact, "almost all public pension funds assume returns somewhere around 7%," which is "highly unlikely due to the debt we've accumulated, and debt is a drag on growth."[24] If that's not alarming, consider that, according to two experts in the area of pension research and retirement, you should not depend on pensions to carry you through retirement. Both Olivia Mitchell, who is a professor of business economics and public policy at the Wharton School, and Leora Friedberg, a professor of economics and public policy at the University of Virginia's Frank Batten School of Leadership and Public Policy, "have some advice for public-sector workers who are counting on a pension: don't."[25]

SOCIAL SECURITY

If you leave your retirement fate to Social Security, things may not work out as well as you thought. Americans who are depending on the decades-old Social Security program to protect them through their retirement years will likely find this plan to be lacking. While it is unlikely Social Security payouts will go to zero, retirees may expect to receive 75% of what they were promised as early as the year 2034.

The problem is with the Social Security Trust, "a surplus that was built up when taxes collected exceeded benefits paid out. The trust makes up the difference between money coming in via the Federal Insurance Contributions Act (FICA) taxes and money paid out. Once the trust is empty, the payments into the system will support payouts at a level of only 75% of current commitments."[26] To put this in perspective, by 2034 Social Security's $3 trillion in asset reserves, which was built over decades, is expected to be exhausted unless measures are taken before then to extend the life of the fund.[27]

The problem for retirees is the stubborn reality of numbers. Consider this: "62% of today's retired workers receiving a Social Security benefit rely on the program to provide at least half of their monthly income. A 23% cut to their benefits would definitely be felt, and would notably increase elderly poverty rates."[28] The lesson here is that if you leave your retirement fate to pensions and Social Security, your future won't look as rosy as you planned.

THE DOUBLE-WHAMMY EFFECT

Some of you reading this will remember that in the 1970s, we were comforted by the belief that pensions and Social Security would take care of us during our retirement years. This belief wasn't grounded in reality. Twenty-five years ago roughly 38% of Americans worked in jobs that promised them pensions; now that number is less than 13%.[29] The pension system has been replaced by 401(k)s, IRAs, and other investment vehicles that have shifted the responsibility of managing those funds from the employer to the employee.[30] Most Americans have savings of less than $1,000 and nothing put aside for retirement, even in 401(k)s and IRAs.[31] To exacerbate matters, some of the remaining pension plans of today are at risk of going broke.[32]

As for Social Security, many of us don't seem to understand how it works. Only 30% of a group of respondents given a 10-question quiz on Social Security were able to pass.[33] Many of you will notice a deduction from your paycheck called FICA, which is an acronym for the Federal Insurance Contributions Act. This deduction represents 6.2% of your gross income for Social Security and 1.45% for Medicare. If you contribute a minimum of $52,000 over your entire working life, you will qualify for Social Security benefits. Of course, most employees contribute far more than this amount. Although this system worked well for many years, Social Security may soon become insolvent. In 2015 the government collected $817 billion from paychecks for Social Security; that same year, they distributed $877 billion.[34] If you do simple arithmetic, you will see a deficit of $60 billion in just one year. At this rate, Social Security will run out of money by 2034, unless Congress acts.

This leads to a double-whammy effect on retirement planning. In many cases, Americans are not saving enough through pension plans or on their own, and the public support system is breaking down. Corporations are no longer offering pension plans, and some of the remaining pensions are underfunded. To make matters worse, Social Security may not be able to take care of our retirement needs as intended. The burden has shifted to you, the average American, to plan for your own retirement. More than ever, you need to protect yourself by taking charge of your financial future.

CORPORATE DEBT

As if that's not enough, government and corporate debt are on the rise, which affects both bonds and the stock market. The Institute of International Finance released a disturbing report in 2018 on the state of global debt, which is worth quoting here:

> U.S. non-financial corporate debt hit a post-crisis high of 72% of GDP: At around $14.5 trillion in 2017, non-financial corporate sector debt was $810 billion higher than it was a year ago [2016], with 60% of the rise stemming from new bank loan creation. At present, bond financing accounts for 43% of outstanding debt with an average maturity of 15 years vs.

the average maturity of 2.1 years for U.S. business loans. This implies roughly around $3.8 trillion of loan repayment per year. Against this backdrop, rising interest rates will add pressure on corporates with large refinancing needs.[35]

What is significant here is that corporate debts reached 72% of GDP, which is in addition to the government debt that now stands at 100% of GDP and household debt that is currently at 77% of GDP.[36] To exacerbate matters, according to Moody's, "37% [$2.4 trillion] of U.S. non-financial corporate debt is now below investment grade."[37] Now, let's connect corporate debt to stocks and bonds. Corporations can borrow money in two different ways: by issuing fixed-income securities or by taking out loans from a bank or other lending institutions. When investors purchase fixed-income securities, whether corporate debt or US Treasuries, they are essentially lending money to a corporation. Corporations may also obtain a line of credit from banks to meet day-to-day operations such as payroll, inventory, and other expenses.

Here is the problem with high corporate debt. When a company takes on a substantial amount of debt, it negatively impacts the company and its shareholders "because it inhibits a company's ability to create a cash surplus. Furthermore, high debt levels may negatively affect common stockholders, who are last in line for claiming payback from a company that becomes insolvent."[38]

In addition, debt that is below investment grade, which is called junk bonds, "are structured with far fewer protections and made prospective investors increasingly uneasy about a trend of eroding standards in that area of the fixed-income market."[39] The point I'm trying to make is that traditional portfolio strategies are susceptible to powerful economic forces that can undermine your investment future. When you factor in household debt, you begin to get an idea of where we are as a society. Consider that "29% of Americans have more credit-card debt than they do emergency savings . . . [and] 41.2% of households carry credit-card debt and the average amount is $5,700."[40] This is why you need to improve your financial literacy.

Debt can also create asset bubbles, as we saw during the 2008 real estate bubble. This bubble "was fueled by credit default swaps that were used to insure derivatives such as mortgage-backed securities and collateralized debt obligations. Hedge-fund managers created a huge demand for these supposedly risk-free securities, which in turn boosted demand for the mortgages that backed them."[41] Asset bubbles typically burst when prices, of real estate, for example, crash and demand falls. This will usually lead to lower business and household spending and potential economic contraction. Prior to the COVID-19 pandemic, we were living through another bubble. According to an article by Ben Reynolds in 2019, he believes that "The global economy is clearly headed for another recession after a decade of lukewarm recovery. The bailouts and loose monetary policy of the post-2008 world did nothing to fix the fundamental causes of capitalism's latest systemic crisis."[42] This possibility offers you a reason why you need to protect yourself against economic forces that will impact your future.

SHIFTING RESPONSIBILITY

One of the consequences of poor financial literacy, beyond the obvious mistakes of poor financial planning, is the inability to understand

and direct that financial future for ourselves. Times are changing, and the responsibility is shifting to us to be active participants in directing our own future. Given the new economic reality facing us, I believe that most people are woefully underprepared for securing a comfortable retirement. What we need today is a fundamental paradigm shift away from our passive dependence on systems—which may or may not still exist when we're ready to retire—to take care of our retirement; instead, we must begin to educate ourselves about the basic economic reality confronting us.

Think of financial literacy as an investment in your own human capital.[43] Inherent in each of us is the untapped potential of financial awareness. The knowledge you gain today is an investment that can pay off in the future. To put this in perspective, the National Financial Educators Council estimates that a "lack of financial knowledge cost Americans $295 billion in 2018."[44] Over a lifetime Americans lose a staggering $2.3 trillion as a result of poor financial literacy.[45] Developing your own knowledge base can help you make informed decisions that have the potential to reduce those losses for your own financial future.

I'm not suggesting that people need to develop expertise in economics or to brave the rapids of investing on their own; rather, we need to develop a basic understanding of the economic forces that impact our financial future. A level of financial literacy adequate to understand and choose your path is crucial—for all of us. This knowledge, combined with a trusted financial advisor, plays an indispensable role in shaping and directing your financial future. The expertise of financial advisors, however, does not absolve you from your responsibility to educate yourself on the basics of the financial world.

Financial professionals have long insisted that investors must take on higher risk to gain potentially higher returns.[46] However, this wisdom did not apply to large institutional endowment funds. The endowment model has shown that with greater diversification encompassing a wide variety of asset classes, an investment plan may deliver "stronger risk-adjusted returns with less volatility."[47] For example, the legendary manager of the Yale University Endowment, David Swensen, demonstrated that over the past 40 years the Yale Endowment beat the S&P 500 by just under 3% per year.[48] And while diversification itself cannot ensure a profit or guarantee against a loss, some of the elements of the endowment approach are now available, with the help of professional advisors, to the individual investor.

Let's look at the traditional 60/40 portfolio, which puts 60% of your investments in stocks and 40% in bonds, then leaves them there to hopefully grow. The idea was to potentially maximize returns while managing risk—according to mathematical models like the modern portfolio theory. The stocks were meant to provide a large return for increased risk while the investment in bonds offered protection for a lesser return. According to Morgan Stanley, the average return for the 60/40 portfolio has been nearly 8% since 1881. However, Morgan Stanley forecasts a 2.8% average annual return over the next 10 years.[49] It is important to remember that investing in stocks is risky and that past performance doesn't ensure future performance or results.

Universities, endowments, and other large organizations have traditionally been able to invest in a much larger array of asset types than the average investor could. However, that field has recently opened to the rest of us, and that opportunity for heightened diversification offers us the chance to replace the 60/40 model with something designed to work in today's digital, globalized world, a new system that offers potentially high rates of return for lower levels of risk.

How we exercise our right to choose will depend on our capacity to think critically about the decisions and choices that have come before us. This is why financial literacy is a social imperative. It is how we navigate, absorb, and engage all the information available to us that determines how prepared we are for retirement. This book should be a wake-up call. Knowledge is power, and today, more than ever before, what is needed to take control of your own financial power is financial literacy.

All these factors are a lesson for all of us: Never surrender control of your financial future. You need to take charge of your finances now, and to do so means you need to educate yourself about the financial world. Financial literacy is not some slogan that I use to inspire you; rather, it is a financial imperative for all of us. The more we learn about the economic forces swirling above us, the better prepared we will be.

Chapter 1

HIDDEN FORCES

"There should exist among the citizens neither extreme poverty nor excessive wealth, for both are productive of great evil."

–PLATO

———

The title of this book is *Redefining Financial Literacy,* which is critical to our understanding of the knowledge and skills we need to effectively plan and manage money. Financial literacy has traditionally been defined in terms of our "ability to understand and effectively apply various financial skills, including personal financial management, budgeting, and investing."[1] This rather simple definition needs to be broadened to include historical, social, political, and economic forces that directly impact our financial planning. What is urgently needed today is the kind of financial literacy that transforms our mindset from passive spectators to active participants.

The question to ask, of course, is what are these hidden forces and why is it important that we should be aware of them? Let's examine for a minute the paycheck you get every month. Who dictates how much you are paid? Is it simply your employer? How much FICA tax is deducted from your paycheck? Where do your tax dollars go? Why do women often make less than men for the same work? The answer to these, and other, questions involves a basic understanding of history, politics, and economics. I'm not suggesting you need a degree in history or economics; rather, the more knowledge you have about these intersecting and overlapping forces, the better questions you will raise about your financial future, which can improve how you plan for your retirement. The more you compare, contrast, and understand parallels in certain historical events, the more you will realize just how important they are to the decisions you make today.

If we look at the hidden economic forces that impact how much you earn, we find that unemployment levels, globalization, industry conditions, and cost of living all contribute to your salary. As an example, during periods of high unemployment, companies are reluctant to hire new employees and may even ask existing employees to work longer hours. In this scenario, given the abundance of workers, wages become stagnant. Globalization enables many corporations to ship high-paying jobs overseas, therefore impacting wages of domestic workers.[2] Let's suppose you have a 401(k) plan, which invests in the 60/40 portfolio. In other words, your retirement allocation is invested 60% in stocks and 40% in bonds. What happens if this strategy is potentially broken? As you keep reading, you will learn about the economic forces that are changing the investment landscape.

These hidden forces are not merely abstract concepts; in fact, they have a direct impact on your financial future. For example, the

Social Security system that our parents and grandparents enjoyed may become insolvent if Congress fails to enact reforms. The pensions that past generations have relied upon to carry them through retirement are becoming extinct. Consider this: "The practice of companies sending monthly retirement checks to their former workers is headed for extinction, and remaining pension funds are in tough financial shape."[3] Again, there are hidden forces that seem to be out of our control, but there is something you could do about them. If you broaden your understanding of the hidden forces that could affect your financial future, you could be in a position to better prepare and plan for your retirement. One of the hidden forces I've mentioned above is history. You might remember taking history classes in high school and saying to yourself, "Who needs history?"

What you must realize is that a meaningful understanding of the financial world must include its history. You see, history is not just some abstract and pedantic study that is removed from our lives. It encroaches on us in ways that are instructive in how we plan our future. As the saying goes, "Those who cannot learn from history are doomed to repeat it." This, as recent history has shown us, is precisely what has happened over the past century.[4] Although history tends to repeat itself, we don't have to acquiesce to the inevitable; we can use the knowledge of past events to shape our own future. This is especially true for women, who now hold more than half of the personal wealth in the United States.[5] It is precisely because we have the freedom to choose that history need not repeat itself. How we exercise our right to choose will depend on our capacity to think critically about the decisions and choices that come before us.

THE GILDED AGE

The Gilded Age in America, the period between 1876 and World War I, was characterized as a time seemingly covered with glitter on the surface but corrupt underneath. It was a time of "greed and guile: of rapacious Robber Barons, unscrupulous spectators, and corporate buccaneers, of shady business practices, scandal-plagued politics, and vulgar display."[6] By 1890 more than 70% of America's wealth was concentrated and controlled by the top 10% of the population. Although it is tempting to believe that our world is far more egalitarian today, in 2016 the top 10% of families controlled 76% of the total wealth.[7] Despite the fact that we are 150 years removed from the original Gilded Age, the economic reality today is just as bifurcated and iniquitous as it has ever been. The American Dream continues to elude the vast majority of Americans, and generational wealth favors a small percentage of the population.

The Gilded Age coincided with the Industrial Revolution, in which factory work replaced farming as the leading source of employment, the railroad introduced a national transportation system, and the corporation revolutionized capitalism. The Gilded Age witnessed a period of unprecedented technological breakthroughs, including the telephone, the phonograph, the radio, the electric light bulb, the automobile, and countless other innovations. This was the beginning of the consumer economy, where technology and culture converged to create popular culture. For example, by the turn of the 20th century, the rise of the mass-circulation newspaper and the monetization of leisure, including sports and entertainment, fundamentally changed how we lived. As a consequence of this dramatic change over a very short period of time, an economic chasm opened between the privileged few and everyone else.

Those who accumulated vast amounts of wealth became known as robber barons. These robber barons created a closed loop, in which wealth, greed, and corruption shaped and defined the political and economic reality of their time. These captains of industry succeeded by paying workers low wages, exploiting children and immigrants, and avoiding government regulations. Men such as John D. Rockefeller, Andrew Carnegie, and J. P. Morgan amassed sufficient wealth to both control and manipulate the economy.

Andrew Carnegie, for example, made his fortune in the steel industry. He "engaged in tactics that were not in the best interests of his workers";[8] in 1892, in response to Carnegie's attempts to lower wages, his workers went on strike. The Homestead steel strike, also known as the Homestead massacre, ended in violence and numerous deaths. Treating workers with disdain and contempt was the result of a lack of government regulations, as well as monopolistic practices. John D. Rockefeller, who owned Standard Oil, controlled 90% of the oil infrastructure in the United States. In the area of banking and finance, J. P. Morgan "invested in Thomas Edison and the Edison Electricity Company, helped to create General Electric and International Harvester, formed J. P. Morgan & Company, and gained control of half of the country's railroad mileage."[9] The amount of power these men wielded, particularly in politics, was extraordinary.

The politics of the Gilded Age involved widespread corruption, where power was concentrated in the hands of a few men who used their money and influence to secure political favors. "Congress was known for being rowdy and inefficient. It was not unusual to find that a quorum could not be achieved because too many members were drunk or otherwise preoccupied with extra-governmental affairs."[10] Congress was filled with men who operated in smoke-filled back rooms and catered to the privileged few who made sure their empires continued to dominate the corporate world.

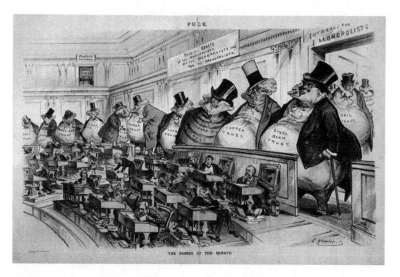

The Bosses of the Senate by Joseph Keppler[10]

Every president from 1876 to 1900 was elected for a single term. This helped establish a system where presidents rewarded those who helped elect them through backroom deals. The most glaring example of this was the 1876 election, which was hotly disputed. The Democratic candidate, Samuel J. Tilden of New York, won the popular vote; however, the electoral votes of three southern states were disputed. This dispute would last four months, during which both the Republicans and Democrats contested the outcome. In January 1877 Congress established a 15-member Electoral Commission to decide who would be president. The commission voted along party lines and awarded the presidency to Rutherford B. Hayes.

This election would set the stage for a series of weak presidents elected into office. Once elected, these one-term presidents spent their time repaying the political favors to those individuals who helped them narrowly win the White House. The patronage system gave presidents wide latitude to appoint friends and supporters to high political posts. This form of corruption occurred across both political parties and at every level of government. Part of the reason the patronage system took hold was that presidents during the Gilded Age had very little power of their own. There was no popular mandate for them to rule or carry out substantive policies. To exacerbate matters, Congress was controlled by corporations that dictated policies favoring their own selfish ends. The end result of the patronage system was that little was accomplished on the federal level, save for the legislation that both protected and encouraged corporate monopolies. In other words, there was no real impetus for change or protections for workers who toiled in sweatshops. The Gilded Age created one of the most bifurcated economies in American history, which exposed some of the flaws of unchecked capitalism. Historian Nell Painter described this corrupt period by arguing that "capitalism makes some people really rich, and democracy is not strong enough to counter the power of great wealth."[11] Although an intervening Progressive Era helped bring about reform, the oceanic problem of bifurcated inequality is far more pervasive today than ever before.

THE NEW DEAL AND FORDISM

The free-market capitalism that marked the Gilded Age benefited a small elite group who manipulated the political system in order to perpetuate their economic dominance. The government failed to intervene when greed and excess, which came at the expense of the vast majority of Americans, was out of control. These hidden forces would continue to dominate the economic landscape well into the 1920s. Let's look at the rampant greed that defined the 1920s. Greed captured the imagination of both the banks and the individual investor. Banks engaged in speculative investing by lending money to people who wanted to buy stocks. At the time there were no regulations, which led to a market bubble. By 1929 the stock market crashed under the weight of its own irrational exuberance. On October 28, 1929, which is remembered today as Black Monday, the Dow Jones Industrial Average plunged nearly 13 percent. On the following day, Black Tuesday, the market fell an additional 12 percent.[12]

President Herbert Hoover advocated for laissez-faire economics, which is the idea, first developed by the philosopher and economist Adam Smith, that governments should take a hands-off approach to the market. Hoover believed "that economic assistance would make people stop working. He believed business prosperity would trickle down to the average person."[13] This noninterventionist belief in economic affairs would lead to the greatest economic disaster in American history as well as Hoover's defeat in 1932. By the time Franklin Roosevelt took office on March 4, 1933, "unemployment had risen from 3% to 25% of the nation's workforce. Wages for those who still had jobs fell. U.S. gross domestic product was cut in half, from $103 billion to $55 billion, due partly to deflation."[14] By his first 100 days in office, Roosevelt had introduced numerous government programs called the New Deal.

One of the first things Roosevelt did upon taking office was to appoint Frances Perkins to be his Secretary of Labor. Perkins would become the first woman appointed to the US Cabinet, the longest-serving Secretary of Labor (1933–1945), and the architect behind Roosevelt's New Deal programs. She was responsible for either introducing or implementing such programs as the Civilian Conservation Corps, the National Industrial Recovery Act, Public Works Administration programs, the Social Security Act, the Fair Labor Standards Act, pensions, unemployment compensation, a minimum wage, the 40-hour work week, and countless other programs.[15] In addition to the New Deal programs, Roosevelt wanted to address the fundamental causes of the financial collapse.

Let's remember that before the stock market crash of 1929, retail banks used depositors' funds for the purpose of investing in initial stock sales, otherwise known as initial public offerings. Many banks facilitated risky mergers and acquisitions and operated their own hedge funds without any governmental oversight. In response to the near collapse of the banking system, Congress passed the Glass-Steagall Act in 1933, which removed and separated investment banks from retail banks. The Glass-Steagall Act "restored confidence in the U.S. banking system. It increased trust by only allowing banks to use depositors' funds in safe investments. Its FDIC [Federal Deposit Insurance Corporation] insurance program prevented further bank runs. Depositors knew the government protected them from a failing bank."[16] Over the next several decades the banking industry fought to repeal what they believed to be excessive government regulations.

Following World War II, a new form of economic growth helped give rise to the postwar boom and, by extension, a strong viable middle class. This mode of growth became known as Fordism. It offered mass consumption, sufficient wages to support families, job stability, and rising incomes. From the late 1940s to the early 1970s, "Fordism extended well beyond the factory walls; it reshaped the spatial and demographic configuration of cities; it ignited bouts of economic development, industrial concentration, and social conflict."[17] Fordism was a broadly defined system of standardized production in which workers were offered a decent wage to afford the very goods they produced. In many ways Fordism gave rise to the American middle class, which, in turn, helped spread the American Dream. The end of Fordism marked the beginning of a new economic philosophy that favored free markets and little to no government intervention. Neoliberalism, as you will see, would prove to be disastrous.

NEOLIBERALISM AND MILTON FRIEDMAN

By the early 1970s a new economic philosophy was starting to take hold. Neoliberalism embraced laissez-faire economics, which is "an economic theory from the 18th century that opposed any government intervention in business affairs."[18] One of the early architects of neoliberalism was the Nobel Prize–winning economist Milton Friedman. In a little-known *New York Times Magazine* article published in 1970, "The Social Responsibility of Business is to Increase Its Profits," Friedman offered a framework for corporate behavior. Friedman wrote, "There is one and only one social responsibility of business—to use its resources and engage in activities designed to increase its profits so long as it stays within the rules of the game, which is to say, engages in open and free competition without deception."[19] In other words, the government should not interfere with free-market competition by imposing regulations that interfere with market competition. As you will soon see, neoliberalism, as championed by Milton Friedman, would contribute to the eventual repeal of the Glass-Steagall Act.

In 1971, a Virginia attorney by the name of Lewis Powell wrote a memo in support of businesses coming together to defend their corporate interests. Powell argued: "Business must learn the lesson . . . that political power is necessary; that such power must be assiduously cultivated; and that when necessary, it must be used aggressively and with determination—without embarrassment and without the reluctance which has been so characteristic of American business."[20] This one fateful memo would catch the attention of President Nixon. Two months later Nixon nominated Lewis Powell to the US Supreme Court. Powell's memo was, in effect, a call to arms for businesses to come together to defend its mission of free and open competition without government regulations. Both Milton Friedman and Lewis Powell set the stage for less government regulation, which would have a dramatic effect on the stock market. It is these hidden forces that have the potential to impact your investment strategy. As you will see, once regulation was removed, the stock market would crash several times. Let's connect the dots.

THE NIXON SHOCK AND THE GOLD STANDARD

On Sunday, August 15, 1971, President Nixon addressed the American people on national television in what became known as the Nixon

Shock. In response to increasing inflation, Nixon committed himself to a series of economic measures that included wage and price freezes, surcharges on imports, and the unilateral decision to take the United States off the gold standard.[21] Nixon's motivation to make these dramatic changes was political in nature. Unemployment in 1971 was at 6.1%, which Nixon believed would undermine his reelection. Although his economic advisor, Milton Friedman, told him these measures would not work, Nixon responded, "I've never seen anybody beaten on inflation in the United States. I've seen many people beaten on unemployment."[22] To better understand the far-reaching implications of taking America off the gold standard, we need to mention the Bretton Woods Conference.

In 1944, as World War II was raging in both Europe and Asia, representatives of 44 nations met at a lodge in Bretton Woods, New Hampshire. The purpose of the Bretton Woods Conference was to construct a set of economic rules for the postwar world and establish an international monetary system. The two tangible outcomes were the creation of the International Monetary Fund (IMF) and the International Bank (later called the World Bank) for reconstruction and development to address the total devastation of Europe following the war.

One of the most fateful decisions of Bretton Woods was the establishment of the US dollar as the world's reserve currency.[23] Given that the United States emerged from World War II as a military and economic superpower, most of the countries at the conference agreed to peg world currencies to the US dollar, which in turn was convertible into gold at $35 per ounce. In other words, all of the major global currencies were pegged to the dollar, and the dollar, in turn, was pegged to gold. This became known as the gold standard. This helped stabilize global currencies and, as result of the agreement, "central banks of countries other than the United States were given the task of maintaining fixed exchange rates between their currencies and the [US] dollar."[24] They did this by intervening in foreign-exchange markets.

The consequences of Nixon's taking us off the gold standard, and effectively killing the Bretton Woods agreements, were dramatic and far-reaching. Consider that since World War II, unemployment averaged 6% and real economic growth averaged 2.9% per year, which represents a full percentage point lower than during the gold standard era.[25]

Remember that Nixon told the American people in his 1971 television address that the measures he was taking were designed to address inflation and the high unemployment rate. If we judge his policies based on the unemployment numbers, then they were disastrous. "The unemployment rate averaged 8.5% in 1975, almost 10% in 1982.... This performance is horrendous compared to the post World War II gold standard era, which lasted from 1947 to 1970. During those 21 years of economic ups and downs, unemployment averaged less than 5% and never rose above 7%."[26]

Now, why is this important for you to know? It is important for two reasons. First, the gold standard clearly illustrates how historical, political, and economic forces converge in such a way as to potentially impact your financial reality. Second, the knowledge you gain will create an awareness about the hidden forces that influence your money, which, in turn, will help you change your mindset and, ultimately, change your investment behavior.

GLOBALIZATION

Globalization is an inescapable fact of modern life. While there are benefits to globalization, including cultural exchange, attention to climate change, dissemination of information, the sharing of technology, improvement of infrastructure for less-developed nations, and so on, there are also glaring problems with it. Some of the unintended consequences of globalization include the concentration of wealth in the hands of a few corporations, the disappearance of entire industries, and the exporting of American jobs abroad. Globalization creates linkage where the economic downturn of one country creates a domino effect through its trade partners. An example here would be the 2008 global financial crisis. Countries such as Portugal, Spain, Ireland, and Greece were severely impacted and required bailouts from the European Union.[27] As much as globalization improved the living standards of less-developed nations, it came at the expense of the American worker.

With the advent of globalization in the 1970s and an expanding international market, the demand for American labor declined. As a result of a global economy, which required "unprecedented labor flexibility, the industrial Fordist workplaces of post-war America that offered long-term job security to gain experienced, long-term employees eventually collapsed."[28] By the 1980s the political, social, and economic ideas of Fordism were changing. The American worker confronted a corporate reality that was no longer linked to a rising standard of living. Globalization also came at a time when the neoliberal idea of free markets started to take hold.

Globalization has sent jobs overseas, thus shrinking the number of decent-paying jobs. Some millennials, and other generational groups, for example, have been told they need to get a college education in order to maximize their potential. The only problem is that many millennials are burdened with a mountain of student-loan debt, which makes it difficult to accumulate any kind of meaningful wealth. Consider that "10 percent of the richest people in the United States own almost 70 percent of the country's total wealth. As of June 2019, the top 10 percent held 69.4 percent of total U.S. net worth (that is the value of all assets a person hold minus all their liabilities)...The bottom 50 percent of U.S. residents only held about 2 percent of all U.S. wealth."[29] In many ways, globalization allowed large multinational corporations to merge to create even larger companies. Such mergers came at a high cost to employees and the average investor.

THE MERGER

By the late 1990s the corporate power and influence that Milton Friedman and Lewis Powell championed in the 1970s had reached a new height. In 1998, Travelers Group, one of the largest insurance and financial services companies in the world, announced a merger with Citicorp, which was primarily a commercial bank. What made this proposed merger unique and unprecedented was not simply the scale of the merger deal, which was valued at $140 billion; rather, it was the fact that Congress had to repeal the Glass-Steagall Act of 1933 in order to facilitate the merger. In other words, Congress had to officially repeal the Glass-Steagall Act so that the merger could be legal. To ensure that Glass-Steagall would be repealed, both companies poured millions of dollars into the campaigns of both Republicans and Democrats. When corporate greed becomes intertwined with politics, the result is a corrupt and broken capitalist system that protects and perpetuates the interests of those who want to maintain a stranglehold on the political establishment. Once Glass-Steagall was removed, it would only be a matter of time before the stock market found itself in a cycle of unsustainable bubbles and corrections.

With government regulations removed, "the value of equity markets grew exponentially, with the technology-dominated Nasdaq index rising from under 1,000 to more than 5,000 between the years 1995 and 2000."[30] Deregulation enabled start-up companies to obtain loans in order to have an online presence. This would contribute to the stock market crash of 2002. As of September 24, 2002, "the Dow Jones Industrial Average had lost 27% of the value it held on January 1, 2001; a total loss of $5 trillion."[31] Without adequate regulation to control the worst impulses of corporate greed and corruption, the stock market crashed.

As a result of the housing bubble and rampant greed, the stock market once again crashed, dropping more than 50% from October 9, 2007, to March 5, 2009.[32] Let's connect the dots. The stock market crash of 1929 taught us that government regulation was needed to control corporate greed. Once regulation was removed, history repeated itself, and we found ourselves faced with market crashes again. It is important for you to understand these hidden forces so that you can make informed decisions about your investment strategy. Once you have this knowledge and awareness about the forces that may impact a potentially outdated 60/40 strategy, you may want to protect yourself by asking the right questions. You need to understand the risks of removing government regulations, so that you can act on this knowledge. How would you know which questions to ask if you are not aware of these hidden forces?

GREED AND FRAUD

In addition to the hidden forces that shape and inform the world around you, there is also a powerful narrative of greed and corruption that affects how we manage our money. The first Gilded Age, if you recall, was a time of extraordinary wealth for a very small minority who used their power and influence to control and manipulate the political system to their advantage. You've seen that without government regulations, banks engaged in speculative investment in the stock market, which led to the 1929 crash and, subsequently, the Great Depression. The Glass-Steagall Act of 1933 helped curb corporate greed and fraud, but its repeal in 1999 contributed to two massive stock market crashes.

Prior to the repeal of the Glass-Steagall Act, the idea of government deregulation had been brewing for many years. During the 1970s the United States experienced a "seemingly contradictory condition described by slow economic growth and relatively high unemployment, which is at the same time accompanied by rising prices."[33] This condition, known as *stagflation*, negatively impacted the savings-and-loan industry. In response, the Federal Reserve increased the interest rate in order to end double-digit inflation. As a result, savers started to put their money into newly created money-market funds, which offered the individual investor "a high degree of safety and a relatively low return in interest."[34] Given the fact that the savings-and-loan industry could not compete with traditional banks, savings-and-loan institutions (S&Ls)

started to lose money. By 1982 the S&Ls were losing as much as $4 billion per year.[35]

In order to ease the pressure on S&Ls, Congress passed, and President Reagan signed, the Garn–St. Germain Depository Institutions Act of 1982. This law allowed S&Ls and banks to use as much as 40% of their assets in commercial loans and 30% in consumer loans. In addition, Reagan cut the budget of the regulatory agency whose job it was to investigate bad loans. Once government regulation was relaxed or removed, it would only be a matter of time before banks and S&Ls engaged in reckless behavior. Between 1982 and 1986, California, Texas, and Florida passed laws that allowed S&Ls to invest in speculative real estate.[36]

As a result of less regulation, coupled with bad loans made by S&Ls, the Federal Savings and Loan Insurance Corporation (FSLIC) declared itself insolvent in 1987. By 1989 President George H. W. Bush had unveiled a bailout plan that provided $50 billion to close failed S&Ls in order to stop further losses. In all, more than 1,000 S&Ls failed at a cost of $160 billion, of which the industry paid only $28 billion; the rest came from taxpayers.[37]

Whenever government regulations are relaxed or removed, corporate greed seems to automatically take over and the taxpayers end up bailing out those who could not contain their inexhaustible appetite for more. Greed, however, was not the only problem during the 1980s; fraud also played a dominant role.

DECEPTIONS AND SCANDALS

Let's look at the case of Charles Keating, who ran the American Continental Corporation and the Lincoln Savings and Loan Association in the 1980s. Keating is remembered today "as the man whose financial empire cost many investors their life savings when it crumbled."[38] What Keating did epitomized the rampant corruption throughout the savings-and-loan industry. Once government regulations were relaxed in 1982, he took advantage of the opportunity to engage in reckless investments. Over the next few years his Lincoln Savings and Loan increased its assets from $1.1 billion to $5.5 billion.[39] Over the next few years, Keating's Lincoln Savings and Loan engaged in "lending and junk bond financing for speculative real estate development that suffered a loss in value due to overdevelopment and lousy business strategy."[40] By the late 1980s, the Federal Home Loan Bank Board (FHLBB) became suspicious of Keating's activities.

To avoid scrutiny, Keating gave $1.5 million to five US senators who sat on the Senate Ethics Committee. These senators included John McCain (R-Ariz.), Dennis DeConcini (D-Ariz.), John Glenn (D-Ohio), Alan Cranston (D-Calif.), and Donald Riegle (D-Mich.), who became known as the "Keating Five." In return for his "donation," Keating wanted these senators to put pressure on the FHLBB to overlook suspicious activity by the Lincoln Savings and Loan Association.[41] Keating's strategy failed, and in April 1989, the FHLBB seized Lincoln Savings and Loan. The bailout "Cost the government $3 billion and left more than 20,000 customers with junk bonds that were worthless."[42] In the early 1990s Keating was convicted in both federal and state courts. He served four and a half years in prison before the convictions were overturned in 1996. The moral of this story is that greed and corruption, when left unchecked, undermine our capitalist system.

Let me remind you that it was Milton Friedman who said that businesses have no other responsibility except for maximizing profits. In other words, if corporations follow the rules of the game, they have no social responsibility. Charles Keating is a perfect example of how corporations can use their wealth and power to rig the rules for their selfish ends. It is important to remember that these hidden forces will remain hidden unless you make the effort to become aware of them. By now you should have noticed a pattern between government regulation and corporate greed. There is an inverse relationship at work here: More regulation decreases corporate greed and vice versa. We've seen this happen in the 1920s and later in the 1980s. During the early 2000s the pattern of greed and deception would continue.

The dot-com frenzy of the early 2000s, fueled in part by the repeal of the Glass-Steagall Act in 1999, created a kind of irrational exuberance never seen before. Greed and deception became an art form as thousands of start-ups raced to join the potentially lucrative online craze. The new game was to get rich by raising public money through initial public offerings (IPOs) regardless of corporate profitability. A case in point is Priceline.com. Its founder, Jay Walker, recognized a problem with the way traditional airline seats were sold. He noticed that approximately half a million airline seats went unsold every day. Priceline entered this space by asking customers what they were willing to pay for these unused seats. This early online model of selling airline tickets worked beautifully. Consumers benefited from cheap airline tickets, and the airlines sold their excess inventory.

Jay Walker wanted to become a ubiquitous brand, just as Yahoo! had become. He would go on to spend more than $20 million on advertising. I'm sure many of you will remember the ads, which featured *Star Trek's* William Shatner. Walker's gamble of creating brand awareness worked, and by the end of 1998 Priceline was fifth in brand awareness, "behind only AOL, Yahoo, Netscape and Amazon."[43] By March 1999 Priceline went public at $16 a share. On the first day of trading, the share price went as high as $88 and finally settled at $69. One of the benefits of this IPO was that Priceline reached "a market capitalization of $9.8 billion, the largest first-day valuation of an internet company to that date."[44] The only problem with the meteoric rise of Priceline was the disconnect between image and reality.

The image that investors bought into was that Priceline could do no wrong. Many investors wanted to get in on the action. The reality, of course, was far different. Within a few months after Priceline went live, it amassed losses in excess of $140 million. Things got so bad that Priceline was losing $30 for each ticket sold. None of that mattered, of course, since the goal was to create the necessary hype so that Priceline would be positioned to make an IPO splash.

In other words, the business strategy for Priceline, as well as other start-ups in the late 1990s, was to employ "a Get Big Fast strategy to reach ubiquity and corner a particular market; a tendency to sell products at a loss in order to gain that market share; a willingness to spend lavishly on branding and advertising to raise awareness; and a sky-high market valuation that was divorced from any sort of profitability or rationality."[45] The question that we must ask is this: Why create all this hype? The simple answer is greed.

These venture capitalists, or start-ups, appeared to care less about market fundamentals. Their motto of "change the world" was designed to grab the attention of investors who were all too eager to buy shares in companies that were founded on hype and image. The purpose of all this was to create an inflated IPO in order to make millions overnight. If Priceline's strategy was based on greed and deception, then outright fraud would define what happened with Enron.

CORPORATE CRIMINALITY

In the early 2000s, Enron was the largest energy company in the world and the seventh-largest corporation in America. Founded by Kenneth Lay, Enron would be responsible for the largest accounting fraud in history. The fact it was recognized as the seventh-largest corporation in the United States was the result of Enron executives cooking the books. "Once the fraud came to light, the company unraveled, and it filed a Chapter 11 bankruptcy on Dec. 2, 2001."[46] As the revelation of such massive fraud reverberated, it accelerated the stock market crash of 2002. Enron shares, which were as high as $90.56 before the fraud was revealed, plummeted to $0.25 in the immediate sell-off.

Kenneth Lay, as well as other executives, faced 42 charges in connection with the accounting scandal. Lay was "convicted on six counts of fraud and conspiracy and four counts of bank fraud."[47] On July 5, 2006, Kenneth Lay died from a massive heart attack two months before he was sentenced. One would think the coordinated deception by Enron executives was enough to discourage others from committing fraud on a massive scale, but the magnitude of the accounting scandal by WorldCom would surpass anything that came before it.

During the late 1990s, WorldCom was the second-largest telecommunications company in the United States. It was the darling of

Wall Street and was on the verge of tremendous growth. In fact, at the height of the dot-com bubble, WorldCom had a market capitalization of $175 billion. The only problem was that WorldCom cooked its books. To hide its losses, "WorldCom inflated net income and cash flow by recording expenses as investments. By capitalizing expenses, it exaggerated profits by around $3 billion in 2001 and $797 million in Q1 2002, reporting a profit of $1.4 billion instead of a net loss."[48] WorldCom's cofounder and CEO, Bernard Ebbers, was found guilty and sentenced to 25 years in prison.

WorldCom's scandal was the largest accounting scandal in American history, surpassed only by the Bernie Madoff investment scandal. The moral lesson here is that when capitalism becomes broken, it creates an environment where greed and deception flourish. It is why you as an investor should always be aware of the historic, economic, and financial forces that not only shape the world around you but also impact your bottom line. You see, the hidden forces that impact your investment portfolio may at first seem disconnected and divorced from your immediate financial reality, but when you dig deeper, you start to realize that you need protection. Following the massive investment and accounting scandals of the early 2000s, one would think that both the corporate world and the government had learned the lessons of greed and fraud, but they didn't.

Following the repeal of the Glass-Steagall Act in 1999, Congress passed the new Commodity Futures Modernization Act in 2000. An important part of this bill prohibited the regulation of derivatives, "which allowed finance gurus to leverage and speculate with other people's money. By using derivatives, credit default swaps and other unregulated financial instruments, the big banks were able to chop up and resell loans and mortgages as repackaged securities or derivatives."[49] Throughout the 2000s a real estate bubble formed, as banks were only too eager to offer subprime loans to people they knew couldn't afford them.

THE HOUSING BUBBLE

While many of us understand that subprime loans played a central role in the housing bubble, there were other important factors as well. In addition to subprime loans, many banks and lending institutions offered what are known as low-doc loans, which in many cases required little to no verification of income. This would prove disastrous for some people who later wanted to refinance high-interest loans. As lenders tightened their requirements, borrowers were stuck with loans they no longer could afford, thus contributing to massive foreclosures. Lenders took advantage of people by offering them questionable loans. In fact, lenders likely knew that some of these subprime loans would default, but they didn't care. These loans were packaged, insured, and sold on the market.

Along with low-doc loans there were adjustable-rate mortgages (ARMs), which many subprime borrowers were eager to take advantage of, "these interest-only loans. As a result, the percentage of subprime mortgages more than doubled from 6% to 14% of all mortgages between 2001 and 2007."[50] When these mortgage rates adjusted, many people found themselves trapped with loans they no longer could afford. Finally, one of the most glaring problems of the real estate collapse was that some home owners seemed to use the equity in their homes as their personal ATM. Baby boomers used their equity to remodel their homes, buy cars, take luxury vacations, or even purchase second homes. As the real estate bubble started to burst in 2007, market prices plummeted. This created a condition where home owners owed more on their home than that home was actually worth. Once again, foreclosure rates went through the roof, as home owners were unable to pay their mortgages when interest rates adjusted upward.

By 2008 the global financial system was experiencing a catastrophic meltdown. This was triggered when Lehman Brothers filed for bankruptcy in September 2008. The numbers were staggering: "With $639 billion in assets and $619 billion in debt, Lehman's bankruptcy filing was the largest in history, as its assets far surpassed those of previous bankrupt giants such as WorldCom and Enron. Lehman was the fourth-largest U.S. investment bank at the time, with 25,000 employees worldwide."[51] What followed was the greatest economic disaster since the Great Depression.

The stock market collapsed, wiping out almost $8 trillion in value between 2007 and 2009. Unemployment climbed to 10% in October 2009, and Americans lost $9.8 trillion in wealth as a result of plummeting home values. In addition, many Americans saw their retirement accounts vaporized.[52] There are lessons here, but only if you change your mindset and realize that these hidden forces impact your investment decisions. The reason history is important is that it has a stubborn habit of repeating itself.

THE GILDED AGE 2.0

Many economists and historians identify the digital revolution of today as the Gilded Age 2.0. The parallels between the Gilded Age and today are both striking and disturbing. Both periods experienced unprecedented technological change. The telephone today is being replaced with the smartphone. The phonograph is now digital music apps, through which we can hear music whenever and wherever we want. Newspapers and books have been replaced with instantaneous access to information in our pockets or on our wrists. The internal combustion engine is disappearing in favor of clean electric vehicles. The Vanderbilts, Morgans, Rockefellers, and Carnegies of the past are today represented by Jeff Bezos, Steve Jobs, Mark Zuckerberg, Elon Musk, and Bill Gates, to name a few.

Our new Gilded Age is beautiful to look at on the outside, but if we inspect more carefully, we will find massive inequity between those who are on the forefront of the digital revolution and everyone else. In terms of the trappings of wealth and the ostentatious display of material excess, the wealthy elites of today are the mirror image of those of a time long past, yet they are ineluctably connected to the failure of capitalism.

Although historians may look back to the second Gilded Age as beginning around 1990, nothing epitomizes the unabashed projection of wealth and corruption as the current political and economic climate. *USA Today* characterized the 2016 election of Donald Trump as personifying "the second Gilded Age as much as robber baron industrialists and financiers did the first."[53] Boston College historian Patrick Maney declared, "It's as if J. P. Morgan had been elected president. Donald Trump puts an exclamation point on this Gilded Age."[54] To further illustrate some of the similarities between the two historical periods, consider this: In 1894 unemployed workers, known as Coxey's Army (named after Jacob Coxey, a politician from Massillon,

Ohio), marched to Washington, DC, to demand that Congress allocate funds to create jobs for the unemployed. In 2011 the Occupy Wall Street movement marched in New York's financial district to protest the preferential treatment of the top 1% in the nation. In both cases, the protestors failed to achieve their objectives.

During the Gilded Age, wealthy industrialists, such as John D. Rockefeller and his Standard Oil Company, dominated entire industries. Today "almost half of U.S. industries are dominated by the four largest companies" and "Google . . . accounts for 87% of all internet searches."[55] The men who dominate the second Gilded Age did not make themselves out of thin air; rather, they had the example of history shaping and informing beliefs about manifest destiny. They believed in their own capacity to reshape the world, to bend history toward their will. They believed in punctuated historical moments. In other words, they believed their actions in the world would help humanity take leaps forward. The only problem is that when you combine money and power, you inevitably produce greed and corruption, with the inescapable outcome of marginalizing both the middle class and the working class.

The parallels between today's wealthy elites and those of the Gilded Age are uncanny. In fact, I believe the power elites of today are tone deaf when it comes to the other 99% of the population. These individuals live in a separate world removed from the rest of us. Once Donald Trump took office in January 2017, the ostentatious projection of wealth and greed became the new normal. Shortly after the new GOP tax bill was signed into law, Trump went to his members-only Mar-a-Lago resort, otherwise known as the "Winter White House," where he reportedly told his guests, "You all just got a lot richer."[56] This attitude is not simply political rhetoric; rather, it epitomizes a culture where the wealthy elites control and perpetuate their generational wealth. For example, at a rally in Iowa in June 2017, Trump responded to criticism over his choices for top economic jobs in his administration. He offered billionaire investor Wilbur Ross the Commerce Secretary position, and former Goldman Sachs president Gary Cohn became his chief economic advisor. Trump told the assembled audience, "I love all people, rich or poor. But in those particular positions, I just don't want a poor person."[57] Trump is not alone here. In fact, both Democratic and Republican administrations have generally overlooked the poor.

LATE CAPITALISM

Late capitalism explores how the wealthiest 1% today have essentially "rigged" the system in order to perpetuate the closed loop of concentrated wealth. The process of rigging the system enabled powerful corporations to hire "well-paid lobbyists to influence politicians. They won Supreme Court cases that gave corporations the same rights as people. This allowed them to spend untold millions on political ads that benefit them."[58] In order to determine if we are today experiencing late capitalism, we must first assess if we have capitalism at all. Let's remember that capitalism demands a free-market economy where goods and services are distributed according to the fundamental laws of supply and demand. The law of demand dictates that when demand for a product or service increases, the price will rise. As supply increases, the price will come down, thus ensuring a competitive marketplace. The problem with capitalism today is that monopolies are undermining the free-market system.

Part of the problem of late capitalism is that people are no longer willing to accept massive inequality. Consider that "a decade ago, 80 percent of Americans believed that a free market economy was the best economic system. Today, that number is 60 percent. Another recent poll shows that only 42 percent of millennials support capitalism."[59] The problem with late capitalism, as it is constituted today, is its inability to accommodate the majority of the American people. Ever-growing income disparity coupled with wage stagnation has effectively created two separate and removed realities—one for the wealthy few and another for everyone else. It is not that people are rejecting capitalism as an ideal; rather, people are now recognizing the moral bankruptcy of a system that has systematically ignored them.

It is when capitalism breaks down that we realize its glaring short-comings. People will need to wake up to the reality that capitalism may not be able to save them during their retirement years. According to the Nobel Prize–winning economist Edmund Phelps, director of the Columbia University Center on Capitalism and Society, the wave of retirement over the next 10 years will see more people "drawing on retirement and medical benefits. More than that, they will be withdrawing their labour services from the economy, and they're not being replaced by a new-wave of young people coming up. Capital is going to find itself with less labour to work with so I'm afraid business investment activity is going to be weak ten years from now—and is weak already in anticipation of that. The decade beginning around 2020 will not be a good time for capitalism."[60] The more knowledge you gain, the more you realize the urgency of preparing for retirement.

These hidden forces you read about matter. They matter because you can do something about them. You can begin by changing your mindset about the importance of investing for your retirement future. Changing your mindset may lead you to change your behavior, which will lead you to ask the relevant questions regarding the appropriate investment strategy for your unique situation. The world today is radically different from 20 years ago. We live in a world where the burden is on you, and your trusted advisor, to plan and prepare for your retirement.

I believe that no one stands to lose more from our broken capitalist system then millennials. I wrote this book in part to inspire them to take charge of their own financial future. Millennials, and other generational groups, inherited a world filled with greed, fraud, and massive inequality. Buying a home and benefiting from the American Dream is more remote and distant than ever before. The good news is that millennials have time to plan and prepare for their retirement. Millennials may not have their mindset fixed like older Americans, which can help them form positive and actionable habits today. It will be up to millennials to address the systemic problems of our broken capitalist system and reclaim the American Dream.

RECLAIMING THE AMERICAN DREAM

Our cultural understanding of the American Dream has always been defined in relation to happiness. It began as the "dream of opportunity to the acquisition of material things,"[61] but by the 1920s the pursuit of happiness was driven by greed and the single-minded purpose of acquiring wealth. The stock market crash of 1929 would put an end to greedy investors who were ruined by staggering losses. The pendulum eventually swung back, and by the 1940s President Roosevelt "defined the pursuit of happiness as decent housing, a good job, education, and health care."[62] President Truman then expanded the American Dream to include entitlements. The Fair Deal program was premised on the idea that if you worked hard and played by the rules, the government should provide you with "financial security, education, health care, and a home."[63]

Prior to COVID-19 the economy appeared, on the surface, to be in good shape. All of the financial indicators showed that we were in a sustained bullish trend. We had low unemployment, a bullish stock market outlook, and steady job growth. However, corporations, governments, and individuals could no longer fulfill their financial obligations. Baby boomers have both contributed to, and are beneficiaries of, the global market meltdown of a decade ago. Millennials, and other generational groups, who inherited the financial mess of their parents, are burdened by student debt and wary of the downside of home ownership, and their spending habits do not perpetuate the consumer economy of past generations. Financial indicators show only part of the picture, and that part is largely concentrated at the top of society's financial pyramid. Capitalism no longer works for the average American; I believe it is a broken system.

Irish playwright George Bernard Shaw said, "Capitalism has destroyed our belief in any effective power but that of self-interest backed by force."[64] The benefits of capitalism are numerous. Capitalism affords us economic freedom, consumer choice, upward mobility, efficiency, and innovation. But when capitalism is broken, it becomes an unjust and unfair system. When capitalism is broken, it tends to favor the elite few who have monopolized its benefits at the expense of everyone else. When capitalism is broken, our democracy suffers, as the powerful few both dictate and rationalize the massive inequality that we see all around us. When capitalism is broken, the American Dream becomes an exclusive club for the wealthy few.

More than at any other time in history, I believe that the American Dream is in jeopardy. The American Dream gave hope to millions of people who wanted the opportunity to make something of themselves, regardless of their background or the class they were born into. But a select few managed to figure out a way to manipulate the rules in such a way as to favor themselves at the expense of countless millions. Reclaiming the American Dream requires the extraordinary task of bridging the gap between rich and poor. One step toward this goal is for people to have an awakening about the financial world around them. The more we understand how the financial world operates, the less tolerant we will be of its excesses. Individual investors who want to protect their hard-earned money and have something for retirement have choices today. Knowledge, coupled with an ethical framework to help us navigate the constantly evolving complexity of the economic world, can serve as a counterweight to the injustice we see all around us.

Chapter 2

WHY THE 60/40 PORTFOLIO IS POTENTIALLY OUTDATED

"Diversifying sufficiently among uncorrelated risks can reduce
portfolio risk toward zero. But financial engineers should know that's
not true of a portfolio of correlated risks."

–HARRY MARKOWITZ

At its most basic level, investing is all about balancing *risk* and *reward*.
For any investment you make, there's a certain level of associated risk:
You might lose part or all of your investment, or you might gain a
return—a profit. The goal of most investment strategies is to increase
that return, your reward, while minimizing your risk. However, risk
and reward typically move together. They *correlate*: The higher the risk,
the higher the reward. A more accurate statement would be "the
higher the risk, the higher the potential return, and the less likely it
will achieve the higher return."[1] To better understand this correlation,

you need to know your risk tolerance and be able to gauge the level of risk of a particular investment. When you invest your money, you run the possibility of experiencing any or all of the following:

- **Losing your principal**: Individual stocks or high-yield bonds, as well as any other market-based investment, could cause you to lose everything.

- **Not keeping pace with inflation**: Your investment could rise in value slower than prices. This is more likely to happen if you invest in cash equivalents, like treasury or municipal bonds.

- **Coming up short**: The chance that your investments don't earn enough to cover your retirement needs.

- **Paying high fees or other costs**: Expensive fees on mutual funds can make it tough to make a good return. Be aware of actively managed mutual funds or ones with excessive sales loads.[2]

As in gambling, if you bet on long odds, you're more likely to lose your bet, but if you win, your winnings will be more substantial than those on a safe bet. But it's rarely that simple. In order to balance risk and reward, rather than putting all their money into a single investment, investors create a *portfolio*, which is a group of investments that work together. The purpose of a portfolio is to spread out both the risk and the reward over multiple investments in an attempt to minimize the risk while maximizing the reward. A portfolio ideally maximizes your return for part of your money, which usually entails some level of risk, while also safeguarding your capital by putting the rest in a less risky place.

This also brings up *diversification*, which means just what it sounds like: You make the investments in your portfolio more diverse in order to better spread out your risk. So you wouldn't put all your money in pork bellies or Apple stock; you would invest in different kinds of things, which makes each individual risk less important to how well you do overall. And although diversification can't guarantee a profit or ensure you won't lose money, it can help smooth out market volatility within your portfolio.

I hope you're not feeling patronized at this point; that's not my intention at all. Statistically, you are—or a reader near you is—undereducated about finances and investing. You shouldn't feel bad about lacking that information if you do; you're doing something about it already: You've made a choice to remedy your lack of financial literacy by picking up this book. If you already know everything in those deceptively dense first paragraphs, you're ahead of the game. If that's the case, please bear with me as we cover a few more key terms before diving in fully.

To keep it fairly simple, let's look at two types of investments—*bonds* and *stocks*. These are the two most common *asset classes*.[3] Assets are the things you own, and in investing that means the things your investment pays for. For example, bonds are a way of lending money to the government. You buy a bond for a certain amount, and the government pays you interest at a certain percentage on that amount over a certain period of time. Because bonds are guaranteed by the government, they offer generally low risk, but they also offer relatively low returns. There are also corporate bonds, which are debt securities issued by corporations for the purpose of raising capital. An investor who purchases corporate bonds is effectively lending money to a company in return for a series of interest payments. Corporate bonds tend to offer higher interest rates than US government bonds, given their higher risk level. Corporate bonds are actively traded on the secondary market.[4]

Whenever you hear *the market*, we're usually talking about the stock market, where your investment pays for a small piece of a business. When you buy stock—or *equity*—in a company, you become part owner of that company, along with all the other stockholders, and you realize your returns when you sell your stock to someone else; if the company does well and its stocks increase in value, your stock value increases. On the reverse, if the company doesn't do well, you may end up losing money. Stocks are riskier than bonds but potentially also yield higher returns.

MODERN PORTFOLIO THEORY

Of course, reality is more complicated than the description above. In order to turn simple concepts into useful investing strategies, investors often turn to theories and models, which are mathematical attempts to describe and predict how investments will behave. This usually applies to the stock market, but theories also address bonds and other asset classes.

In 1952, Nobel-winning economist Harry Markowitz hypothesized that, given a certain level of market risk, it is possible to construct a portfolio that maximizes your expected return.[5] What made this modern portfolio theory attractive and a bedrock of modern economics is the level of mathematical rigor devoted to proving Markowitz's hypothesis. The idea was that if the math was sufficiently rigorous, it could predict the rise and fall of the market, giving an advantage to investors who follow the theory.

Americans embraced the wisdom behind modern portfolio theory, and over the years financial advisors have focused on the binary interactions between diversification and risk. Properly constructed, a diversified portfolio can help minimize risk, and this direct relationship is something people generally understand: If you want the potential for greater rewards, you must accept greater risk. Think of risk, diversification, and correlation as the moving parts of an investment strategy: Increasing diversification helps you reduce risk while maximizing rewards, but only if the assets correlate in a predictable way.

THE 60/40 ALLOCATION STRATEGY

Because stocks and bonds *did* move together (but in opposite directions) for a long while, the traditional approach to diversification defined an allotment of 60% of assets to stocks and 40% to bonds. This 60/40 mix should, theoretically, balance your portfolio both when the stock market is performing well (stocks are high) and when it drops (stocks are low), such as during a recession. It was designed to minimize risk by placing a portion of your money in "safe" government bonds while generating a higher return from the other portion, in the riskier stock market; ideally, the combination would result in a consistent rate of return over time, even during periods of market volatility.[6]

On the face of it, the 60/40 portfolio looks quite promising. And the approach worked well for a while. But when the COVID-19 pandemic jolted financial markets in March 2020, "the balanced [60/40] fund dropped more than 20% from its peak in February [2020]."[7] If history is any guide, we could very well experience other collapses, which raises the question: Can you trust the 60/40 portfolio to protect you? Consider that since 1900 we've had seven decades where "the annual real [after inflation] return was less than 1%."[8] That's not enough for the typical investor to retire on.

With that range of results, you might be wondering why the 60/40 portfolio is so popular. Part of the answer is marketing. Many on Wall Street use "a well-crafted marketing pitch [to sell] this over-simplified, excessively aggressive strategy."[9] There are those who might argue that the 60/40 portfolio is likely to repeat some of its strong performance in the past. The only problem is that this is not a likely scenario: "Bond rates are too low, and stocks are near all-time highs. This is a toxic combination not seen since the 1970s, way before 60/40 was a way for investment firms to build scale in their businesses by herding people into a unified asset allocation."[10]

Another part of what makes the 60/40 allocation appealing is its simplicity. There isn't much to think about. According to David Koch, senior wealth advisor at Halbert Hargrove, the simplicity of this binary portfolio is "Set it, forget it, and rebalance annually."[11] But a limited asset allocation strategy like 60/40 fails to consider the modern financial landscape of today's investor:

- Increased longevity shifts the focus to growth.

- Diversification potential is limited.

- The market is evolving.

- Investors' needs aren't static.

The 60/40 allocation model is also easy to deal with in retirement—at least in theory. William Bengen, a financial planner from California, created a straightforward guideline for retirement withdrawals in the 1990s. This simple rule governs withdrawals from your portfolio. The rule simply states that you can withdraw 4% of your portfolio each year in retirement. The rule allows retirees to "increase the rate to keep pace with inflation."[12]

Research conducted by Wade Pfau of the Retirement Researcher suggests that you may only be able to withdraw 2.9% (adjusted annually for inflation) from a portfolio that is 50% stocks and 50% bonds.[13] Although this is based on a 50/50 stock/bond portfolio, 2.9% may not give you the protection or income to sustain the stable retirement you need. In addition, financial markets are far more volatile than ever before. International trade, globalization, and the instantaneous speed of communication have converged to create rapid change. The 4% rule was also developed when we assumed a retirement length of less than 30 years, which now may not be a reasonable assumption, and when interest rates were much higher.

CORRELATION RISK

Correlation risk has often been taken for granted. Stocks and bonds are assumed to be inversely correlated assets, which means they are expected to move together—at the same time but in opposite directions—in response to economic cycles. Until recently, this statement was strongly predictive: When stocks rose in value, bonds languished. Conversely, when economic conditions drove stock values down, the value of bonds predictably rose.

This inverse correlation model was bound by certain assumptions, which may no longer hold true. Since 2008 the correlation between stocks and bonds—if it still exists at all—is no longer predictive and no longer meaningfully inverse. This movement away from an inverse correlation negates the very reason we entrusted our diversification strategy.[14]

VOLATILITY RISK

Volatility is the tendency for the market to fluctuate. It is important to remember that the purpose of the 60/40 strategy—60% stocks to 40% bonds—was to produce "stable growth, with bonds 'cushioning' the risks of the volatility in the stock market."[15] But the stock market tends to fluctuate much more rapidly and widely than the bond market does.[16] In other words, on one side of the investment equation, you have stocks, which are susceptible to volatility and unpredictable market corrections. On the other side of the equation are bonds, which are designed to cushion the risks of volatility but are experiencing artificially low interest rates. What happens if the volatility of stocks is too high to be offset by these potentially weak performing bonds? When you factor in inflation—where the price of everything goes up but those interest rates stay right where they are—then the problems of the 60/40 model become even clearer.

One way to think of stock market volatility is in terms of market corrections. A *market correction* is traditionally thought of as a decline of at least 10% from a recent peak, with a bear market representing a minimum 20% pullback from a high.[17] Consider that over the past 50 years, there have been 29 market corrections (a decline of 10% or higher). Of these 29 corrections, six of them were declines greater than 25%.[18] If you apply simple math, it would suggest that the stock market experiences a market correction once every two years, on average (although averages are just that—an average, and not exact). Prior to COVID-19 the most recent major market correction was from 2007 to 2009, where the market declined 57%. The following table shows the number of market corrections since 1968, the percentage decline, and the number of days the market declined.

Volatility has increased over time. According to a study by Kenneth Washer, Randy Jorgensen, and Robert Johnson, volatility, when measured on a daily basis, has more than doubled. To make matters worse, according to Christopher Hyzy, chief investment officer for Bank of America, "we're looking at continued high volatility all the way in to the next election [2020]."[19] How should you deal with heightened volatility? Omar Aguilar, chief investment officer for US equities at Charles Schwab Investment Management, says, "A diversified portfolio of assets is the best long-term strategy."[20] This is why I developed my multi-asset REALM model designed to help protect you against heightened market volatility.

Given such frequent market corrections, I don't believe that a stagnant bond market offers enough protection to offset your losses. For example, "during the financial crisis of 2008, stocks lost 37% of their value while bonds gained about 5%. So if you had a mix of 60% stocks and 40% bonds, on average, you would have seen the value of your portfolio drop about 20%."[22] Again, the 60/40 model is potentially ineffective in the face of stock market volatility and low bond yields. If we factor in inflation, then the return on investment from our 60/40 model can potentially become zero: If your portfolio rises by 5% but inflation is also at 5%, you essentially earn nothing. Worse, you'll be taxed as if you earned that 5%.[23] Again, the 60/40 portfolio strategy is vulnerable to something as basic as inflation.[24]

Date	% Decline	Duration of Correction in Days
1968-70	36%	543
1971	11%	103
1971	11%	76
1973-74	48%	630
1974	14%	29
1975	14%	63
1976-78	19%	531
1978	14%	63
1979	10%	33
1980	17%	43
1980-82	27%	622
1983-84	14%	288
1987	34%	101
1990	10%	28
1990	20%	87
1997	10%	52
1997	11%	20
1998	19%	45
1999	12%	91
2000-02	49%	929
2002-03	15%	104
2007-09	57%	517
2010	16%	70
2011	19%	157
2011	10%	28
2012	10%	60
2015	12%	96
2015-16	13%	100
2018	10%	13

Data source: Yardeni Research. [21]

In addition, financial markets are far more volatile than ever before. International trade, globalization, and the instantaneous speed of communication have converged to create rapid change. According to Bloomberg,[25] volatility isn't what it used to be. Volatility introduces disruption to the market, which can "affect confidence, causing companies to delay expansion or other plans and for consumers to cut back on spending."[26] In addition, according to Lara Rhame, chief US economist at Franklin Square Investments, you "should plan for volatility and focus on building well-diversified portfolios designed to withstand the inevitable return to a higher-volatility world."[27] With financial markets experiencing more frequent and sharper moves up and down, it is impossible for investors to count on reliable, consistent returns. Keep in mind that any strategy can be undermined at any point in time by a burst of volatility. I don't believe that diversification and correlation no longer offer a reliable balance.

THE 60/40 MODEL IS POTENTIALLY BROKEN

The 60/40 portfolio approach leaves 60% of your investments at risk due to volatility—the fluctuations of the market. At any moment, the market could decrease or even crash, and you could potentially lose part of, or your entire, stock investment. On the other hand, if the market surges, you stand to make a windfall profit. That's the point of the 60/40 approach. The 60% in stocks moves in jumps and spurts to hopefully earn you a positive return over a long period. The other 40%, which you've socked away in bonds, is meant to provide protection for your investment by balancing the stock market's constant volatility with bonds' hypothetically conservative returns for lower risk.

But what if stocks and bonds both have a bad year?[28] The days when bonds can offer you absolute protection against the volatile stock market are long gone. "In the past, investors were able to rely on income provided by their bond investments to support their portfolios during periods of market stress. Unfortunately, today's low-yield environment means the diversification benefit from bonds will not be as large as in the past."[29] Bonds can also be risky when you factor in inflation. If the cost of living and inflation increase, you may actually earn a negative rate of return. When it comes to corporate bonds, you must understand that such bonds "aren't guaranteed by the full faith and credit of the US government but, instead, depend on the corporation's ability to repay that debt."[30] As you can see, the 60/40 portfolio may no longer be relevant in today's economic climate.

The 60/40 model has been losing traction over the past several years, both in its ability to safeguard a financially sound retirement and—thankfully—in its use by financial advisors. According to Clifford Stanton, CFP, the preponderant opinion of financial experts is that the 60/40 model is broken.[30] Some of the underlying reasons include the lower yields on bonds, market volatility, and the global economy. This is not what the average investor has envisioned for retirement, particularly when we are living longer today than ever before.

One of the criticisms of modern portfolio theory, in general, is that the investment decisions made based on it would work for a static market, but the real-world stock market is constantly in flux, and the theory fails to adapt to those changes.[31] Modern portfolio theory is too inflexible to adapt to the ever-changing market landscape of today's complex world. Add to that the inconsistently correlated risk of having 60% in stocks and 40% in bonds, and this binary model of investing has potentially created a false sense of reality. In fact, since 1938, this type of portfolio "actually went backwards in relation to inflation."[32] A key problem with the 60/40 asset allocation has always been the lack of diversification; it offers only two kinds of assets.

I'm not the only one, of course, who believes the 60/40 allocation is potentially outdated and ineffective. Consider that "no less than three major firms have issued reports in the last few weeks [November 2019] declaring it dead or ailing: Bank of America Merrill Lynch, Morgan Stanley, and JP Morgan."[33] The primary reason for the need to replace the 60/40 strategy is lower returns from bonds. In other words, "bonds not only deliver less yield in developed markets than they have historically—including negative yields in many European countries—but they also have less potential for capital gains because rates are already so low. The 10-year US Treasury note is currently [November 2019] yielding 1.94%; the 10-year German bond, −.25%."[34] This belief that the 60/40 strategy is "dead" is widely shared by financial advisors.

Suze Orman, who is the founder of the Suze Orman Financial Group and author of several best-selling books, has declared, "60-40 is dead."[35] According to Orman, "bonds will probably keep going down."[36] It is important to remember that Bank of America, Morgan Stanley, JP Morgan, Orman, and others made these statements prior to the COVID-19 pandemic. The current (as of May 13, 2020) 10-year Treasury note is 0.648%, which offers little to no protection to the stock side of your 60/40 portfolio.[37] It is important now, more than ever before, to reevaluate your portfolio, as we are living through a time of heightened volatility.

A final problem with the 60/40 model, a problem that too often creates that false sense of reality, is that, prior to COVID-19, the stock market, if we use the Dow Jones Industrial Average as an index, was "up over 300%"[38] from March 2009 to January 2018. These gains have masked an underlying problem of the 60/40 model, where returns were only 4% to 5% over the past 17 years.[39] As a result, many investors have started to feel a sense of frustration and anxiety about an uncertain future. Some are realizing they may have not planned properly, which, of course, means they may not have enough money for retirement. If you invest in a 60/40 strategy, you potentially expose yourself to higher risk due to the nature of the correlation between stocks and bonds.

Modern portfolio theory may no longer be relevant in today's complex, globally interconnected world. The solution is a paradigm shift in terms of how diversification, coupled with strategic asset allocation, may minimize volatility while potentially providing you with the best possible retirement outcome. Relentless volatility also confuses investors and forces them to react emotionally, which clouds perspective and judgment. It is time for a new strategy that offers investors a wide array of investing possibilities.

THE FEDERAL RESERVE AND INTEREST RATES

One of the ways the government can affect investing is by the Federal Reserve's raising or lowering the national interest rate, which is the rate at which banks lend money. When interest rates are low, people tend to borrow more and buy more things, which increases spending, thus increasing GDP. This works for stocks, too: People borrow to buy more stocks, although this process has the potential to lead to stock bubbles, which eventually burst.

When interest rates drop, that's a signal that the Federal Reserve wants to stimulate spending, to raise the GDP. The end result is that the stock market typically goes up. However, when interest rates go down, bond prices go up; lower interest rates make bonds pay out less. If you buy a $500 bond at 1%, you will make less over the same amount of time as a $500 bond at 4%, so the investment costs more in lost returns.

This lost money can make other investments more attractive; even if investments initially cost more, if their returns are higher, they may negate that extra cost. If stocks are more attractive, more people want to buy them, which pushes their cost up. This can cause stocks and bonds to move in the same direction—the prices of stocks and bonds both increase or decrease, instead of one rising as the other falls. When stocks and bonds move in the same direction, you have little to no protection when the market declines sharply or even crashes, as we've seen over the last 40 years; it is a possible sign of trouble on the horizon.

There are three key factors that may cause stocks and bonds to trend together. These factors include political, social, and economic forces, which may converge to create more risk and less return for the average investor. The political factors occur when the government intervenes in the market by artificially keeping interest rates low in order to boost the economy. This creates a social dimension of concern and uncertainty, particularly among millennials, who now represent the largest demographic. In my experience, many millennials don't care for high-risk investments, which can cause downward pressure on both stocks and bonds, strengthening their correlation—but in the wrong direction. The economic consequence can be increased global debt, slower growth, falling productivity, and inflation, which further affect stocks and bonds, creating a dangerous cycle.

According to Katina Stefanova, CEO of Marto Capital, we need the "right balance between government intervention [meaning interest rates] and a free market."[40] It is the absence of this balance that is causing a cascading effect on the political, social, and economic forces, creating an unnecessary sense of uncertainty among investors. In other words, investors continue to buy stocks for growth and bonds to protect against risk, assuming the 60/40 model works, but for many, the protection is now only wishful thinking. We've created a self-perpetuating false sense of reality.

In addition, government control of interest rates has skewed returns for government bonds, as well as most types of debt. The end result is that, for the past 10 years, the 10-year Treasury bonds are yielding 2% to 3%.[41] If you compare that to the historical level of 4.6%, bond yields are quite disappointing. It is clear that bonds are not delivering the same returns today as they did for your parents and grandparents. What we are experiencing today is a disappointing mix of an overvalued stock market coupled with record-low bond yields.

You might be asking yourself, if bond values are held low while stocks are high, isn't that an inverse correlation? It's a good question, but no. The point is that if bond values aren't moving, they're not correlated at all with the stock market, and nowadays, when they do move, they tend to *directly* correlate with stocks (to move up together or down together). Both of these situations reduce the capability of bonds to protect against fluctuations in the stock market.

Today's low interest rates contribute to "ultralow yields on safe bonds."[42] Consider that in 2018 "the 10-year Treasury yield was at 3.25%, the highest since 2011 . . . Many, including Jeffrey Gundlach, Wall Street's so-called bond king, predicted a 4% 10-year Treasury yield. Instead, the 10-year Treasury yield [dropped] as low as 1.45%."[43] Low bond yields will not offer you any protection against the volatility of stocks. To exacerbate matters, as of the writing of this book, the global bond market is now offering negative interest rates. For example, in July 2019, Swiss two-year bonds yielded negative 0.91%, which were "close to their all-time lows below negative 1.0% [back in 2015]."[44] Negative interest rates are spreading, and as a result of the interconnected nature of global markets, the yields on 10-year US Treasury notes could go lower as investors flood the US bond market.

Consider for a moment that "some $13 trillion in bonds are paying negative interest rates, which means bondholders actually pay for the privilege of holding an issuer's bonds. That represents more than 20% of a total global bond market value of $55 trillion, according to Bloomberg. Other bonds are paying positive rates so low they carry a real (after-inflation) negative yield."[45] The impact of all this is that investors, particularly retirees, are finding it much more difficult to find low-risk vehicles that pay decent returns. In fact, the possibility of saving cash, which for a long time was the most secure investment option, might become risky. The important point here is that there are economic consequences that directly impact your investment future. Think of it this way: These hidden forces work behind the scenes to either positively or negatively impact your investment strategy. Let's look at an example of how keeping interest rates low may favor the wealthy few.

Keeping interest rates artificially low, which is commonly referred to as monetary easing, promotes economic growth by boosting stock prices. When stock prices go up, the wealthy benefit, as they own more stocks than the poor, which further widens the disparity of wealth. In fact, according to former Federal Reserve chairman and current distinguished fellow at the Brookings Institution Ben Bernanke, "the claim that Fed Policy has worsened inequality usually begins with the (correct) observation that monetary easing works in part by raising asset prices, like stock prices. As the rich own more assets than the poor and middle class, the reasoning goes, the Fed's policies are increasing the already large disparities of wealth in the United States."[46] What Bernanke is saying is significant in that inequality and lack of social mobility are often considered "issues of first order significance for economic policy in general."[47] Now, while inequality is considered a long-term systemic problem that is the result of structural changes, such as technological change, globalization, and so on, monetary easing does contribute to the problem.

Let's look at the conditions that led to the global financial crisis in 2008 and the role of the Federal Reserve in addressing this crisis. Throughout the early 2000s "Americans brought home ceaseless volumes of iPods and cashmere sweaters, never mind their declining incomes and dwindling savings. Banks lent staggering sums of money to home owners with dubious credit, convinced that real estate prices could only go up. Government spent as it saw fit, secure that foreigners could always be counted on to finance American debt."[48] In response to the looming financial crisis of 2008, "many economists have concluded that the appropriate medicine is a fresh dose of the very course that delivered the disarray: Spend without limit. Print money today, fret about the consequences tomorrow."[49] In other words, the answer to the global financial meltdown was to simply spend more money. In 2008 the Federal Reserve, which has the authority to "print dollars from thin air . . . expanded its balance sheet from about $900 billion to more than $2.2 trillion, creating $1.3 trillion that did not exist to replace some of the trillions wiped out by falling house prices and vengeful stock markets."[50] To exacerbate matters, many of the banks whose reckless behavior contributed to the financial crisis of 2008 were rewarded with trillions of dollars in bailout money.

The more you understand how the Federal Reserve works, the better questions you will ask regarding your investment portfolio. Whenever the Federal Reserve "sets the target for the federal funds rate—the rate at which banks borrow from and lend to each other overnight—it has a ripple effect across the entire U.S. economy. This also includes the U.S. stock market . . . Understanding the relationship between interest rates and the stock market can help investors understand how changes may affect their investments, and how to make better financial decisions."[51] Again, the hidden forces that you may not have thought much about have an impact on your money. Interest rates also have an effect on bond prices and return on CDs, Treasury bonds, and Treasury bills. For example, when the Federal Reserve raises the federal funds rate, Treasury bills and bonds are seen as a "safe" investment. A decrease in the federal funds rate means bond yields will be less.

THE FEDERAL RESERVE AND CORPORATE BUYBACKS

As you've already read, the Federal Reserve has extraordinary power to influence the economy. The Federal Reserve can impact inflation, employment, and economic production by indirectly setting monetary policy. It can affect the money supply by setting the federal funds rate. If this is not enough power, the Federal Reserve can also offer its own stimulus program, independent of Congress, which includes direct cash aid to corporations.

In response to the COVID-19 pandemic, the Federal Reserve has approved a program to "provide hundreds of billions in emergency aid to large American corporations without requiring them to save jobs or limit payments to executives and shareholders. Under the program, the central bank will buy $500 billion in bonds issued by large companies."[52] Now, on the surface, one might argue that the pandemic has created an extraordinary situation, particularly affecting the airline industry. However, if you dig deeper, you will find that many corporations have created the mess they find themselves in today. One such company is Boeing.

In 2017 Boeing secured $23.4 billion in military contracts— that's taxpayer money. Additional contracts from both foreign and domestic airlines brought the company's total revenue to $100 billion.[53] In April 2020 Boeing announced a $641 million loss in the first quarter of 2020. In addition, it has "burned through $4.3 billion in cash. Revenues dropped 26 percent from the first quarter of last year, to just shy of $17 billion. It will cut payroll 10 percent, through 'voluntary measures' and layoffs in its 160,000-person workforce."[54] As a result of these unprecedented circumstances, Boeing is seeking $60 billion in relief.

Boeing would not need "anywhere as big a bailout as it's likely to get if it hadn't spent almost $60 billion . . . for dividends and stock buybacks from 2014 to 2019."[55] Here is the problem of corporate buybacks: It contributes to social inequality. The practice of "Increasing cash dividend and buying back stock in the open market are classic ways of 'returning money to shareholders,' as Wall Street calls it, and putting upward pressure on share prices . . . keeps not only shareholders happy but often helps enhance top executives' personal wealth and compensation."[56] Now that Boeing and other large corporations find themselves strapped for cash, the Federal Reserve is ready to step in.

Congress is finally waking up to this practice of buybacks by adding conditions to their stimulus package to help businesses during the pandemic. Companies cannot use federal money to buy back their own stock. President Trump has lent his support for this provision in the stimulus bill by saying: "I don't want to give a bailout to a company and then have somebody go out and use that money to buy back stock in the company and raise the price and then get a bonus. OK?"[57] According to Goldman Sachs stock market analysts, "First, politicians are denouncing repurchases given the impending recession. Second, from a practical perspective, as revenues evaporate firms will be looking to preserve cash."[58] The question, of course, is why did it take a pandemic for Congress to take action?

Let's remember that although Congress added a provision barring buybacks in its stimulus package, the Federal Reserve's emergency relief program, which was set up jointly with the Treasury Department, has no restriction on how corporations spend the money. There is no directive to companies limiting stock dividends, executive compensation, stock buybacks, or to maintain a certain employment level. Without these safeguards, this program permits companies to reward shareholders and executives at the expense of employees who stand to lose the most. Let's connect the dots. The Federal Reserve has considerable power to influence the movement of the market, which can create higher volatility and uncertainty. During this pandemic, you need, more than ever before, to reevaluate your portfolio in order to protect yourself.

Chapter 3

INVESTING IN THE DIGITAL AGE

"True wisdom comes to each of us when we realize how little we
understand about life, ourselves, and the world around us."

–SOCRATES

———

Modern portfolio theory, despite its mathematical rigor and predictive
power, is deductively valid only if we accept certain assumptions—
namely, that investors are rational agents in the market—that they
make financial decisions based purely on numbers and what is best for
their portfolio. But that's not how people are. This idealized view of
market participants is based on an unrealistic assumption of human
behavior. As investors, "we have cognitive biases such as loss aversion,
being emotionally affected by losses much more strongly than a profit
of equal value."[1] In short, modern portfolio theory fails to capture

not only the complexity of the market itself but also the multivariable complexity of the real-world investor.

There are two broadly defined approaches to investment philosophy: quantitative analysis and fundamentals. Those who believe in quantitative analysis accept that mathematical models (like modern portfolio theory) alone are sufficient to both describe and predict market behavior. Those who accept the fundamental approach, such as Warren Buffett and others, believe there are political, social, and economic forces that defy the logic of mathematical formulas. Warren Buffett famously said, "Beware of geeks bearing formulas."[2] According to the fundamental approach, mathematical formulas (the quantitative approach) are not sufficiently powerful to capture market movement, given that those formulas require certain assumptions to be made about investor behavior.

Investors' emotions cloud their judgment, often leading to overreactions to shifts in the market. These emotional overreactions can cause "illogical investment decisions."[3] This sort of emotional investment is often worse during times of personal stress, when the economy slows, or when it matters most—like when you're near retirement.[4] Overconfidence can also lead investors to believe they can predict future events. These investors are often under the mistaken belief they possess "above average abilities that enable them to predict market movements into the future."[5]

INVESTOR EMOTIONS

In many ways, the human brain is a marvel of evolutionary biology. The brain is an extraordinary piece of biological engineering. It has helped humanity tame fire, cultivate food from the earth, put a man on the moon, and create the internet. However, for many of us our brain does not necessarily perform well when calculating statistics, understanding risk, or comprehending uncertainty, which is a problem when it comes to investing.

Let's look at a simple coin flip to illustrate why many of us have a difficult time understanding statistics. Imagine you flip a coin 10 times and you want to predict whether the coin will land on heads or tails after each flip. If the first two flips land on tails, you might be tempted to conclude that the next flip will land on heads. The reason is that the normal human reaction is to assume that, since the coin has landed on tails twice already, it is due to land on heads. This, of course, is wrong.

INDEPENDENT EVENTS

Part of our misunderstanding of probability stems from the concept of independent events. You have a 50% chance the coin will land on heads each time, and this chance is entirely independent of the previous toss. What if you toss the coin 1,000 times? The probability will still be a 50% chance *for each toss* that the coin will land on heads. It's not 50% of 1,000 flips; it's 50% of each individual flip. Although this is a simple mathematical principle, our brain struggles to absorb it. Part of the reason is emotional. If we toss a coin 10 times and 7 out of those 10 tosses turn out to be tails, our emotional, instinctive expectation is that the next toss will be heads.

Numerous studies have shown that "uncertainty sends the human brain into a state of stress and anxiety."[6] This emotional response can lead us into making bad decisions. This is one of the reasons so few investors were able to predict the dot-com bubble and subsequent stock market crash in 2000 or the housing crisis in 2008.[7] This emotional response to rationally explainable events creates a powerful aversion to risk.

THE POWER OF DISSATISFACTION

One reason humans are so risk averse is that the dissatisfaction we experience from losing is more powerful than the satisfaction we feel from winning. For example, "if you went to the casino and lost $100, you would feel much more emotion than if you won $100."[8]

Researchers in psychology[9] have proposed that "losses cause a greater emotional impact on an individual than does an equivalent amount of gain, so given choices presented two ways—with both offering the same result—an individual will pick the option offering perceived gains."[10] For instance, say you have two groups: One will receive $20 straightaway. The other will receive $40 but then lose half of it. The end result is the same: Both groups end up with $20. But people are more likely to choose the first option—to just get $20. For the other option, the perceived loss of half their initial $40 gain is felt emotionally as a loss of $20—even though they actually ended up with a gain of $20.[11]

This irrational but instinctive perception can lead to irrational investment decisions. Being aware of your own risk aversion can help you avoid some of the effect, but a safer bet is to work with a qualified financial advisor. Their training, certification, and professional distance (it's your money, not theirs) can help you make more rational decisions based on the numbers rather than your perceptions.

CONFIRMATION BIAS

Another natural human tendency that gets in the way of rational investment decisions involves our expectations, much like our inability to instinctively understand the statistics of individual events. *Confirmation bias* is the tendency to interpret input from the world in a way that justifies our preconceived notions about it. We don't tend to look at data and interpret it from a blank slate; we all have ideas about the way things work, and confirmation bias leads us to see our version of how things work in our observations of the world, even if they don't necessarily match. It also leads us to prefer hearing information that we already agree with; this is why your dad, for example, likely watches one particular news channel. This form of bias makes it difficult for many of us to challenge our thinking or entertain new ideas.

Let's say you hear or read somewhere that some particular stock is about to skyrocket. When you look into the company, you discover that it just purchased another company. That could be a sign of growth—the corporation is branching out into a new area or reducing competition. But it doesn't *indicate* that growth; the company could just as easily go out of business next week because the purchase was a terrible decision. In this scenario, you have very little information, and the information you do have doesn't clearly predict anything. But your brain tells you that it does, because that's the result you expected.

Confirmation bias can be a huge problem for investors, especially if you're making decisions without the support of a professional. It can cause you to see information that bolsters your beliefs and you may fail to pay attention to information that contradicts those beliefs. This can lead to poor decisions, based on only half of the bigger picture. "Confirmation bias can . . . cause investors to make poor decisions, whether it's in their choice of investments or their buy-and-sell timing."[12]

As with our other inherent human flaws, being aware of your own biases can help you avoid them, but we all let down our guard at times. One good way to avoid succumbing to confirmation bias is to distance yourself from the process. Again, working with a financial professional can help: By having someone else guide your decisions, with your specific goals in mind, you may be able to avoid the natural pitfalls of your own brain.

INVESTOR OVERCONFIDENCE

The profound irony of our worsening financial literacy is that we live in the information age, but information alone is not the path to knowledge. We live in a Google-ized world with a near-infinite supply of information, but we don't necessarily know how to interpret that information or, often, how to determine whether it's even true.[13] Digital technology gives us the false impression that we are far more enlightened today than in generations past, but I don't believe we are actually any more enlightened; rather, I believe that we are bombarded with trivial information. For example, we consume information, but we don't necessarily engage in substantive ideas. Within this digital landscape, financial literacy has become a glaring problem. For those who do not rely on a financial advisor, a lack of basic understanding of how the financial world operates can reduce the chance of investment success, and for those who do, it can affect the ability to ask relevant questions.

Rapid technological change is fundamentally reshaping our lives with sweeping social, political, and economic consequences. Progress is never synchronized with our ability to adapt. "Technologies change faster than cultures, and cultures change faster than genes, [which] is why any extended periods of strong growth and progress create divergences in incomes and values that eventually become unsustainable."[14] One of the great ironies of the digital age is the ever-widening inequality created by the oceanic gulf between those who understand and strategically utilize information and those who struggle to make sense of a world that is seemingly changing all around them. Despite the fact that we are enveloped by endless information, I believe that knowledge in general, and financial knowledge in particular, is diminishing.

We are today living in a world in which a near-infinite supply of information is just a click away. Our smartphones are massive libraries, where information is available to us anytime and anywhere. The rapid and concentrated technological advancements we've made in a single generation seem to dwarf all other technological leaps that have come before. You might expect that our collective wisdom would have increased in direct proportion to our technological sophistication, but in my experience, this is not the case. In fact, I believe that our capacity to think and reason, to recall basic information, has been compromised by the convenience of infinite and infinitely accessible information. Our ever-increasing dependence on technology has created a phenomenon known as the *Google effect,* which is defined as, "our tendency to forget information which can be promptly Googled."[15] Also called *digital amnesia,* the Google effect describes how easy it is for us to forget information simply because we can easily search for every conceivable fact.

The Google effect has the potential to affect our thinking in such a way that we may no longer flex our mental muscles: We don't need to remember things that are easily available. A study by the Kaspersky Lab showed that "more than 70 percent of people don't know their children's phone numbers by heart, and 49 percent have not memorized their partner's number."[16] Why memorize a bunch of numbers when our smartphone puts an entire database of contacts—and the phone number, address, and website of every business online—at our fingertips?

What is particularly troubling about the Google effect is that it acts as an extension of our memory; therefore, we rely less upon our own memory. According to Maria Wimber, lecturer at the University of Birmingham's School of Psychology, the Google effect "makes us good at remembering where to find a given bit of information, but not necessarily what the information was."[17] The Google effect can affect how we read and internalize the knowledge we gain.

Today, as a result of the ubiquitous nature of information, our capacity to read and absorb ideas appears to be diminishing. College students, for example, "actively avoid" the classic literature of earlier centuries because they no longer "have the patience to read longer, denser, more difficult texts."[18] Some of us no longer read the way we did for thousands of years. Rather than read and engage dense layers of texts, some skim for information. This seemingly benign act—skimming—means "we don't have time to grasp complexity, to understand another's feelings or to perceive beauty."[19] If the internet knows everything, why should we bother cluttering our brains with unnecessary information that is easily accessible? This idea is both disturbing and consequential.

THE GOOGLE MIND

In many ways, the digital age is changing us in a fundamental way. Let me introduce and define a new term: the Google mind, which is the existential state of being immersed in a world of information and falsely believing that we possess a great deal of knowledge by simply relying on our smart devices. The Google mind tends toward narcissism, as is evidenced by the ego-driven behavior of many on social media. One of the unflattering aspects of the Google mind is that we no longer read the same way as in previous generations. The tragic irony, of course, is that the very technology that made it easy for us to access endless books and articles has made us consumers of information. In fact, "our ability to interpret text, to make rich mental connections that form when we read deeply and without distraction, remains largely disengaged."[20]

To better understand how the Google mind today has fundamentally changed the approach to reading, let's look at how one author describes his own transformation. Nicholas Carr is the author of such books as *The Shallows: What the Internet Is Doing to Our Brains*, *The Glass Cage: Automation and Us*, and *Utopia Is Creepy: and Other Provocations*. A critic of the digital revolution, Carr, in *The Shallows*, writes in intimate detail about his own transformation, which is the result of the digital mind.

Over the last few years, I've had an uncomfortable sense that someone, or something, has been tinkering with my brain, remapping the neural circuitry, reprogramming the memory. My mind isn't going—so far as I can tell—but it's changing. I'm not thinking the way I used to think. I feel it most strongly when I'm reading. I used to find it easy to immerse myself in a book or a lengthy article. My mind would get caught up in the twists of the narrative or the turns of the argument, and I'd spend hours strolling through long stretches of prose. That's rarely the case anymore. Now my concentration starts to drift after a page or two. I get fidgety, lose the thread, begin looking for something else to do. I feel like I'm always dragging my wayward brain back to the text. The deep reading that used to come naturally has become a struggle.[21]

What Carr is describing is the gradual change that can happen to the human brain as a result of being bombarded with information. We don't have the temperament to immerse ourselves in reading and to absorb the dense layers of ideas. It is the density of ideas, and not surface information, that gives rise to substantive knowledge. Now the question that I'm sure you are asking yourself is how all of this is connected to financial literacy. The short answer is that the Google mind can give the false impression that we know far more about the financial world than we actually do—and that can be dangerous for your financial future.

If so many of us are exhausted from skimming through endless bits of information, when do we have time to absorb the social, political, historical, and economic ideas that shape our world? Despite the massive amount of financial information available, the Financial Industry Regulatory Authority Foundation "estimated that nearly two-thirds of Americans couldn't pass a basic financial literacy test."[22] Think about this statistic for a minute: 66% of all Americans lack the necessary knowledge to understand basic financial concepts.

THE DUNNING-KRUGER EFFECT

One of the disturbing consequences of our Google-ized world is the Dunning–Kruger effect, a "cognitive bias in which people believe that they are smarter and more capable than they really are."[23] The massive amount of information that is immediately accessible lulls us into a false sense of overconfidence. Charles Darwin, in his book *The Descent of Man*, observed that "ignorance more frequently begets confidence than does knowledge."[24]

The Dunning–Kruger effect is named after two social psychologists who discovered that people often underperform simply because they are not aware of their own ignorance. One possible explanation for people's exaggerated sense of knowledge is a lack of *metacognition*, "or the ability to step back and look at one's own behavior and abilities from outside of oneself."[25] In other words, all of us evaluate ourselves from our own limited perspective. When we arm ourselves with information, we often overinflate our sense of understanding. This false equivocation between knowledge and information is at the heart of the digital world we find ourselves in.

The Dunning–Kruger effect tells us that a "tiny bit of knowledge on a subject matter can lead people to mistakenly believe that they know all there is to know about it."[26] Disconnected and disjointed pieces of information engender in people the illusion of knowledge. The current general lack of financial literacy, coupled with an exaggerated sense of confidence, often causes people to exhibit poor judgment.

This is a profound and disturbing irony: Many of us are simply unaware of our own incompetence. In fact, "incompetence does not leave people disoriented, perplexed, or cautious. Instead, the incompetent are often blessed with an inappropriate confidence, buoyed by something that feels to them like knowledge."[27] In other words, our own incompetence may mask itself as overconfidence. That overconfidence can lead investors to mistakenly believe they can predict the future of the market.[28]

Let's suppose for a minute that you have the time, inclination, and critical thinking skills to make sense of all the information available to you. You see, "financial planning is a process, not an event. Investors are too easily distracted by all of the underlying assumptions involved in creating a comprehensive plan. Yes, those assumptions are important, but how you react when life invariably gets in the way is far more crucial. A real-world plan rarely plays out like it does on a spreadsheet."[29] How will you react to unexpected changes, which are certain to happen?

THE GOLDILOCKS PRINCIPLE

The Goldilocks Principle derives its name from the children's story about a girl who takes a walk in the forest. Upon encountering a house, she finds three bowls of porridge. The first bowl was too hot to eat, the second bowl was too cold, but the third bowl was just right. The Goldilocks Principle has been used in several fields, including psychology, economics, astronomy, and medicine. In astronomy, we have the Goldilocks Zone, or habitable zone, which is "the region around a star where temperatures on a rocky planet allow liquid water to exist."[30] If a planet is too hot or too cold, it will not be able to support life.

Aristotle called this principle the Golden Mean, which refers to a desirable middle between two extremes. Let's use the Goldilocks

Principle to describe the mindset of two types of average investors. On one end of the spectrum is an investor who is either too busy or unwilling to learn about investment strategies. This person may purchase some random stocks and hope for the best. On the other end of the spectrum is an investor who reads a great deal of information and believes he knows all there is to know about investing. Both extremes are risky. The investor who doesn't care about learning anything about the financial world might make ill-advised decisions and squander his or her retirement benefits. The investor who believes he knows all there is to know about the financial world may be suffering from the Dunning–Kruger effect and could potentially make ill-informed decisions.

The Goldilocks Principle is about finding moderation instead of polarization. This is particularly useful to people who tend to see the world as black and white. Once you recognize this psychological quirk, then you need to begin to find your way toward the middle. You need to remember that the world is much more nuanced than the black-and-white interpretation you've relied upon in the past. Here is an actionable habit: If you find yourself at one end of the spectrum, then challenge yourself to gradually move toward the middle ground. If you believe you know all there is to know about finance and investing, then pick up the phone and call a qualified professional for the purpose of exchanging ideas. If you happen to be on the other end of the spectrum, where you constantly put off learning about the financial world, try picking up a book on financial literacy. Having an awareness that our thinking sometimes gravitates toward extremes is the first step toward changing your mindset.

THE EDELMAN TRUST BAROMETER

Our world today is radically different from previous generations. In the past we placed a great deal of trust in government and corporations. Following the 2008 global financial meltdown, our trust declined. For the past 20 years the Edelman Trust Barometer has gauged the public's trust. Despite a strong economy over the past decade, Edelman's 2020 Trust Barometer reveals that trust in government and business is declining. The CEO of Edelman, Richard Edelman, calls this phenomenon the "trust paradox." Trust is "based on competence (effectiveness) and ethics (purpose, honesty, vision, fairness)."[31] The trust people have of corporate competence accounts for only 25% of a company's "trust capital," while ethical behavior accounts for 75%. In other words, people are far more concerned with honesty and integrity than with ability.

The lesson here is that both government and businesses need to act with an ethical impulse toward positive change. In this sense, we need to have a more ethical capitalism that no longer tolerates rampant greed. Ethical capitalism should look to build deep, trust-based relationships. Businesses need "to look to their past as well as the future. They must use their organizational history and data to develop authentic storytelling content that highlights past instances of competent and ethical behavior, and share this authentic content to effectively share their values and character."[32] When it comes to the financial sector, trust is magnified.

According to the Vanguard Group, which is one of the largest investment-management companies in the world, "clients were more likely to trust their advisors when they believed that their functional, emotional, and ethical needs were being met."[33] When it comes to your money, trust is of paramount importance. The trust clients are interested in is not simply competence but more importantly ethical trust. According to Billy Lanter, who is a fiduciary investment advisor at Unified Trust Company, advisors reveal how they act in their clients' best interest in a tangible way. "Ethical trust is like a sixth sense—clients usually know when something doesn't feel right."[34] In today's financial landscape, with automated investing and people trying to go it alone, a trusted advisor is more important than ever before.

AUTOMATED INVESTING

Another aspect of our interconnected world that takes agency and power away from investors is the preponderance of algorithm-based automated investing. In general, algorithms make our lives easier—making online searches better and automating tasks. These conveniences, of course, come at a cost. When we surrender our mental abilities to automated systems, we give up an important part of who we are. In fact, "if we let computers think for us and the underlying input data is corrupt, they'll do the thinking badly, and we might not ever know it."[35]

Automated—or *robo*—advisors are algorithm-based programs designed to offer the retail investor investment advice. Part of what makes these automated advisors popular is their convenience, but convenience can make us lazy. While Robo advisors may be just fine for some folks, one financial expert[36] offered three clear reasons to consider avoiding automated advisors:

- "Automatic rebalancing isn't perfect."
- "Robo advisors can be tax inefficient."
- "There's no personal touch."[37]

One of the problems I see with automated rebalancing is that it may not work with large market corrections. Robo advisors, which are simple algorithms, use a risk-tolerance score to rebalance your portfolio, but they are incapable of accounting for other critical pieces of your financial plan. Also, "robo investing makes your portfolio performance average, rarely giving you superlative returns relative to the market."[38] Beyond these problems with automated investing is the broader implication of using algorithms to plan your financial future.

All of these cultural forces and practices converge in such a way as to potentially cause you to make poor decisions when it comes to your financial future. There is also the circular effect where technology unwittingly contributes to your diminished level of financial literacy. As technology becomes more sophisticated, we have the tendency to become lazier. Why would we want to read about financial matters if a robo advisor can make the decision for you? Why should we bother to read books about the political, economic, historical, or financial world if Google and robo advisors can tell us all that we need to know? The short answer is that an automated and algorithm-driven technology could cause us to surrender a certain component of our humanity. We surrender a part of ourselves when we transfer our mental functions to machines. This act of surrendering dramatically has the potential effect of reducing our financial literacy, thus continuing the cycle.

EMOTIONS, OVERCONFIDENCE, AND INVESTING

Today the individual investor has access to a seemingly endless supply of information and real-time news. In fact, the individual investor has the very same information available to Wall Street professionals. On one hand, this access to information levels the playing field, but on the other hand, having information alone is not enough to suddenly make the average person a competent investor.

Individual investors do not have a great track record. According to a recent study by Dalbar, for the years 1988–2019, the annualized S&P 500 return averaged 9.96% a year. A pretty attractive historical return. By contrast, over the same time period, the average equity fund investor earned a market return of only 5.04%.[39] The lesson here is that having information without the necessary knowledge to make sense of it—and without a strategy different from the traditional 60/40 model—can be costly.

When it comes to investing, the problem with emotional reactions to changes in the market and overconfidence is overreaction. In other words, our "emotional reaction causes illogical investment decisions. This tendency to overreact can become even greater during times of personal uncertainty; near retirement, for example, or when the economy is bad."[40] The stubborn nature of our emotional response to uncertainty, combined with the possible overconfidence induced by vast information at your fingertips, can prevent us from having an objective perspective about our financial future.

This is why I encourage people to seek out the help and guidance of a professional financial advisor. A professional advisor "can serve as an intermediary between you and your emotions."[41] If you have a natural tendency to make emotional decisions based on insufficient data or a cursory understanding of the markets, then it would be prudent and wise to seek the help of a professional advisor.

Chapter 4

THE HISTORY OF ALTERNATIVE INVESTMENTS

"We should remember that good fortune often happens
when opportunity meets with preparation."

–THOMAS EDISON

———

Investment wins are often described as home runs. Lucky investors will boast of their dramatic gains in individual stocks, which they believe could become the next Facebook or Amazon. Home runs are about taking a large risk and (hopefully) claiming the large prize. However, as any baseball player will tell you, you will have a better chance of winning a game with a balanced and defensive team of players who consistently hit singles and doubles. If you count on one superstar to carry you to victory, you will risk greater failure. A strategy of offense can win games; a strategy of defense can win championships. Investors may also extol the virtues of conservative asset classes, such as municipal bonds, which offer a level of protection for their portfolio. But protection only gets you so far; you have to take some risk to gain a greater reward. The key to these two extremes, risk and reward, is balance. If you carefully construct an investment strategy suitably designed for your age, circumstance, and defined goals, you should not have to suffer the emotional ups and downs of change or the lower return potential of a "safe" investment strategy that might not grow enough to support you in retirement.

The average investor has often been advised to invest according to the 60/40 stocks-and-bonds approach for many years. Although in the past stocks have generally produced stable long-term growth, with bonds offering a hedge against the risk of stocks, this strategy may no longer be relevant in today's world. This autopilot approach was reasonable under ideal conditions, but we live in the real world. Investors today need trained advisors to navigate an increasingly complex world filled with uncertainty and unpredictable conditions. Many retail, or individual, investors have become accustomed to a set-it-and-forget-it approach, where algorithms and esoteric formulas are used to rebalance portfolios. Algorithms, however, do not account for changing economic conditions and individual circumstances.

This is why I believe a different approach is critically important; it must offer customizability and flexibility while managing risk. While so many working Americans have quietly accepted the same tired investment advice, the largest endowment funds have systematically implemented a strategy that goes beyond stocks and bonds. As we noted earlier, the result has often been a consistently better rate of return than those of individual investors. These endowments manage billions of dollars. Now an institutional model can be adapted to your individual portfolio.

THE ENDOWMENT MODEL

Foundations and universities had benefited for decades from multi-billion-dollar funds managed by professionals and using investment instruments that are often unavailable to the average investor. Through these endowments, the investor institutions have often succeeded in achieving better returns, have managed risk better, and have created sustainable income on a much larger scale than the individual investor has been able to do.

Now the individual investor can implement some aspects of the endowment approach, which potentially offers increased and sustained returns. Over the past decade a growing number of financial advisors have successfully adapted the endowment model for individuals. These advisors incorporated certain strategies in order to make the endowment model more suitable to the retail investor. Endowments invest in stocks, counting on the long-term growth of the market, but they also employ protection strategies—beyond bonds—to help minimize losses. The funds they invest are professionally managed and offer the potential for substantial long-term gains.

Today you have choices. Tap the knowledge and expertise of endowment managers who can offer you a scaled and customizable strategy. With the endowment approach, you devote money to three categories: stocks, bonds, and alternative assets, some of which will entail greater risk. You select assets with unique and uncorrelated strengths. You will be expected to buy and hold some of these assets, letting their value mature, depending on predicted returns for each asset class. Your financial manager will also adopt additional strategies based on assets whose growth potential is not correlated to the performance of stocks and bonds. Your endowment strategy may include some types of assets to gain certain tax advantages while other assets are designed to potentially yield healthy returns, and yet others are designed to potentially generate steady income for the foreseeable future. The point here is that you do not want to put all your money in a single asset class; rather, you want balance.

Certain aspects of the endowment model will sound familiar to you, as you have undoubtedly heard and read bits and pieces of it in the financial news. Given its track record, diversification, and relative stability, why aren't most financial advisors recommending it? Part of the reason is the simplicity and familiarity of the 60/40 model.

ENDOWMENTS VERSUS 60/40

Let's compare how the 60/40 stock/bond portfolio performed in relation to the multi-asset-class endowment models used by colleges such as Yale, Harvard, and Stanford. The following graph illustrates how major university endowments performed in relation to the 60/40 model. From 2003 to 2019, Ivy League endowments have outperformed the 60/40 portfolio for 12 out of the past 17 years, which is 70.5% of the time. It is important to remember that past performance is no guarantee of future performance or results. You must also be aware that Ivy League endowments utilize alternative investments, which are considered high risk and, therefore, not suitable for everyone.

Ivy League Endowment Fiscal Year Performance
2003-2019

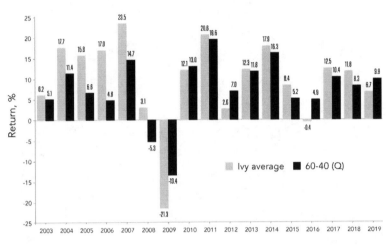

Source: Markov Processes International Inc., "Ivy League Endowments Fail to Make Grade in Fiscal 2019," markovprocesses.com, October 13, 2019, https://www.markovprocesses.com/blog/ivy-league-endowments-fail-to-make-the-grade-in-fiscal-2019/.

If you continue with the traditional stocks-and-bonds investment strategy, as with any investment approach, you might lose ground. According to Daniel Pinto of JPMorgan, "It's normal for there to be a correction at the end of an investing cycle, and . . . markets could be heading for a 'deep correction' of between 20% and 40%, depending upon the market values at the time the downturn starts."[1] In fact, both the American economist and Nobel laureate Robert Shiller and Jeremy Siegel of the Wharton School argue that "stocks are overvalued on a long-term basis."[2] If the stock market is ripe for a "correction," which could reduce your portfolio, you may not be able to minimize risk by simply moving your money to bonds. The endowment model offers an alternative.

DAVID SWENSEN AND THE IVY LEAGUE PORTFOLIO

David Swensen was the first to adapt the modern portfolio theory for Yale's multibillion-dollar university endowment. Prior to 1985 Yale largely followed the 60/40 investment model, which offered predictable results without significant growth. Swensen understood that "the decision whether to invest in specific asset classes matters much more than picking the right stock."[3] For the last 30 years Yale has invested mostly in alternative assets "like natural resources, venture capital, real estate, and foreign stocks."[4]

In his 2005 book, *Unconventional Success,* Swensen wrote that "asset-allocation decisions play a central role in determining investor results. A number of well-regarded studies of institutional portfolios conclude that approximately 90 percent of the variability of returns stems from asset allocation, leaving approximately 10 percent of the variability to be determined by security selection and market timing."[5] In other words, asset allocation is at the heart of the endowment model.

Asset allocation is the decision to distribute your money into certain sets of investments, called *assets*. You and your financial advisor choose a proportion of your total investment to go into each of several classes of assets.[6] This proportion may work over the long term or it may need to change with market fluctuations.

The endowment portfolio philosophy is to allocate a high proportion of the total investment into alternative assets, which is largely responsible for Swensen's success.[7] Although Swensen allocates a high proportion of Yale's total investment in alternative assets, it is important to remember that the endowment portfolio is based on diversification. According to Swensen, "if you diversify your portfolio for a given level of return, you can generate that return at lower risk. If you diversify for a given level of risk, you can generate higher returns."[8]

The net result is that endowment managers have the potential to reap income from multiple asset classes, as well as multiple strategies. If one asset or strategy falters, it can be adjusted. The magnitude of success of university endowment funds has been impressive. Consider that "from 1990 to 2020, the market value of the 20 largest college endowments grew at an average annual rage of 8.5%—faster than the 6.6% average annual growth rate for the Fortune 500 over the same period."[9] Keep in mind that past performance is not a guarantee of future performance. Given that endowment strategies rely heavily upon alternative investments, they can be high risk and not suitable for the average investor.

Endowments plan for and anticipate timely exits within the parameters of each type of investment while seeking to fulfill the income needs of the investor. They do this by reallocating asset classes—which you might hear referred to as *rebalancing*. For example, the Yale endowment fund "dramatically reduced the endowment's dependence on domestic marketable securities by reallocating assets to nontraditional asset classes."[10] This forward-thinking strategy enables endowments to support both income and longevity. The endowment strategy is predicated upon a wide variety of asset classes, which are designed and managed to deliver results across different time horizons; rebalancing helps protect the endowment portfolio against market turbulence and unforeseen punctuated moments of market volatility.

Part of the reason Swensen created the endowment approach was to mitigate against the inherent risk of stock market fluctuations, as well as to hedge against inflation due to low interest rates on bonds. What makes the endowment strategy a powerful investment approach for some investors is the flexibility and malleability of its multi-asset-class allocation structure. In other words, endowments offer institutional investors customizable strategic balance designed to help meet long-term needs.

One of the reasons Swensen's multi-asset strategy worked so well is the changing face of the stock market. Beginning in the late 1990s, the number of public companies started to shrink. As a result of corporate monopolies and technological changes, fewer companies are listed on stock exchanges. Consider that "about 3,600 companies were listed on the U.S. stock exchanges at the end of 2017, down more than half from 1997."[11] This shift raises certain questions: Is the traditional purpose of public ownership at risk? Are people being excluded from attractive investment opportunities?[12] Having fewer public companies means that "investors are consigned to a less diverse universe than they may realize."[13] As far back as the mid-1980s Swensen was able to see a shift in how the stock market was structured and introduced his endowment model as a means of creating greater diversification.

In a very similar way, the retail investor may potentially benefit from a customized model, which can be uniquely suitable for long-term retirement goals. While the retail investor may be encouraged to pursue potentially outdated investment strategies, large university funds and foundations have quietly adopted a new approach. These institutions' fund managers have successfully transitioned away from the 60/40 strategy and have moved toward a much more diversified model. This type of portfolio relies on its allocations being highly skewed toward alternative assets—investments other than stocks and bonds.[14] Institutional investors have long "benefited from the liquidity diversification, which results from the alternative assets' staggered maturity date."[15] Today the retail investor can potentially benefit, just as large institutional funds do, from incorporating different strategies with different assets and staggered time frames if their individual risk tolerance allows for it.

The individual investor today has access to a variety of noncorrelated asset classes. Under the guidance of experienced managers, these asset classes, which were previously available only to institutional investors, are now available to all of us. It is important to underscore the point that you must consult with a qualified and experienced financial advisor before adopting the endowment model. It is also incumbent upon every financial advisor to confirm that individual investors are suitable for the endowment model as a complement to a broader portfolio.

A THREE-PRONGED APPROACH

Endowment managers have successfully designed institutional strategies for everyday Americans, which is why I believe you should consider strategically changing how you invest for the future. If endowments work for institutional funds, then they may offer potential for individual investors as well.

One of the important benefits of the endowment approach is the possibility of offering individual investors more income over a longer retirement. Given that we are living longer, we must start to think like the large institutional endowments, who operate under the assumption they will be around forever. As an individual investor, your goal is to support your own sense of forever. To do that, you need a diversified approach, which could include three fundamental strategies: passive, tactical, and alternative strategies. Below is a summary of each of the strategies.

- The passive strategy aims to capture market growth by risk-adjusted reward against volatility and low-yielding bonds with limited inflation hedge.

- The tactical strategy positions you to move quickly, if required, to protect your assets in the event of a downturn.

- The alternative strategy provides a buffer zone of assets that are not correlated to the stock or bond markets.

The passive approach involves both liquid and limited liquidity assets, the tactical approach has a high degree of liquidity, and the alternative approach makes use of both limited liquidity and illiquid assets. This diversification strategy offers flexibility to potentially fuel sustained results that could potentially support retirement withdrawals of 4% to 5% per year, which is similar to the institutional endowments. In fact, Matthew Tuttle, who is the author of *How Harvard and Yale Beat the Market,* recommended in August 2020 that you can "safely withdraw 4% to 4.5% without eating into your money."[16]

The power of diversification affords you the breathing room to pursue specific investments within each type of investment. You might choose very low-risk stocks and bonds and gradually increase the risk with alternatives. In other words, there is enough flexibility to construct a balanced portfolio in terms of how much liquidity you want, the protection you need, and the amount of growth you require to replenish your portfolio, which can support consistent withdrawals. These withdrawals represent the income you need for the retirement you want.

A BRIEF HISTORY OF ALTERNATIVE INVESTMENTS

Although alternative investments gained momentum in the past few years, the historical underpinning of this once-radical new approach to investing was established during the early part of the 20th century. Benjamin Graham (1894–1976) was a British-born American investor, economist, and professor. He is widely known as the "father of value investing, and wrote two of the founding texts in neoclassical investing: *Security Analysis* (1934) with David Dodd, and *The Intelligent Investor* (1949)."[17] His philosophical view of investing explored investor psychology, buy-and-hold investing, fundamental analysis, minimal debt, concentrated diversification, margin safety, and contrarian mindsets. Graham is also acknowledged to be the father of alternative investing.

He was "an early adopter of the concept of alternative investing; garnering higher risk-adjusted returns than the market by doing things differently, rather than following the crowd."[18] Graham was the first to introduce hedge funds in the 1920s. By the 1940s, Alfred Winslow

Jones had "ushered in a new era by launching the first hedge fund which exploited leverage and derivatives to enhance performance."[19] The next several decades would bring regulations and technological innovations that expanded the types of alternative investments available to the individual investor.

Beginning in 1958, the US Small Business Investment Act "enabled the creation of venture capital, which was attractive to investors who benefited from the fact that fund profits could be taxed at lower capital gains rates."[20] By 1978 the US Department of Labor updated "the Employee Retirement Income Security Act of 1974 (ERISA): This update lifted an earlier restriction placed on pension funds from investing in privately held securities, thereby enabling them to invest in alternative investments."[21] The history of pension funds prior to ERISA is a fascinating story with intersections of corruption, organized crime, and mismanagement.[22]

It is important to understand that prior to ERISA, many private pensions suffered from gross mismanagement and outright fraud. A case in point was the 1963 closing of the Studebaker automobile plant in South Bend, Indiana. As a result of mismanagement, more than 4,000 employees lost some or all of their promised pension plan benefits.[23] Pensions also suffered from corruption when James Hoffa, who was the president of the International Brotherhood of Teamsters, along with six others, fraudulently arranged $25 million in pension loans and diverted $1.7 million for their own personal use.[24]

The 1978 US Department of Labor update to ERISA allowed pensions to utilize alternative investments. ERISA was enacted to address fraud and to protect employee benefit-plan participants and beneficiaries. The three pillars of ERISA include:

- Loyalty: Putting client needs first.

- Education: Managers must be educated and have expertise to manage portfolios.

- Diversification: Portfolio protection for plan participants.[25]

One of the important features of ERISA is that institutional managers have to be educated in how to build and manage complex, multi-asset portfolios. It is my opinion that retail managers and financial advisors also need to be educated in alternative investments. Consider that "about 67% of advisers say lack of understanding is one of the main reasons why they don't invest more heavily in alternatives."[26] In my opinion, this lack of understanding is partly the reason retail investors haven't been informed about alternative investments.

For many years, access to alternative investments belonged almost exclusively to large institutions and wealthy individuals. Over the past several years the alternative investment industry has grown from a handful of firms in the United States managing a few billion dollars to thousands of firms spread across the world, and are on track to exceed $14 trillion by 2023.[27] One of the reasons for this shift was that pensions were becoming underfunded, which forced large investment companies to shift their focus to the retail investor. For example, in 2018 Moody's Investors Service estimated that "public pensions are underfunded by $4.4 trillion, which is the equivalent to the economy of Germany."[28] Alternative investments became popular with retail clients in response to underfunded pensions and large investment companies shifting their focus to the individual investor. Let's not forget that many pensions use the 60/40 portfolio, which is potentially broken. In many ways, underfunded pensions, coupled with a questionable 60/40 investment strategy, helped give rise to the popularity of alternatives for the retail client.

Another reason alternative investments became available to the average investor was technological innovation. The digital revolution, more specifically computing power, has "transformed financial markets and made it possible to record, track, move, store, and analyse previously unmanageable and unthinkable amounts of data."[29] Mathematical innovations, such as the Black–Scholes options pricing formula, enabled investors to quickly and easily price complex financial products such as derivatives and structured securities. In many ways the convergence of several forces helped open up alternative investments to the general public. These forces included massively underfunded pensions, technological sophistication, and mathematical innovation.

ALTERNATIVE INVESTMENTS GAIN POPULARITY WITH RETAIL CLIENTS

The growing popularity of alternative investments for the retail client has changed how average Americans are able to plan and prepare for retirement. Although alternative investments have been around for several decades, they have been exclusive to institutions and large university endowments. It was only 20 years ago that alternatives started to become available to individual investors, and with that the financial landscape changed. You see, "many people are not even aware of what is really driving their retirement savings and have little or no control over how their future is invested."[30] When you consider that in today's pandemic environment, with heightened uncertainty, inflation, the high cost of health care, and a potentially broken and unreliable 60/40 strategy, you can begin to appreciate the opportunities available to you today.

As alternative investments started to become popular in 2002, several important changes and innovations occurred. For example, competition increased as a result of fewer companies going public. Alternatives offer durability, since they "tend to behave differently than typical stock and bond investments . . . adding them to a portfolio may provide broader diversification, reduce risk and enhance returns."[31] Technological innovation, as I've stated earlier, has enabled companies to become more transparent and more efficient. Finally, the government has recognized the importance of alternative investment strategies.

In 2012 Congress passed the Jumpstart Our Business Startups (JOBS) Act, partly to encourage private funding of small businesses. Over time, the JOBS act evolved to allow more investors to participate in investments that "were only accessible to wealthy, accredited investors, a term defined by federal securities law which includes individuals earning $200,000 or more annually or holding at least $1 million in assets, minus their private homes."[32] The JOBS Act has opened the door to all investors, regardless of being accredited, to invest in certain private offerings such as business development companies (BDCs).

When you consider the results of university endowments, you start to appreciate the potential benefits of adding alternatives to your multi-asset-class portfolio. Take Yale's endowment as an example. Managed by David Swensen, the endowment returned 11.1% per annum over the 10 years ending June 30, 2019.[33] This world of institutional investing is now available to you. The potential benefits of alternatives, when used as part of a diversification strategy, can be eye opening. Alternatives are "uncorrelated with traditional investments. Where stocks must weather the ups and downs of the market, alternative investments respond differently. The effects of market fluctuations will still be felt in alternative investments, and they often involve the similar or even greater risks, but in a different way than many traditional assets."[34] Although alternative investments have grown in popularity, they are complex assets, which is why education for financial advisors is critical.

Although alternative investments for the retail client are changing how average Americans are able to prepare for retirement, education has been slow. The kind of education I'm talking about here is for advisors, which I feel is woefully inadequate. Just as ERISA mandated that pension-fund managers be educated in the often-complex instruments of alternative assets, financial advisors also need to become educated. I think we need a kind of ERISA 2.0 for financial advisors to learn about alternative investment strategies. If advisors are not versed in these complex instruments, how will they explain them to their clients when they could be a good fit for their portfolio? Here is an actionable step. If you believe that alternatives might be a good addition to your portfolio, and your advisor doesn't offer them, you may want to consider finding an advisor who not only understands them but also has experience with alternative investments.

Here is something else that you need to know. Over the past 20 years there has been a convergence of events that opened up opportunities for the individual investor that were unheard of a generation ago. Look at the forces that have come together just at the right time: Technology made it possible to carry out complex investment strategies with ease, innovation in mathematical formulas made pricing of these instruments much easier than ever before, and we are living longer. We are in many ways living through exciting times, filled with possibilities. This is why you need to take charge of your financial future.

REAL ESTATE

Commercial real estate has become one of the most popular forms of alternative investments in recent years. This is in large part due to historically stable returns and reliable cash flows. Given that only "about 3,600 firms were listed on U.S. stock exchanges at the end of 2017, down more than half from 1997," commercial real estate has offered the potential for powerful stability and diversification to any portfolio.[35] Large university endowments and pension funds have long utilized commercial real estate. In fact, "on average, this vast institutional cadre invests 10% of their assets in real estate and yet the average investor overall has 3%."[36] As with all investments, the COVID-19 pandemic has impacted commercial real estate. Although it is too early to determine the full impact of this pandemic, history can serve as a guide.

Over the past century, external shocks to the economy, such as sudden market corrections or pandemics, have been followed by an economic downturn with immediate to short-term impact on commercial real estate. For example, the 2008 recession "resulted in a more protracted recovery. As a rule of thumb, the industry has historically lagged the broader economy by six months."[37] Prior to COVID-19, the commercial real estate industry was in a strong position, as evidenced by healthy balance sheets, capital availability, and liquidity. Rather than the typical six-month lag, the commercial real estate industry has affected more immediately by COVID-19. For example, the pandemic has directly impacted "the demand for space through quarantines, social distancing, shutdowns, supply chain disruptions, employment loss, and a shattering of consumer confidence."[38] According to industry experts, commercial real estate, as well as the overall economy, will rebound. The speed of the recovery will depend on several factors, including the development of a vaccine and the magnitude of monetary stimulus.[39] In my opinion, once the economy recovers from the pandemic, commercial real estate will be a powerful source of alternative investments.

Prior to the COVID-19 pandemic, "commercial real estate has provided income and generated a total return that are well above those of stocks and corporate bonds."[40] Now obviously this is based on past performance only and we are not suggesting that we, or anyone, can ensure the same strong performance going forward. The following figure shows how commercial real estate compared in both income and total return to stocks and bonds over a 20-year period. The data is from December 31, 1999, to December 31, 2019. When you factor in the volatility of the stock market, you begin to appreciate why real estate might be a potentially attractive alternative.

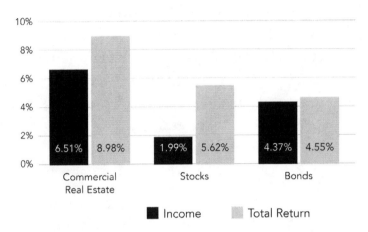

Comparison of income and total return of commercial real estate with stocks and bonds.

Source: Griffin Capital, "Commercial Real Estate: Six Potential Benefits," griffincapital.com, retrieved March 4, 2020, https://www.griffincapital.com/investor-education/commercial-real-estate-six-potential-benefits.

In addition, commercial real estate tends to offer lower volatility, inflation protection, and enhanced risk-adjusted returns. If you recall the chapter on hidden forces, you may recall that I stressed the importance of understanding how historical, political, and economic forces impact your investment. "Movements in the broad markets, corporate announcements and analyst actions can cause large fluctuations in prices of stocks and bonds."[41] Given that commercial real estate is not publicly traded, it has historically exhibited "volatility that is substantially lower than stocks and closer to bonds, which may help reduce portfolio volatility."[42] Another important feature of commercial real estate is inflation protection.

One very simple way to understand inflation is that it erodes the purchasing power of your money. Real estate growth has outpaced inflation over the last 10 years. From March 31, 2009, to March 31, 2019, the 10-year average annual growth rate in net operating income has outpaced inflation. For example, the 10-year average annual growth rate (2009 to 2019) for net operating income was 2.72% versus an inflation growth rate of 1.60%.[43] Again, keep in mind that past performance is not an indication of future performance.

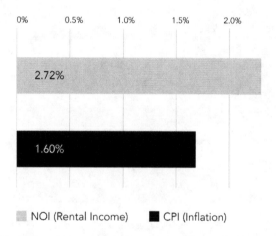

10-year average annual growth rates (March 31, 2009–March 31, 2019).

Source: Griffin Capital, "Commercial Real Estate: Six Potential Benefits," griffincapital.com, retrieved March 4, 2020, https://www.griffincapital.com/investor-education/commercial-real-estate-six-potential-benefits.

Real estate also offers the potential for risk-adjusted returns. In other words, if you add commercial real estate "to stock and bond holdings [it] may be able to boost your portfolio performance and lower risk."[44] The following figure shows the impact of adding commercial real estate on both return and volatility from 1999 to 2018. Notice the increase in return and decrease in volatility. As I've stated elsewhere in this book, past performance is not a guarantee of future performance. You must also keep in mind that investing in commercial real estate is both risky and not suitable for every investor.

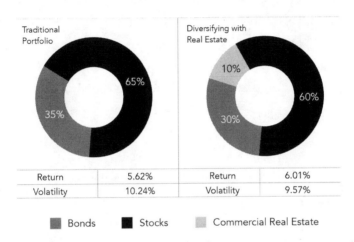

Traditional Portfolio		Diversifying with Real Estate	
Return	5.62%	Return	6.01%
Volatility	10.24%	Volatility	9.57%

Bonds   Stocks   Commercial Real Estate

Commercial real estate may lower risk and improve portfolio return (1999–2018).

Source: Griffin Capital, "Commercial Real Estate: Six Potential Benefits," griffincapital.com, retrieved March 4, 2020, https://www.griffincapital.com/investor-education/commercial-real-estate-six-potential-benefits.

Real estate today has become the fourth asset class, according to a report by David Funk, who is the director of the Baker Program in Real Estate at Cornell University. Real estate has come a long way since the 1980s, when it made up only about 2% of institutional investor portfolios. Most portfolios back then were made up of three asset classes—stocks, bonds, and cash.

Some of the reasons as to why real estate became a more popular asset class include noncorrelated diversification, inflation hedge, and greater return potential. Real estate is not correlated with the movement of the stock market, which helps reduce risk. In other words, real estate adds a level of diversification to your portfolio that is not as susceptible to the volatility of the stock market. Real estate also has the potential to respond well to inflation. When values of stocks and bonds decline, real estate often remains more steady. Over the years real estate has evolved in such a way as to become available to the average investor.[45] Real estate may pose higher risk than investing in stocks and bonds and may not be suitable for the average investor. You need to take these disclaimers seriously. I'm here to inform you of the facts, and part of the facts are these disclaimers, which are designed to protect you.

Let's look at the three generations of real estate classes. These asset classes were introduced "because of the potential diversification (reduced risk) and higher portfolio returns when added to a portfolio of traditional investments."[46] The three generations of real estate include:

- First generation: traded real estate investment trusts (REITs)

- Second generation: nontraded REITs

- Third generation: interval funds, which are a form of closed-end funds

The first generation of REITs was introduced in 1960 when President Eisenhower signed legislation that introduced a new vehicle for investors to benefit from income-producing commercial real estate. In the beginning REITs were available only to large financial institutions and wealthy individuals. Over time REITs have "grown to a $1 trillion equity market capitalization representing nearly $3 trillion in gross real estate assets."[47] First-generation REITs were traded. For example, Continental Mortgage Investors became the first traded REIT on the New York Stock Exchange in 1965.

The second generation of real estate includes nontraded REITs. Nontraded REITs, as the name implies, are not listed on a public exchange like the NYSE or NASDAQ. What makes them attractive is that their value does not fluctuate with the stock market. In other words, nontraded REITs are not correlated with stocks. Nontraded REITs sell shares based on their net asset value (NAV), which is the total value of its assets minus liabilities. NAV is important because investors can usually buy shares based on actual value of the real estate instead of market price. Nontraded REITs have a long holding period, typically more than a year.[48]

Part of what makes nontraded REITs attractive to the retail investor is the low barrier of entry, requiring "only a few thousand dollars as a minimum investment."[49] For example, the Blackstone Group, which is the largest alternative investment firm in the world, offered the average investor "a 2017 non-traded real estate investment trust with an entry point of $2,500."[50] Nontraded REITs have attracted $70 billion in investments since 2013.[51] According to investment banking firm Robert A. Stanger & Co., shares of nontraded REITs totaled $1.4 billion for the month of August 2019.[52] Some of the benefits of nontraded REITs include:

- Diversification
- Potential hedge against inflation

• Access to high-quality and professionally managed real estate

Robert A. Stanger & Co., which is one of the largest investment banks to offer nontraded REITs, along with the Institute for Portfolio Alternatives (IPA), recently (2019) launched "the IPA/Stanger Monitor, a new report that tracks the total return of 58 non-traded REITs, including seven NAV REITs, with a combined market capitalization of more than $49.5 billion."[53] According to the report, both the Stanger NAV REIT and the Stanger Lifecycle REIT indexes had "cumulative returns (distributions and capital appreciation) of 22.2% and 18.2% respectively, for the three-year period ending December 31, 2018."[54] For 2018 alone, the Stanger NAV REIT had returns of 7.35%, compared to 3.48% from the Dow Jones Industrial Average.[55] One of the reasons nontraded REITs performed so admirably is noncorrelation.

As a low-correlation asset class, real estate is not directly affected by the uncertain movements of the stock market. Nontraded REITs can provide long-term capital appreciation and rent increases that can help address rising inflation. The average investor today has access to the same portfolios that were once exclusive to institutional and wealthy investors. When you "couple this access with the professional property management and leasing capabilities of REITs . . . you have a truly passive form of income-generating, recession-proof investing."[56] REITs have a unique set of risks that you must be aware of. These risks include restrictions and excessive costs and limitations regarding early redemption, excessive fees, lack of diversification, unspecified properties, and potential tax consequences. You need to familiarize yourself with these risks before adding REITs as part of your portfolio.

BUSINESS DEVELOPMENT COMPANIES (BDCS)

Another asset class that started to become popular in 2009 was business development companies. A BDC invests in small- and medium-size companies. What made BDCs popular with the retail investor were the high profit potential, diversification, and transparency. Some of the larger companies, such as Owl Rock and Franklin Square, introduced BDCs to the retail investor because of the return potential. Consider this: "Owl Rock Capital Corporation sold 10 million shares to investors during its initial public offering on July 18, 2019."[57] In short, REITs and BDCs are "regulated investment companies that must distribute 90% of their taxable income to shareholders. They are very popular among investors and rightfully so."[58]

Although BDCs were first introduced in 1940, when Congress passed the Investment Company Act, they didn't start to take off until the early 2000s, which is why I'm identifying them as second-generation real estate. Following the 2002 tech wreck, BDCs started to become attractive because fewer companies were trading on the stock market. In 2002 Congress passed the Sarbanes–Oxley Act to protect investors from fraudulent financial reporting by corporations. Sarbanes–Oxley was enacted in response to the greed and corruption of the dot-com era. Remember Enron and WorldCom? As a result of the more stringent conditions of Sarbanes–Oxley, such as senior corporate officers personally certifying the company's financials with the SEC and rules regarding record keeping, among other requirements, fewer companies went public. This created a space for BDCs to offer lending solutions to midsize companies.[59]

Following the financial crisis of 2008, banks significantly curtailed lending to middle-market businesses. BDCs benefited from this by offering financing to these businesses at attractive rates.[60] In addition, BDCs have "established due diligence and underwriting practices that are specifically tailored to middle-market lending, and understand the extensive ongoing monitoring required by the lender."[61] Many of these BDCs "can be profitable if you get the timing right."[62]

Let's look at the performance of the Cliffwater BDC, which is called the Cliffwater Direct Lending Index (CDLI). From June 2004 to June 2020, the total annualized average return was 9.11%.[63] For comparison, the S&P 500 annualized average return over the same time period was 7.99%.[64] Please remember that investing in BDCs is risky and speculative. The portfolio companies in which BDCs invest may have limited financial resources and may be unable to meet their obligations on the debt securities held by the BDCs, causing them to default. I'm giving you the knowledge that you need to be able to determine if BDCs are suitable for you. There are also suitability requirements. Please speak to a qualified and experienced financial advisor so that you can make an informed choice.

To make matters worse, today there are five companies that make up 20% of the S&P 500. These companies include Microsoft, Apple, Amazon, Google, and Facebook. According to Goldman Sachs, that's a bad signal for future market returns.[65] The point I want you to understand is this: There are opportunities available to you now that were once exclusive to institutional or wealthy investors. Let's delve a little deeper into BDCs.

As closed-end investment companies, BDCs invest in small and midsize businesses. They invest shareholders' money to generate income and hopefully turn a profit.[66] BDCs are both traded and non-traded. Traded BDCs are public companies whose shares trade on major stock exchanges. Given that BDCs are regulated investment companies (RICs), they must distribute 90% of their profits to shareholders. The advantage is they don't pay corporate income tax on profits before they distribute them to shareholders.[67]

Nontraded BDCs were first introduced by Franklin Square Investments in 2009. Some of the advantages of nontraded BDCs include access to investments that were once dominated by wealthy and institutional investors. They also offer a potentially reduced risk through diversification and a regulated investment vehicle with transparent disclosure and periodic reporting.[68] One of the most popular BDCs available today is the Cliffwater BDC Index.[69] There are other unique risks associated with BDCs. For example, BDCs are illiquid, are often not investment grade, are sensitive to interest rates, and can have high management fees.

INTERVAL FUNDS

The third generation of real estate is interval funds, which are a type of closed-end fund with shares that do not trade on the secondary market. You give up liquidity in exchange for the potential for higher yields. Interval funds "give investors a greater exposure to higher-yielding credit markets while avoiding the lower realized returns that can result from investor psychology, promoting longer-term investment periods."[70] Because interval funds do not have daily liquidity, portfolio managers can invest interval fund capital in more illiquid assets than they could in mutual funds.[71]

Although the structure of interval funds was adopted by the SEC in 1993, the industry was slow to adopt interval funds, largely because fund managers, distribution partners, and clients were unfamiliar with them. Interval funds started to become popular in 2016 as more funds were launched. For example, in 2014 there were eight new interval funds launched, and by 2016, that number climbed to 27.[72] One of the advantages of interval funds is "that they offer yields that can be potentially higher than most other mutual fund options."[73] Large institutions like Morningstar started to offer interval funds to retail clients, which made the funds more popular. It is important to note that these funds are often more expensive than regular mutual funds. Again, consult your qualified financial advisor for a more detail explanation of the risks involved. The more you are aware of the unique risks for the asset classes, the smarter investor you will become.

Let's summarize some of the reasons why alternatives became popular with retail clients. For much too long alternative investments were exclusively reserved for institutional investors, such as large university endowments and wealthy individuals. Over the past several years many alternative products became available to the retail investor, which is you. I cannot emphasize enough how important this shift has been for the average investor. It allowed the individual investor to potentially benefit from the same opportunities as large institutions.

It is important to understand that alternative investments are not for everyone. There are suitability requirements that include age, income, net worth, liquidity needs, investment objectives, risk profile, investment experience, and time horizon. In addition, there are state and federal laws and guidelines that you need to be aware of. When clients come to me for portfolio evaluation and recovery, I spend quite a bit of time with them going over the benefits and risks of adding alternative asset classes to their portfolio, as well as ensuring that their portfolio is in line with their risks tolerance and future goals. I do this before any recommendations are made. Below is a summary of benefits and risks:

Benefits	Risks
Not correlated to stocks and bonds	Illiquid
A potentially durable source of income	Complex instruments
Potentially stronger returns	Risk of losing principal
Added diversification	Management experience (or lack of)
Tax benefits	Loss of principal

TACTICAL INVESTING

Tactical investing is designed to protect investors against the unexpected swings of the market. The important thing to remember about tactical asset allocation is that it "is an active investment approach that attempts to capture superior returns due to predicted underlying shifts in market fundamentals, opportunities or risks."[74] The key phrase here is "active investment approach," which is the ability to adapt to, and opportunistically capitalize on, changing market conditions. Tactical investments became popular following the global financial meltdown of 2008. The stock market crash, in particular, created a great deal of uncertainty, and investors wanted a hedge against sudden market swings.

Large university endowments have long used tactical assets because they have large teams of in-house investment managers conducting research.[75] As an active form of portfolio management, tactical strategies are designed to help investors maximize profits while minimizing risk. As someone who has spent years adapting the endowment model to the retail investor, I can tell you that it requires not only adding multiple asset classes, but also the management of each of my clients' portfolios. I use outside managers, as well as my own research, to help maximize profits while minimizing risk. Examples of tactical products include absolute-return funds and structured products.

ABSOLUTE-RETURN FUNDS

As the name implies, *absolute-return funds* refer to the performance of an asset class or strategy without comparison to any benchmark. The aim of absolute-return funds is to generate positive returns "year after year no matter what happens to the S&P 500 or any other benchmark index."[76] What makes absolute-return funds part of a tactical strategy is the freedom "to invest in a wide variety of securities as well as a variety of strategies to hedge specific types of risk. The funds may have lower volatility over time and may operate independently of market direction."[77] Absolute-return funds are different from mutual funds that "seek to produce returns that are better than its peers, its fund category, and the market as a whole."[78] This is why mutual funds are known as relative-return funds. You will read more about absolute-return funds in Chapter 5.

STRUCTURED PRODUCTS

Structured products are prepackaged investments that "normally include assets linked to interest plus one or more derivatives. They are generally tied to an index or basket of securities and are designed to facilitate highly customized risk-return objectives. This is accomplished by taking a traditional security such as a conventional investment-grade bond and replacing the usual payment features."[79] Structured products are sometimes referred to as market-linked investments because they are linked to the performance of one or more underlying benchmarks, such as interest rates, equity markets, commodities, or corporate credits.

Structured products started to gain popularity in 2006. In fact, according to the American structured products industry, "an estimated $45 to $50 billion worth of products placed in the United States in 2005."[80] Also, in 2006 a significant innovation to improve liquidity in certain types of structured products came in the form of exchange-traded notes (ETNs), which were introduced by multinational investment bank Barclays.

One of the things that gave rise to structured products was the need for companies to issue cheap debt. The advantage of structured products is "their ability to offer customized exposure to otherwise hard-to-reach asset classes and subclasses," which means they are ideal tactical assets.[81] The issuers of these structured products, or notes, pay returns upon maturity. Let's look at an example of a structured product in the form of bank-issued notes. Let's say you purchase a bank note with a face value of $1,000. The note is "fully principal-protected, meaning you will get your $1,000 back at maturity no matter what happens to the underlying asset."[82] The note is linked to an underlying equity instrument such as common stock or an ETF that mimics a popular index like the S&P 500. If the underlying asset is positive at maturity of the note, the investor will earn a profit with minimal risk. It is important to understand that, "should you need to sell your structured note before maturity, it is unlikely the original issuer will give you a good price—assuming they are willing or interested in making you an offer at all."[83]

Structured products are complex instruments, which is why it is critical you discuss their benefits and risks with a qualified financial planner. There are three unique risks associated with structured products which include credit risk, market risk, and inflation risk. In terms of credit risk, "the security backing your investment plan will be issued by a financial institution, usually a bank. In the unlikely event of default or bankruptcy of the bank, investors will receive back less than they invested."[84] The point here is that you need to protect yourself by seeking out the services of a qualified professional to advise you.

ADAPTING TO A NEW WAY OF THINKING

Until recently it was nearly impossible for individuals to adopt the endowment approach. Endowments are complex financial vehicles requiring high minimum investments, offer less liquidity than individual investors typically need, and involve the implementation of a wide variety of asset classes. It can all be confusing and overwhelming at first, especially if you, like most Americans, are accustomed to stock-and-bond strategies. The chances are that you have been making investment decisions for years based on safe yet unchallenged assumptions.

Remember that you can no longer avoid market risks by simply shifting to bonds; those days are gone. That may have worked for your parents and grandparents, but it will likely not work for you. According to Lara Rhame, chief US economist at Franklin Square Investments, you "should plan for volatility and focus on building well-diversified portfolios to withstand the inevitable return to a higher-volatility world."[85] In addition, because of government control of interest rates, which has skewed returns for bonds, as well as for most types of debt, bonds are not delivering the same returns today as they did for your parents and grandparents.

An endowment-like portfolio, on the other hand, includes illiquid assets with bond-like features, with potentially better returns, which offers the individual investor a buffer against the emotionally draining churn of the market. Moreover, the endowment approach has the potential to deliver a sufficient and reliable income, which could allow you to withdraw 4% or more. Prior to COVID-19 we were living through a bull market, but you shouldn't be complacent. You need to investigate and learn about other investment options that could potentially offer you better returns while managing risk. As we have seen so far, the endowment model is flexible enough and sufficiently diversified to potentially offer you a powerful alternative.

In order for you, the individual investor, to better understand how to prepare for the retirement you've earned and deserve, I believe that you'll need to adopt this new way of thinking, regardless of how much money you have. You'll need to work with your advisor to see if it makes sense to restructure your portfolio to potentially achieve a better outcome. Don't let algorithms control your financial future. The financial literacy you're investing in now can help keep you from being solely at the mercy of the whims of the market, the fallibility of algorithms, and false or misleading information.

Chapter 5

THE REALLOCATION EFFECT: ASSETS IN ACTION

"You should have a strategic asset allocation mix that
assumes that you don't know what the future is going to hold."

–RAY DALIO

———

Merriam-Webster defines the word "reallocate" as "to apportion or distribute (something) in a new or different way."[1] Let me now introduce the *reallocation effect* so that you can better understand why I developed the Retail Endowment Allocation Like Model (REALM). I define the reallocation effect as the fundamental process of simultaneously expanding asset classes in a portfolio while potentially reducing exposure of existing allocations, such as stocks and bonds. I spent years thinking about, and painstakingly researching, what I believe is a better model to potentially protect my clients from powerful forces that can derail their retirement years. These forces include globalization, greed, inequality, monopolies, fraud and corruption, a potentially broken 60/40 investment strategy, and systemic failures in pensions and Social Security.

The REALM model could *potentially* provide you the following benefits:

- Better results with five core investments versus two asset classes.

- Reduced sequence-of-return risk due to less volatility.

- Higher durable income sources.

- Equity-like returns with bond-like volatility.

- Protection for investors from things they can't control.

Now what happens if you limit your core asset classes to stocks and bonds? First, you are likely increasing your exposure, which increases your risk. I've already stated that exposing yourself to 60% in stocks increases your risk, especially when bond yields are at historic lows. What does this mean for the average investor? It means that you may not be able to afford 60% exposure to a stock market that experiences frequent volatility. Investors may need protection, which is what the REALM model potentially offers you.

The REALM model is built around three fundamental pillars—passive, tactical, and alternative strategies. The passive approach involves both liquid and limited liquidity assets. The tactical approach has a high degree of liquidity, while the alternative approach incorporates both limited liquidity and illiquid assets. The three moving parts of REALM—passive, tactical, and alternative—work together in synergistic harmony. The passive strategy includes stocks and bonds, mutual funds, index funds, exchange-traded funds (ETFs), annuities, and structured notes. The tactical strategy includes absolute-return funds. Finally, the alternative strategy includes business development corporations (BDCs), private or public commercial real estate funds, nontraded real estate investment trusts (REITS), and private placements. Let's explore each of these strategies in detail.

THE CONSTRUCTION OF REALM

Think of the word "realm" for a minute. It refers to an area of knowledge or expertise in some field. Knowledge itself is something we accumulate from reading about particular subjects as well as by experiencing the world. Innovation, however, is the result of epiphanies, which are these sudden bursts of insight or inspiration that come to us. Think of epiphanies as aha! moments that help us become aware of deeper insights about certain areas of knowledge or a way of doing things. As I said in the preface, following the market crash of 2002, which was the result of the dot-com bubble, I was devastated. My clients lost a great deal of money, and I questioned whether I should continue working in the financial world. After a brief period of experiencing the kind of existential fear that freezes you into inaction, I decided not only to resume my work in the financial world but also to fully immerse myself in it by engaging in a rigorous study of the hidden forces that may be impacting my clients' money. It would be during this time that I experienced deep insights into what would later become the foundation of my REALM model.

In order for innovation to happen, one must first recognize and understand why the old way of doing things didn't work. Throughout the 1990s and early 2000s, I utilized the 60/40 portfolio. The market crash of 2002 hit me hard. I suppose I could have justified the losses as many other financial advisors did, by simply saying, "That's the nature of the market: It's always unpredictable and risky." But that was not me. I couldn't, and didn't, accept the idea there was nothing one can do when the markets behave in a wild and unpredictable manner. I knew at an intuitive level there was something wrong with the accepted wisdom. I knew there was something wrong with a portfolio strategy that exposed people to 60% in stocks and 40% in bonds. I spent the next several years engaged in rigorous study of the 60/40 portfolio in order to understand why it was potentially broken.

I had a powerful sense something was wrong almost 20 years before some major banks and other experts officially declared the 60/40 strategy obsolete. It was in October 2019 when Bank of America strategists Derek Harris and Jared Woodard, wrote, "'The end of 60/40 keyed in on the changing role of bonds in portfolios."[2] The following month, JP Morgan suggested that investors incorporate "other income generating assets, like real estate."[3] Morgan Stanley gave a more ominous warning: "that returns on a traditional balanced portfolio with 60% stocks and 40% bonds could approach 100-year lows and drop by half versus the last 20 years."[4] In addition, best-selling author Suze Orman stated in February 2020, "Actually, the 60-40 is dead."[5] Although I appreciate these affirmations of what I recognized many years ago, I sometimes wonder why it took these experts so long to acknowledge it.

Having an intuitive sense that the 60/40 portfolio was potentially broken was not enough. In order to create an entirely new investment model, I needed to understand why this tried-and-true strategy was vulnerable to market swings. I started reading books and journals that ranged from the technical to the historical. I read "Portfolio Selection," a paper by Harry Markowitz; I read books and articles on modern portfolio theory, the first Gilded Age, income inequality, the Great Depression, the New Deal, portfolio construction, risk, diversification, globalization, the Federal Reserve, and so on. I learned about the hidden forces that can impact any portfolio strategy. I learned that a portfolio composed of stocks and bonds, which have historically been inversely correlated, is potentially problematic when stocks and bonds start moving in the same direction, which is what is happening today. Knowledge, as I've stated in the preface, is hollow and empty if it is not applied.

I spent years studying and researching ways to improve upon the 60/40 portfolio. I was on a mission to find a solution to protect my clients. Unfortunately, I didn't find a ready-made solution out there. That's when I realized that I had to find my own solution. I began with the fundamental premise that any meaningful portfolio in today's complex, globally interconnected world must be based on diversification. I started to construct a multi-asset-class model that would potentially offer my clients better returns while managing risk. I knew early on that I had to incorporate alternative asset classes, but that was not enough. I needed to find a way to try to create a level of protection for my clients' portfolios. And I need to state again that diversification, as well as asset allocation, are strategies—they are not guarantees that you can't lose money or that you will always realize a profit. Rather, these are time-tested strategies that we use to help manage risk and reduce volatility.

I was told by several financial advisors and money managers that the 60/40 portfolio already had a built-in protection with the bond side of the equation. I, of course, rejected such advice, as bonds were offering less protection. I searched for other means of protecting my clients' money without sacrificing returns. As I was doing research into portfolio construction, I came across the book *Pioneering Portfolio Management: An Unconventional Approach to Institutional Investment* by David Swensen. At the time I almost didn't read the book, as the topic was relevant to institutional investment. I was doing research, after all, on portfolio construction for the individual investor. For some reason, however, I decided to read the book.

As I started reading, I became excited. The introduction alone paralleled my thinking in such a way that I felt vindicated. Swensen wrote, "The knowledge base that provides useful support for investment decisions knows no bounds. A rich understanding of human psychology, a reasonable appreciation of financial theory, a deep awareness of history, and a broad exposure to current events all contribute to the development of well-informed portfolio strategies."[6] I couldn't put the book down. Although it was more than 350 pages long, I stayed up all night reading it. By the time I finished, I was dizzy with possibilities. Prior to reading Swensen, I had felt I was the only one who noticed the need for a more diversified portfolio.

Swensen has enormous credibility. When he started as Yale's endowment manager in 1985, the endowment had $1 billion under management. Within 14 years, Swensen increased Yale's endowment to $7.2 billion, and by 2018 the endowment ballooned to $29.4 billion.[7] When I started building my REALM model, many of the products that were available to institutional investors had not been made available to the individual investor. Over time, however, the doors would open up, and in the last 10 years several products have become available. The challenge, of course, was how to adapt a multibillion-dollar endowment fund to the individual investor. While on the surface it may sound simple—just use the same products the endowments use and everything will be fine—it proved to be incredibly challenging and time consuming.

The challenge was not only adapting the endowment model, taking into consideration that individuals have a different time horizon and levels of risk, but also making my model adaptable enough and flexible enough for the individual investor. Another significant difference between the REALM and endowment models is that I don't get institutional pricing like the large endowments do. Although adapting the model was a herculean effort, I pushed on. I spent 16-hour days studying different products. For diversification, I added alternative asset classes such as BDCs, which are noncorrelated asset classes, to help smooth volatility. I used tactical strategies to help my clients protect their portfolios against market declines.

The architectural blueprint of my multi-asset-class strategy was coming into focus. The challenge was not simply finding suitable products; I also had to create an easy-to-understand model for my clients. After spending years on study and research, my multi-asset-class model was born. As I noted previously, it rests on three pillars: passive, tactical, and alternative strategies. My model also had to be fluid, meaning it had to be flexible enough to accommodate different levels of allocation based on each client's needs. I didn't want to have a fixed percentage allocated to passive, tactical, and alternative asset classes; rather, I wanted the flexibility to customize a multi-asset-class strategy based on client needs, investment profile, liquidity needs, and financial circumstances.

Next was naming the model. I needed a name that would convey all the knowledge and research that went into the construction of my strategy. In addition to being a CFP', with numerous licenses, I also believe in educating my clients. I knew my model had endowment-like qualities, with certain allocations in different asset classes. I also knew it was designed for the retail—individual—investor. The acronym was staring me in the face: **R**etail **E**ndowment **A**llocation **L**ike **M**odel. Once my REALM model was born, I proceeded to undertake the monumental task of meeting with hundreds of my clients to determine if it made sense to convert their portfolios to this model. My Cinergy team and I worked 12-hour days, perhaps more, to make sure my clients held suitable products according to my innovative REALM model.

Over time, more products became available to my clients, and today I have more than 50 products to choose from, which increases the availability and flexibility of what I can offer the individual investor. I have the freedom to offer my clients products that include nontraded REITs, interval funds, private placements, nontraded preferred stock, BDCs, structured products, and traditional stocks and bonds. Through my broker-dealer I have access to and utilize products offered by some of the most reputable companies used by large institutions and endowments. These companies include Fidelity, Owl Rock, and Franklin Square. Let's now look at the various passive, tactical, and alternative products available to clients.

PASSIVE INVESTMENT

As the name implies, passive investing is a buy-and-hold strategy where investors take a hands-off approach. Passive investing is a strategy in which you try to maximize your returns but also minimize buying and selling, because these can have fees associated with them, require supervision or a professional advisor, and involve complicated portfolio management. Investing in a market index is a common passive approach; with this strategy, investors purchase a representative benchmark fund, such as the S&P 500 index, and hold it for a long time.[8] This longer time frame is crucial; it allows the index to absorb day-to-day fluctuations in the market to take advantage of the general trend. This is a simple strategy to apply in strong markets, when every stock fund seems to have a tailwind; however, it proves far more difficult in a down market. Many individual investors have traditionally shifted their buy-and-hold strategy from volatile stocks to more "reliable" bonds as they approach retirement age, but stagnant interest rates make this a potentially costly strategy if the returns on those bonds are not adequate to reach your retirement needs.

One of the main problems with passive investing is that investors are exposed to market risks. For example, index funds track a significant portion of the entire stock market (depending on the specific companies and industries they track), so if the stock market falls, the index fund often falls as well. Another problem with passive investing is the lack of flexibility. For example, the managers of index funds are often prohibited from using defensive measures to offset market losses. "Passively managed index funds face performance constraints, as they are designed to provide returns that closely track their benchmark index rather than seek outperformance."[9]

In some respect, passive investments don't require much thought, which can also create a false sense of security; one concern is that the complacency could result in unnecessary risk. In fact, Robert Shiller, who teaches economics at Yale University, compares passive investing to "seeing a green light at an intersection and crossing the street without looking both ways."[10] Shiller believes that passive investing is a chaotic system where investors are focusing on fees rather than beating the market.[11] The term *alpha* represents an investment strategy's ability to beat the market and is often used as a measure of the active return on an investment. Alpha "gauges the performance of an investment against a market index or benchmark that is considered to represent the market's movement as a whole."[12]

Passive assets include mutual funds, exchange-traded funds, index funds, structured notes, and annuities.

MUTUAL FUNDS

Mutual *funds* allow you to make investments you might not be able to make on your own by pooling your money with that of others to buy multiple investments together. The fund is often named after the underlying investment it is in, such as *money market funds, bond funds*, and *equity* or *stock funds*.

A mutual fund's price is determined by its net asset value, or NAV, which is the price of its assets (with all of its liabilities subtracted) divided by the number of shares. The determining factor of the price of a mutual fund is the growth of its assets. Most mutual funds include stocks in numerous companies. As the individual companies rise in value, so does the price of the mutual fund.[13] Mutual funds offer some advantages over, for example, buying individual stocks or bonds. They are more diversified, of course, since you're buying into more than one bond, and they're more affordable, since you are buying in a pool rather than on your own. They can be "bought and sold with relative ease, making them highly liquid investments."[14] Mutual funds must be managed by a professional manager, so they offer the benefit of expertise, but that comes along with added fees and expenses.[15]

There are three ways a mutual fund will earn you money: First, the fund may pay *dividends* (a portion of their profit periodically paid out to shareholders). Second, you might also earn capital gains, which come from the fund's selling parts of its investment at a profit. Finally, if the market value of your fund increases, the value of your investment increases. These returns are passed on to you and the other investors in the fund—minus fees.[16]

If the assets held within your fund drop in value, so will your investment. Like that coin toss—or **any other** market-based investment—a fund's performance in the past doesn't predict how well or badly it will deliver returns in the future, but you can use its past performance to help estimate its volatility—how much it has fluctuated—which helps determine the level of risk involved.[17]

EXCHANGE-TRADED FUNDS

An exchange-traded fund, usually referred to by its abbreviation ETF, is similar to a mutual fund in that you pool your investment with those of others. However, they differ from mutual funds by being traded directly on the market, and their market value may not match the value of the combined parts. You can think of these as somewhere between mutual funds and normal stocks—pooled but tradable.[18]

Unlike mutual funds, you cannot directly buy into an exchange-traded fund as an individual investor; they are sold through financial institutions (called "authorized participants"), so you will need to have an account with a financial advisor to take advantage of this investment type. Most exchange-traded funds are based on an index of the market, but some fit more into the "tactical" category below.[19]

INDEX FUNDS

An index fund is a "type of mutual fund or exchange-traded fund (ETF) with a portfolio constructed to match or track the components of a financial market index, such the Standard & Poor's 500 index (S&P 500)."[20] Index funds are often named for what they index. For example, the S&P 500 indexes the stock and performance of the 500 largest companies on the US stock exchange.[21]

Like other passive investment strategies, index funds are designed to benefit from an upward trend of the market. However, they may not always match that potential growth because of fees, costs, or errors in alignment with their indexed stocks. They are also subject to the same risks as the stocks they index.[22]

STRUCTURED NOTES

A structured note is a debt security—a tradable asset—issued by a financial institution, like a bank. A note includes two pieces: a bond and a *derivative,* a sort of payout that changes in value based on the value of the main part of the note.[23] Structured notes, like funds, allow you to use an investment strategy that might not otherwise be available to you.[24] A structured note, if used appropriately, can help "retail investors to access parts of the market that they ordinarily might not see."[25] Some of the benefits of structured notes include flexibility, liquidity, cost efficiency, capital protection, and growth.[26] The risk level of the note is determined by the credit risk of the bank issuing the note. The rate of return is typically linked to an equity index. The notes may or may not include a variety of bonds, equities, and derivatives. It is important for you to understand that structured notes have a higher risk of default.

The rate of return on a structured note is typically "based on equity indexes, a single equity, a basket of equities, interest rates, commodities or foreign currencies." Your potential return will be linked to the performance of these underlying assets or indexes.[27]

The risk level of the note is determined by the credit risk of the bank or other institution issuing the note. Certain types of notes, such as buffer and principal-protected notes, are complex and may not be suitable for individual investors. The risks associated with structured notes are complex and they may not be insured by the FDIC.[28]

ANNUITIES

Annuities offer income for life; they offer assured, guaranteed income to balance the growth (and risk) of other investments. Annuities are sold by insurance companies and act like other types of insurance: You pay for them in advance, and then the insurance company pays out a certain amount for the rest of your life.[29] How much income the annuity pays will depend on the type of annuity. The amount of guaranteed income you will need depends on your age, the size of your portfolio, and the amount of money you will need to support the life you envision after retirement. By increasing the amount of income that comes from guaranteed sources such as annuities, you can "significantly reduce your sequence of return risk."[30] Annuities have "one big advantage over stocks and bonds which is guaranteed income (as long as the insurance company stays in business—the guarantee is based on the company's financial strength and ability to pay claims). The stock market has been volatile and [one] wouldn't want to depend on it too much in retirement. Bonds have very low interest right now and they are riskier than annuities."[31]

Annuities are often appealing to people who are risk averse. As we approach retirement, many of us are concerned with protecting our assets. Given the unpredictability of past market corrections (quick rises and falls), we become more cautious with our assets. In general, an annuity is a conservative vehicle that can provide an income floor that gives you breathing room to take on a little more risk over the balance of your portfolio.

Annuities are largely intended for people who are in or near retirement. Typically, annuities offer tax benefits, but investors younger than 59½ will face a 10% early withdrawal penalty if you make a withdrawal during the early years of the contract, referred to as the surrender charge period. Most annuities also include a death benefit, such as a return of your original premium payment minus withdrawals. Annuities involve fees and expenses, like any other financial product or investment. In addition, they assess surrender penalties if you withdraw funds before the end of what's called the "surrender charge period," so they are designed to be long-term products.

Typically, annuities fall into one of four categories, based on how they are designed to deliver income: variable, immediate, fixed, and fixed indexed.

Variable annuities seek to capture market gains, so the value of the account can grow before you start taking withdrawals. Most variable annuities allow the policyholder to choose some of the underlying investments. This has the potential to raise the amount on which your withdrawals are based, but you can also lose money since variable annuities are market-based products. However, you may be able to purchase optional riders that assure you that, even if market returns erode the value of the account, you are still assured a minimum amount of value. In this case, the income base continues to grow and that minimum increase is called a *living benefit,* which typically involves an extra charge.

Immediate annuities require that once you purchase it, you start drawing income right away, generally within one year at the latest. Immediate annuities are not designed to keep up with inflation. You continue receiving the same amount of money regardless of what inflation does to your purchasing power and how the economic conditions change.

Fixed annuities require that you commit your money for a specified (fixed) time, and you, in turn, will receive a specified interest rate.

Fixed indexed annuities allow you to receive interest that is tied to the performance of an external market index without the threat of losing your principal (the amount you've invested), because you are never invested in the market itself. The annuity is pegged to a market index which you select, and then each year the issuing company calculates any potential interest based on changes in the index. Interest will be subject to limits set by the company, such as caps, spreads, or participation rates. In return for these limits, if the index declines, the annuity is guaranteed not to lose money due to market declines. Your money is committed for a specified period of time, making the annuity an illiquid investment.

By definition, an annuity offers the closest thing to a guaranteed income. But it is important to remember that all investment decisions should be grounded in caution. Annuities are complex instruments, so you will need to consult a qualified financial planner to help you navigate the different features and associated costs.

TACTICAL INVESTMENT

Tactical investing is active rather than passive: a hands-on approach. It requires someone—either you or a professional financial advisor—to actively manage your portfolio.[32] Tactical investment requires rigorous analysis and a certain level of expertise because the portfolio manager will need to use both fundamental and quantitative analysis in order to anticipate price movements and react to them by actively changing strategies and assets.

Some of the advantages of active investing include flexibility, hedging (a complicated way to help protect your investment), and risk management. Active portfolio managers are not required to hold specific stocks or bonds, as a passive portfolio would, which gives them more flexibility.

Tactical assets also offer *liquidity*—the ability to sell an investment and take your funds out. This can help balance the stability of debt securities, like bonds, that require a certain period of time before your potential return materializes. Tactical investment is proactive, designed to zig when the market zags, in order to help protect your assets while delivering opportunistic growth opportunity in short bursts. Tactical allocations also adjust, which means that you could potentially sidestep a market crash that could undermine your financial goals.

The objective of active portfolio management is to beat the market, to earn a return higher than the market average. It is also meant to fully embrace the fluctuations of the market, taking advantage of rises and drops in the prices of stocks to maximize your return.[33] Tactical product offerings include absolute-return funds, market-neutral funds, and managed futures.

ABSOLUTE-RETURN FUNDS

An absolute-return fund is a kind of mutual fund that includes investments that are less traditional than a typical mutual fund. They involve complex strategies designed to seek a positive return even when the stock market falls.[34] The term *absolute* is in contrast to *relative,* meaning that the fund earns returns based on its own performance and not as an index of the market.[35] The techniques used in absolute-return investment include short selling, futures, options, derivatives, arbitrage, leverage, and unconventional assets.[36]

MANAGED FUTURES

Futures, as the name implies, involve a transaction in the future. A *futures contract* is an agreement to buy or sell a defined quantity of a commodity or financial instrument at a certain price on a date specified in the agreement.[37] A *commodity* is a real physical material or agricultural product, such as pork bellies or wheat—or a financial instrument like bonds, stocks, or even cash. You would earn a return or loss based on the difference between the market value on the future date and the value of the contract at the time of purchase.

Given the sophisticated nature of futures contracts, they must be managed by regulated specialists, called *commodity trading advisors.*

These managers "use sophisticated technology and quantitative modeling to systematically identify the trends they wish to follow."[38]

Managed futures are the same as regular futures but they are necessarily managed by a professional.[39] "Managed futures are considered an alternative investment and are often used by funds and institutional investors to provide both portfolio and market diversification."[40] By buying the right to buy and sell commodities, regardless of market direction, managers can capture returns in bullish (high) or bearish (low) markets. Managed futures involve a wide array of liquid exchange-traded contracts, which include futures and forward contracts.

Incorporating managed futures into a portfolio has, over the last 40 years or so, "resulted in higher returns, reduced drawdowns, and lower volatility."[41] As the following chart illustrates, a portfolio that is half dedicated to managed futures far outperformed more conservative models.[42]

Tactical Strategies
Consider Reallocation of Stocks to An Absolute Return Fund

Potentially Allocating to Managed Futures May Enhance Risks-Adjusted Returns[1]

Growth of $10,000 for Equities, Managed Futures, and Blended Portfolios
Based on monthly return data from 12/31/1979 to 10/31/2018. Source: Bloomberg LP.

RISKS — Futures trading is not suitable for all investors, and involves the risk of loss. Futures are a leveraged investment, and because only a percentage of a contract's value is required to trade, it is possible to lose more than the amount of money deposited for a futures position. (2)

Source: 1. https://catalystmf.com/adding-alternatives-top-managed-futures-research-of-2018-ml-version/
2. https://www.keloniacapital.com/site/Frequently_Asked_Questions_About_Managed_Futures_2011pdf-en-6-2.html

MARKET-NEUTRAL FUNDS

Market-neutral funds are another kind of mutual fund. In this case, they involve a balance of short selling and holding long in equal measure—so that they become "market neutral."[43] *Short selling* is selling something you don't yet own and that you think will drop in value so that you can profit from that drop. The long position is the opposite: You hold a stock you do own with the expectation that it will increase in value.

Tactical assets are critical for minimizing risk, reducing volatility, and creating a dynamic strategy for investors, but they lack the traditional long-term stability of passive investment.

SIMPLE MOVING AVERAGE

The 200-day simple moving average is a technical indicator that can be used to detect both short-term and long-term trend opportunities.[44] This technical indicator is used to time when to buy or sell a security. When the market is trending upward, you or your advisor buy the security when its monthly closing price rises above the simple moving average. Your goal then is to wait until the market trend reverses—tips back down—and sell the investment at a profit.[45]

Certain specialty funds are based on types of moving averages, which allow investors to go long (buy) or short (sell) when the simple moving average is favorable. A simple moving average fund complements a buy-and-hold stock strategy. If the market is rising, the fund shifts more money into rising funds. Conversely, money is shifted away in declining funds.[46]

ALTERNATIVE STRUCTURES

As you've already read, alternative assets have been gaining momentum with individual investors since 2003. Some investors discovered alternatives as a way of trying to protect themselves from the 2002 stock market crash. These brave investors were pleasantly surprised to learn that alternatives generally offered potential growth opportunities, respectable income, and noncorrelated risk to the stock market. Please keep in mind that alternatives can only be purchased through a qualified advisor. Let's explore some of these alternative assets.

Alternative investing includes several products or structures that you need to be aware of. These structures include illiquid and limited liquidity assets. For example, BDCs and interval funds that are priced daily at net asset value (NAV) offer limited liquidity. Qualified opportunity zones and private placements are illiquid. Commercial real estate and BDCs offer a range of liquidity. To better understand the liquidity of alternatives, we need to distinguish between traded and nontraded alternative structures.

Unlike stocks that trade on an exchange, alternative structures invest more directly in a company or project. Most traditional investments "are publicly available to any investor who has money to pay for them, and liquid, which means they can be bought and sold when you wish, though not at the price you would like."[47] Due to their complex nature, most alternatives are sold through broker-dealers or financial advisory firms. Many alternative structures offer limited liquidity or are illiquid. It is important to understand what liquidity means. Some of the attraction of illiquid alternative investments is they can help diversify your portfolio. Also, alternative investments tend to have a low correlation with the stock market.

Let's summarize the potential benefits of alternative structures:

- They help diversify your portfolio.

- They potentially increase income and total return.

- They can hedge against inflation, recession, or both.

- They capitalize on access to a broader range of assets than previously available.[48]

REAL ESTATE INVESTMENT TRUSTS

Let's begin with the basics. Real estate investment trusts (REITs) are alternative structures that own and manage large portfolios of real estate. REITs consistently create categories of income-producing real estate that include hospitality, senior housing, student housing, storage, professional buildings and hospitals, offices, multifamily housing, industrial buildings, and select categories of retail. Some REITs include funds that back commercial mortgages, and others are hybrids of real estate ownership and mortgages.

Shares in nontraded REITs are not available on exchanges and usually have limited liquidity, but newer types of nontraded REITs enable investors to buy in and exit at any time; these are known as *continuously offered* REITs. REITs may also return certain tax advantages to some investors.

These trusts have the ability to generate money in two different ways: from rent and from the realization of property appreciation. In order to qualify as a REIT, each trust must pay 90% or more of its taxable income each year to its shareholders, and most of them distribute 100% of their taxable income.[49]

Nontraded REITs are generally insulated from the daily fluctuations of the stock and bond markets (unlike traded REITs). In the past, high fees and long wait times have eroded both returns from and trust in REITs. However, some of the newer versions of REITs offer reasonable fees and terms, which can be suitable for investors who are comfortable with holding an asset over a longer time horizon. Your financial advisor should assess both the underlying drivers of the properties in the REIT and the track record and qualifications of the professionals managing the trust.

BDCS

As its name implies, *BDCs*, also known as *secured corporate debt*, consist of loans made to corporations, collateralized by assets such as the corporation's property or its receivables (money owed to it).[50] This type of debt is also known as *senior secured loans* because it is the first (senior) debt to be reimbursed by the borrower corporation.[51]

In essence, investors pool money to loan, and companies borrow from these pooled funds instead of borrowing from banks. The companies pay more for these loans as a result of unique circumstances and timelines. The investor commits money for a certain period of time and can expect to earn somewhere between 5% and 7% (which is not guaranteed), which is well above the current returns of the bond market.[52]

Secured corporate debt is organized and managed into funds generally by highly experienced teams of managers and can be either illiquid or limited liquidity. The fund may or may not pay out on predetermined dates in the interim. The potential advantage of adding BDCs to your portfolio is that it has "low to moderate correlation to traditional investments and the market inefficiencies associated with increased volatility."[53] Some of the factors financial planners and managers consider when adding this alternative structure include targeted return, risk, and liquidity. For example, some investors may want to minimize risk and others may opt for maximizing return. Liquidity is an important consideration, as BDCs typically offer limited or quarterly liquidity.

BUSINESS DEVELOPMENT CORPORATIONS

Nontraded BDCs are the structures of private credit. They provide capital to private American companies valued at $250 million or higher. A BDC is an investment company that helps small companies meet their capital needs and grow.[54]

BDCs became more popular as banks were somewhat forced out of middle-market lending due to regulatory changes in the wake of the 2008 market crash. BDCs offer the individual investor the opportunity to invest in a wide range of fast-growing industries, such as energy, technology, and health.

As with REITs, BDCs must distribute 90% of taxable net income as dividends to investors; this high-dividend yield makes them popular with income-seeking investors.[55] Furthermore, regulations require that BDCs be well diversified, with no more than 5% of their total assets in any single investment. Depending on the type of BDC, investors may buy in with as little as $5,000. The typical time frame for BDCs are long-term investments designed to yield income. It is important that a financial advisor confirm that most of the loans in the fund are collateralized for more protection.

Some of the benefits of nontraded BDCs include: access to investments that have historically belonged to high-net-worth individuals, professional management, potential reduction of risk by diversifying your portfolio over a broad range of asset classes, and the fact that they are a regulated investment vehicle with transparent and periodic reporting.[56] Nontraded BDCs offer advantages to shareholders when compared to traded BDCs. For example, most publicly traded BDCs experienced extreme volatility during the 2008 global financial crisis. As a result, publicly traded BDCs were unable to access capital for many years. Nontraded BDCs, such as FS Investment Corporation, are able to raise capital based on NAV.[57]

INTERVAL FUNDS

An interval fund includes shares that do not trade on the market.[58] Interval funds are illiquid, invest in a diverse set of assets, and are classified as *closed-end* funds, which means they issue a fixed number of shares. The assets that make up an interval fund might include hedge and private equity funds; commercial property, such as farmland or forestry land; business loans; catastrophic bonds; and REITS securities.[59] Interval funds allow investors to get in on potentially lucrative opportunities with a clearly defined exit point. The value of the fund is determined for each exit date, and no more than 5% of the total amount of the fund can be cashed out annually. This means that individual investors must plan their own access to their cash in the fund accordingly. Interval funds are listed on national exchanges, which means investors can monitor their value on a daily basis. Some of the benefits of interval funds include:

- Returns have the potential to be significantly higher than those of open-ended mutual funds.

- Access to institutional-grade alternative investments with relatively low minimums.

- Funds are often less volatile and market reactive since investments are not tied to equities.[60]

NONTRADED PREFERRED STOCK

Preferred stock is a type of corporate ownership (like regular stocks) that involves a priority claim on the company's earnings and assets over that of regular stockholders, although it typically does not entail voting rights. For example, preferred stock dividends must be paid out before payments to common shareholders.[61] A preferred stock is valued by the issuer on factors generally not related to the stock market. Given that the companies issuing the stock are publicly held, investors can see the companies' financial statements, which is not the case with privately held companies. Investors hold the stock for a period of time and expect to receive dividends in the interim. It is possible to exit early, but you will incur a penalty.

Nontraded preferred stocks offer certain advantages in that they offer regular income payments, "which are generally higher than the interest you'd earn on a bond from the same company. They are called preferred because a company must pay dividends on its preferred shares before any dividends on its common stock."[62] Preferred stocks are one of the few places where you have the potential for a reasonable income stream. For example, preferred stocks, while there is no guarantee, can "often yield 5% or more—well above the 3% you'd get on a typical investment-grade corporate bond."[63] Another benefit is that preferred stocks often have a low correlation with stocks.

PRIVATE EQUITY AND VENTURE CAPITAL

Private equity is an investment in stocks—but not through the stock market. Instead of purchasing a piece of a company through the stock exchange, competing on price with every other investor out there, private equity is negotiated directly with the company. This usually involves smaller or younger companies; *venture capital* is a type of private equity used to support start-ups. Of course, that entails risk: A new company that is not yet listed on the stock exchange may have less of a track record of past performance. However, the company's size may also allow you to purchase a larger stake in the organization, giving you a larger share of their profits if they succeed.

Private equity from individual companies is not often available to lone investors unless they have extremely large amounts to invest. However, there are funds that specifically deal in private equity, allowing you to pool your capital with that of others.

REGULATION D PRIVATE INVESTMENTS

Regulation D (Reg D) is a regulation by the US Securities and Exchange Commission (SEC) that governs exemptions for private placements, which means that the investment is not required to be listed with the SEC. These private placements entail more risk, because they are not subject to some of the regulations that protect investors, but that can also mean higher returns.[64] Reg D allows smaller companies to raise capital through the sale of equity or debt securities when registering those securities with the SEC might be more costly or prohibitive.[65]

Only accredited investors are allowed to buy into these riskier investments. The broker–dealer industry's guidelines indicate that no individual should invest more than 5% of his or her assets in Reg D private placements. It is essential to work with a financial advisor for this class of asset, and they must thoroughly vet the quality and credibility of Reg D offerings and the related investment recommendations.

REGULATION A PLUS PRIVATE INVESTMENTS

Regulation A investments are also exempt from registration with the SEC, but this class refers only to public offerings of debt securities that do not exceed $5 million per year.[66] Under SEC Regulation A, companies may raise up to $50 million in equity from investors and investors must have at least $70,000 in annual income and $250,000 in investable assets.

As with Reg D, the SEC's standards recommend that no individual invest more than 5% of his or her assets in Reg A private placements due to the smaller size of the offering, lower diversification, and higher risk. It is essential to work with a financial advisor for this class of asset, and they must thoroughly vet the quality and credibility of Reg A offerings and the related investment recommendations.

THE ILLIQUIDITY PREMIUM

One of the most important considerations of alternative structures is liquidity. Think of liquidity as the ease by which you can convert an asset, or security, to cash. Liquid assets are typically seen as cash, as they can usually be redeemed for their full value without the deduction of fees or penalties. Investors have different liquidity needs. For example, someone who is working and in the accumulation phase may have less liquidity needs versus someone who is near or at retirement. Assets that tend to be more liquid, such as those invested in the stock market, are typically more volatile than assets that offer limited liquidity or illiquidity. To better understand the relationship between liquidity and volatility, I need to introduce the concept of *standard deviation*.

Although standard deviation is a mathematical concept, it is actually quite simple to explain. Take, for example, a number that represents an average. Any movement away from the average is a deviation. Let's suppose a student takes five tests and his average test score is 93%. (This is a hardworking student.) On his sixth test the student earns a score of 79%. This represents a significant deviation from the average.

Any investment you make will have an average return. Standard deviation is, simply, "a measure of how much an investment's returns can vary from its average return."[67] In this sense, standard deviation is a measure of risk. The smaller the deviation, the less volatile and less risky it is. Conversely, the higher the standard deviation, the more volatile, and therefore more risky, the investment becomes. Standard deviation is the measure of a portfolio's volatility, which in turn is the measure of a portfolio's risk. We will look at the standard deviation of various asset classes.

Another important concept to consider is the idea of *alpha*. This is a simple concept that will help you ask the right questions about your investments. Alpha measures "the amount that [an] investment has returned in comparison to the market index or other broad benchmark that it is compared against."[68] *Beta,* on the other hand, measures the volatility of an investment, which is an indication of risk. You may have heard that investors are always seeking alpha, meaning they want to outperform the benchmark. An alpha of 1.0 means the investment outperformed its benchmark by 1%. Conversely, an alpha of −1.0 means the investment has underperformed its benchmark by 1%. It is important to understand that alpha is a historical number. It tracks an investment's performance over time in relation to an index, but it is not predictive of future performance.[69] Let's go back to standard deviation to see how it is used to compare alternative investments with the stock market.

Stocks of large companies typically have a standard deviation of 16%, which reflects the high volatility of equities. Nontraded REITs, on the other hand, have a standard deviation of 2%. Traded REITs have a high standard deviation, in fact more than large stock. The standard deviation for traded REITs is 22%, which makes them highly volatile. The reason traded REITs are volatile is that they are subject to the same public sentiments as stocks. This is why I incorporate only non-traded REITs, since they have a lower correlation to the stock market.[70] Nontraded REITs are illiquid, meaning that investors typically have a required holding period of one to 10 years. The illiquidity premium tells us that nontraded REITs can offer the potential for better returns than stocks. In fact, "since the early 1970's real estate has beat the stock market nearly 2:1."[71] Of course, I have to note that their historical performance is no assurance of repeat performance in the future.

Similarly, BDCs offer illiquidity premiums with a lower standard deviation versus stocks. Goldman Sachs offers BDCs with a "current Standard Deviation of 9.76%."[72] Remember that BDCs have a low correlation to the stock market, which makes them less risky. Consider that BDCs "have notched an average annual return of nearly 20% over the last 30 years, while the S&P 500 has returned an average of just under 10% each year over the same period."[73] For a long time investors favored liquid asset classes such as stocks. Liquidity, after all, ensures that cash can be generated quickly to meet spending goals. Long-term investors wanted liquidity in order to liquidate one asset for a more appealing one.

While this may sound counterintuitive, "a growing base of research suggests that in reality, the prospective returns of highly liquid investments are impaired compared to those that are illiquid."[74] In other words, it turned out that illiquid investments (illiquid asset classes) have a higher expected return than more liquid assets. One of the things that often holds investors back from adopting alternative structures is their desire for more liquidity. There is this almost irrational belief that illiquid assets somehow perform worse. However, illiquid investments offer the potential for "an outsize return premium."[75] This concept became known as the "illiquidity premium," which means that the potential for excess returns appear to be significant and stable enough that "a recent Ibbotson paper suggests it should be a factor which itself receives a long-term allocation, similar to having tilts towards size, value, or momentum stocks."[76]

The idea of an illiquidity premium was made popular by David Swensen, who, you will recall, is the chief investment officer of the Yale endowment fund. Swensen was one of the first institutional investors to see the potential of illiquid investments. It was Swensen's willingness to invest in especially illiquid investments, including asset classes like real estate, and private equity that contributed to his extraordinary success.

It is important to understand that illiquid asset classes are complex instruments that generally have a longer time horizon than more liquid assets. An endowment fund, such as Yale, can afford an indefinite time horizon, but the individual investor may not have the luxury of time. This is why it is important to discuss illiquid alternative structures with a qualified and experienced financial advisor. One of the things I do at Cinergy Financial is construct a customized portfolio for each client based on their unique circumstances, suitability, goals, time horizon, and several other factors. I add the illiquid portion where it's appropriate to a multi-asset-class strategy that takes into account my client's needs.

As with any investment, alternative structures come with certain risks that you need to be aware of. There are liquidity risks, as well as the risk of losing your principal. You also need to be aware of concentration risk, which occurs when all of your investments focus on one region, industry, or product type. You also need to be aware of high costs and fee structures. Although alternative investments have historically low correlation with traditional investments, during economic downturns the correlation may increase.

TAKE THE WHEEL OF YOUR FINANCIAL FUTURE

The average investor has often been advised to adopt the 60/40 stocks-and-bonds rule for many years. But that strategy is on autopilot, which may make it difficult to land in retirement. Although stocks have produced stable long-term growth, with bonds no longer always offering a hedge against the risk of stocks, this strategy may no longer be relevant in today's world. The autopilot approach may be suitable under ideal conditions, but we live in the real world.

Investors today need trained advisors to navigate an increasingly complex world filled with uncertainty and unpredictable conditions. It is critically important to embrace a variety of investment strategies that offer customizability and flexibility while managing risk. A qualified investment professional can help you combine passive investment with tactical strategies where suitable, designed to increase your investments' growth before you need to begin withdrawing in retirement. Adding in alternative investment opportunities could further diversify your portfolio and can offer reasonable growth potential.

Chapter 6

APPROACHING RETIREMENT

"You are never too old to set a new goal or dream a new dream."

The old idea of working to the age of 65 and heading directly to the golf course is a distant memory from a distant past. The number of older Americans who are still working is rising and is projected to pass 30% of those between the ages of 65 and 74 by 2026.[1] Let's also not forget that millions of baby boomers and Gen Xers suffered significant losses as a result of the Great Recession of 2008. The magnitude of these losses has forced many hardworking individuals to work longer or to reevaluate their investment strategies in order to make up for the massive losses they suffered.

- The number-one fear of many older Americans is not having enough money for retirement. In fact, 49% of Americans worry about outliving their savings."[2] By the time you enter your 50s, retirement planning takes on an urgent tone. With only a decade or two left to work, your financial planning becomes far more focused, as is evidenced by the type of questions my clients typically ask:

- How much money can I withdraw from my investment?
- How can I make course corrections along the way to avoid taking out money too early and potentially running out of money?

The average retiree will likely face three to five bear markets, in which they are likely to suffer losses, in retirement.[3] If that is not disturbing enough, consider that "there have been 23 corrections since 1945 and 12 bear markets, not including the current near-bear market."[4] In addition, "it takes more than two years (25 months on average) to claw back the losses."[5] You must also deal with certain risks associated with how and when you withdraw your hard-earned investment income from your accounts: "Taking withdrawals during a bear market will accelerate the depletion of retirement savings, adversely affecting a portfolio's ability to provide lifetime income."[6]

What does this very reasonable concern mean for the average investor? It means that you may not be able to afford 60% exposure to a stock market that experiences frequent volatility. You need greater protection. You need a solid plan for retirement—*before* you retire. You may even need to delay retirement in order to better secure your financial future. These are decisions you can make only with adequate knowledge about financial planning and, most likely, with a professional advisor to guide you through.

SHOULD YOU CONTINUE WORKING?

One of the first questions to ask yourself as you approach retirement age is whether you actually can—or want to—retire yet. Do you need to continue adding to your savings, either because you started saving late or because the market is down? Working for a few more years will allow your investments to continue to help build or to recover from a recession or other market hiccup.

What additional factors might you change that could free up funds to funnel to your investments? If you become self-employed, for instance, you might be able to take business tax deductions, like the home-office deduction, which could free up some additional funds to contribute toward your retirement. I believe that one of the most important things you can do as you approach retirement is to talk to a qualified financial planner and, if appropriate, a qualified tax specialist about your unique situation.

You'll also want to consider what additional financial goals you want to achieve in your final years of working. These might include adding to your emergency fund, designing a giving plan that is most advantageous while you are in a higher tax bracket, or earning enough to buy a substantial long-term care insurance policy.

Finally, think about your bucket list. What do you want to achieve both now and after you retire? For example, have you always dreamed of climbing Mt. Kilimanjaro? You may not have time now, but you will after retirement—but will you have the money to fund it? Figure out how much you'll need not just for your retirement living expenses but also for the big events or activities you want to enjoy. If your portfolio won't necessarily provide that extra cushion as it is now, you may be able to pad it enough with a few more years of income.

Evaluate whether your goals are better achieved while you're still employed. Ideally, you'll have planned for these events early, so you don't have to stay in your job longer than you would otherwise choose to. But even if you haven't, a few extra years can push your portfolio and your goals far enough to support the kind of retirement you want.

SOCIAL SECURITY

To what degree will additional contributions to Social Security—from working longer—increase the amount you can eventually start claiming? Your Social Security benefit is based on your age and on the year you were born. You can apply for Social Security benefits as early as age 62, but you will receive a reduced percentage of your full benefit depending on your birth year.

If you were born in 1955, you'll get only 74.2% of your full retirement benefit if you start withdrawing at age 62 and only 92.2% at age 65. And this percentage doesn't increase; you'll always receive that lower payout for taking early distribution. You won't get the full benefit until you hit age 66 and 2 months.[7]

However, if you are younger, those numbers are worse: If you were born in 1960, you'll receive 70% if you apply at age 62 and 86.7% at age 65, and you won't receive the full benefit until age 67.[8] Working longer and delaying your benefits will increase your benefit until the age of 70.[9] It's crucial that you plan your retirement age with this information in mind: Is it worth a few extra years in the office to increase your benefit?

If you were born in the 1970s or later, there's no telling what Social Security will look like when you are finally ready to retire. In that case, you'll need to ensure that your investment portfolio is robust enough to maintain your lifestyle without help from Social Security.

EMPLOYER BENEFITS

Some seniors will continue to work in order to retain their employment benefits, such as employer-subsidized health care. However, with more older people in the workforce, some employers make adjustments to your benefits package as you age.

If you work for a very small company (fewer than 20 employees), for example, you may be required to enroll in Medicare at age 65, whereas larger companies may continue to provide you with health coverage, although you'll likely have to maintain a minimum number of work hours.[10] However, even with a larger employer, your work-based coverage may interact with Medicare, such as supplementing or switching to secondary coverage, and your plan may not cover prescriptions at all.[11]

Other parts of your employer's plan may phase out completely after you hit 65. The only way to be sure is to determine your specific employee coverage. You should ask your HR department or the provider of your health-care plan before you get locked into a situation you didn't plan for.

MEDICARE

Shifting to Medicare can dramatically affect your health-care budget. Not only will your coverage likely change, whether you continue to work or not, but you must also be aware of the requirements for applying so you can avoid being charged a penalty.

People who are newly eligible to enroll in Medicare and are no longer working have a seven-month initial enrollment period to sign up for Medicare. If you miss that window, you may be subject to a 10% increase—a late fee—to your premiums. If you're still working, your window will open once you lose your workplace coverage.[12]

As we discussed earlier, your employer-subsidized coverage may supplement or be supplemented by Medicare, and it may even make financial sense to drop your employer's plan and rely fully on Medicare coverage. You'll need to compare your options to determine the best path for you.[13]

SYNCHRONIZING WITH YOUR PARTNER

All of the advice so far has been geared toward an individual—you alone—on their way to retirement. But if you have a spouse, you'll need to consider how your retirement plans—investments, timing, medical coverage, and so on—work together.

Do you and your partner have the same mental picture of what retirement looks like? For example, if you're a homebody looking forward to more time in the workshop, but your spouse wants to travel eight months a year from grandkid to grandkid, those are very different lifestyles with very different financial requirements. You'll need to determine what your joint retirement will actually be and whether your combined portfolios will be enough to cover those goals and that lifestyle.

Will your partner resent you if you retire early, and they're stuck working for another decade? It may be worth putting off your retirement or for them to retire early to make life easier for both of you. Either way, you'll need to make sure your financial plan is ready and adequate to support you.

WHEN TO WITHDRAW

At some point, you'll have to start withdrawing from your accounts. However, that date is not based only on when you retire and how much money you'll need for your expenses.

For example, the government mandates *required minimum distributions* from many types of retirement accounts, such as IRAs and 401(k)s. You must withdraw a certain percentage from your retirement account, starting at age 72, or else face a penalty.[14] Roth IRAs do not require withdrawals until after the death of the owner. You must remember that whenever you take a distribution from your IRA or 401(k), that money is considered taxable income. Under some circumstances, there is an additional penalty tax, as high as 25%.[15]

There are a lot of moving parts that you'll need to coordinate to ensure that you're prepared for retirement. It will require you to know not only what the entire puzzle of your retirement future looks like but also the partial picture of each piece and how they all fit together. Your investment now in understanding withdrawal rates and penalties will help you cultivate lifelong economic independence.

KNOW YOUR RIGHTS

Financial regulators have instituted new rules intended to protect senior citizens from predatory and high-pressure financial advisors.[16] Some states now require financial advisors to operate as *fiduciaries*— that is, to make decisions in your best interest—regardless of how the advisor is paid (fees or commission).

DRAWDOWN

A drawdown is a high-to-low decline in a specific period of an investment or trading account. Drawdowns are quoted as a percentage of the high and the subsequent low. For example, if a trading account has $10,000 and it drops to $9,000 before moving back up to $10,000, then the trading account witnessed a 10% drawdown.[17] Lower withdrawals mean that your capital is reduced more slowly, and your portfolio then has the potential to better withstand negative returns and benefit from positive returns. However, you will have less money to live on.

It is, therefore, often advised that you take minimal or no withdrawals, if possible, during bear markets. If, however, the market is up, it might be permissible to withdraw some funds without affecting the long-term performance of your portfolio. In other words, in order to offset your portfolio's depletion when the markets are down, "retirees can set up strategies for taking minimal or no distribution from their equity portfolios during times of equity market underperformance and instead withdraw from bond or cash buckets."[18] This strategy tends to work better when you have another source of income to rely upon.

DYNAMIC WITHDRAWALS

A dynamic withdrawal strategy involves modulating your withdrawals to reflect market conditions. When the market drops, you withdraw less; when the market surges, you can increase your yearly withdrawal.

As you might imagine, this strategy is potentially risky for an individual investor: If the market slumps for several years, those will be lean years for you, too, because your income will be reduced in parallel.

The market is also unpredictable, so, without significant experience and knowledge about investing, you could be behind the trend.

DEEPER DIVERSIFICATION

Diversifying your portfolio can offer a buffer against sequence-of-return risk. A robust mixture of passive, tactical, and alternative investment strategies may help reduce the effects of a down market. In fact, "empirical evidence suggests that in periods of heightened volatility, stocks and bond markets often move in tandem with one another. Changing economic conditions that push one market downward can pull the other with it, thereby increasing the correlation between stocks and bonds. For that reason, it's important to pursue diversification on multiple levels."[19] It is easier to lessen the effects of a stock market crash if other asset classes of your portfolio, such as real estate and private debt, consistently generate stable monthly income. In addition, if you are retired and rely on investment income, "having too much exposure to the stock market may open [your] portfolio up to excessive risk in a protracted market downturn."[20]

This is especially true of assets not correlated with the stock market. For instance, real estate investments might not suffer the same downturns—or, at least, might not suffer losses of the same magnitude—as the stock market. By ensuring that your portfolio is well diversified, you may be able to continue growing your investment, even during an economic downturn, and safely withdraw a steady income.[21] As I noted earlier, we need to remember that diversification of your assets does not guarantee a profit or that you won't lose money, but it's been a time-tested strategy for smoothing out market volatility and reducing risk.

You've surely noticed this repeated message by now: Complex investment strategies are best executed with the help of a professional advisor. It is imperative that you seek out the advice of an experienced and knowledgeable financial advisor who understands market conditions. Your advisor can help you determine the best time to begin withdrawing funds, how much to withdraw, and how to adjust your retirement income to maximize the amount of money you'll have—and to maintain the best possible standard of living—during your retirement.

CREATE A PLAN

The more you understand how the financial world works, the more flexibility you will have when important decisions need to be made about your retirement future. Whether on your own or with a financial advisor, you should make a plan now, so you're not caught off guard when you're ready to retire—or, worse, a decade later when you run out of money.

Start by projecting your likely required income and lifestyle in retirement. It's best to use multiple investment and retirement timelines that can help achieve your financial and lifestyle goals so you can compare and find the best fit for you. You'll also want to understand your aspirations for legacy and giving, both in retirement and for your heirs.

Review the asset allocations of your employer-sponsored accounts. These allocations are likely set by computer models, with little regard for protection. You'll also want to closely review the actual impact of fees on your portfolio's performance. If you pay a higher fee but see much higher returns, your net gain may well be greater than low fees for low returns. By comparing your accounts' asset allocations and the fees associated with your portfolio, you can assess the potential impact of consolidating into a different account or shifting to a different fee model.

With your advisor, you can identify a plan for adjusting your asset mix to help maximize your chances of success. You should identify triggers for capturing gains and moving them to more conservative assets for protection and anticipate likely risks to your retirement income, especially the possibility that your retirement will coincide with a bear market. Make sure you understand the decisions you make and make them in collaboration with a fiduciary advisor to find a suitable approach for your specific situation.

Chapter 7

A REALM OF POSSIBILITIES

"In all realms of life, it takes courage to stretch your limits,
express your power, and fulfill your potential. . . .
It's no different in the financial realm."

–SUZE ORMAN

At the heart of the endowment strategy is managed risk. This allows the endowments' investment managers, like David Swensen, to manage their endowment to their specific goals that might include the potential for durable income, which means they strive for higher withdrawal rates, risk-adjusted returns, and less volatility than the stock market. This is, of course, what the retail investor may want, depending on their needs—a powerful strategy that can manage risk while potentially offering durable income with less volatility.

Durability implies that the firms "can take a financial punch in one year and come back swinging the next."[1] Although it may not be predictable for any given year, it can help even out over a longer period—like any good investment.[2] What can make it durable is its potential to survive the fluctuations of the market and perhaps even continue to grow.

Durable income is a key ingredient in addressing that all-too-common concern we talked about earlier—that you may outlive your money in retirement. If you know that your portfolio will most likely survive whatever pits and valleys the market throws at its investors, you'll know better what to expect, and knowledge is the greatest enemy of fear.

Returns from the durable income provided by a more diversified portfolio may also come at lower risk. *Risk-adjusted returns* are a way to compare investment risk: If two investments deliver the same return (you earn the same amount of money), but one was a risky investment while the other was relatively conservative, the conservative investment has a higher risk-adjusted return—same profit but with less of a chance of losing it.

Carefully choosing assets to include in an investment portfolio—outside of stocks and bonds alone—can also expose your investment to less volatility than the stock market.

But all of this requires that the risk be somehow managed, reduced to a level that can help offset the stock market's inherent volatility while maintaining your portfolio's growth potential during the accumulation phase—and potentially even during your retirement. The endowment model strives for that managed risk by going beyond modern portfolio theory with uncorrelated assets. Remember the correlation between stocks and bonds? In the old days, when stocks were down, bonds tended to go up and vice versa, giving you a simple way to help protect your money from all of the volatility of the stock market. But because that correlation is no longer always both inverse and predictable, that strategy is often not as effective as consumers would like. By intentionally diversifying their portfolios with assets uncorrelated with the stock market, endowment managers have often been able to find opportunities for growth without the same volatility as stocks but with potentially greater rewards—and for potentially less risk.

Alternative assets expand our investment options, increasing our ability to grow and diversify our portfolios.[3] However, this is true only if the alternative asset is not perfectly correlated with public equity. The diversification benefit comes from the uncorrelated nature of additional asset classes. The benefit of uncorrelated assets is that they are not necessarily affected by market swings, which means you have the potential to grow your portfolio independent of the fluctuations of the stock market.[4]

The Yale endowment still uses stocks and bonds, but at a much lower percentage of their entire portfolio than the traditional respective 60% and 40%. They are instead diversified into assets like BDCs, real estate (including REITS), absolute-return funds, venture capital, and other forms of private equity. By strategically choosing which assets can work best for their investment goals, endowments have been able to manage their risk exposure while using risk-adjusted return strategies.

For many years, access to these alternative investments belonged almost exclusively to large institutions and wealthy individuals. But by the late 20th century the alternative investment industry had "grown from a handful of firms in the US managing a few billion dollars to thousands of firms spread across the world that now manage more than $7 trillion on behalf of investors."[5] Although many of these assets are still not available directly to individual investors, you can access them through funds and with the help of a professional financial planner.

There are regulatory requirements for investors who wish to reallocate their portfolio into certain investments, such as interval funds, nontraded real estate investment trusts (REITs), business development corporations (BDCs), and absolute-return funds, as well as those who want to use hedging strategies. However, jumping through regulatory requirements does not automatically equate to a significantly riskier approach than the stocks-and-bonds approach.

CAN YOU DIG IT?

I do not typically recommend to my clients that they blindly invest exactly like any particular endowment. You are not a university. The goals of a large organization are likely entirely alien to those of an individual who just wants a nice life in retirement, and the sums of money you have to invest are probably much more modest.

To help retail investors like you, my firm focuses on three interlinked targets: diversification, income, and growth—or DIG. Like the three legs of a stool, these three goals meet in the middle and work together to support the weight of your investment needs.

Diversification, you'll remember, is the process of managing risk with a greater spectrum of asset classes in your portfolio. Diversification has become the "battle cry for many financial planners, fund managers, and individual investors alike."[6] The purpose of diversifying your portfolio is to attempt to spread your risk out over multiple investments, the idea being that the return of one investment compensates for the risk of the others. Ideally, those multiple opportunities for returns with diffused risk are designed to lead to reliable growth of your investments.[7] In addition to managing risk, the retail investor wants, and deserves, a strategy that can potentially offer durable income with less volatility.

The REALM® Approach
Based on Three Integrated Strategies

A Multi-Strategy approach aimed at providing STRENGTH and STABILITY to withstand uncertain markets

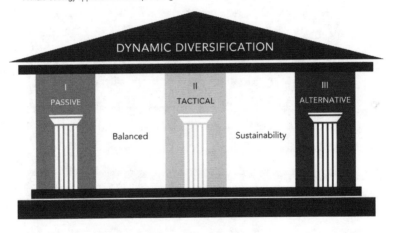

How the three integrated strategies form dynamic diversification.

That diversification will potentially lead to durable income to support you during retirement. A diverse, well-allocated, and well-managed portfolio has the potential to continue earning returns, which can be used to balance your portfolio against your income withdrawals. With a solid plan of asset allocation designed for your personal needs and goals, you'll potentially be able to count on withdrawals from your portfolio that will sustain you through retirement.

Finally, if your investments are allocated properly and are well managed—and with a little luck—your portfolio will address your income goals during your retirement, but also your portfolio may continue to grow, despite your income withdrawals. This excess income can then be used to create a legacy: You can start thinking about leaving an inheritance, giving back to your community, or supporting causes you believe in.

A diversified portfolio can include a durable income stream while seeking growth of your portfolio, a strategy focused on future capital appreciation and designed to offer a hedge against inflation. The DIG conceptual approach—focused on diversification, income, and growth—is designed to help you, as an individual investor, achieve a much more certain retirement by potentially offering less risk. The three considerations of DIG can be derived from a multi-asset portfolio, with both dynamic and tactical asset-allocation strategies. It is critical that you are aware that the DIG approach is not an assurance that it will achieve its objectives or that your portfolio will have certainty or less risk in your portfolio.

ASSET CLASSES FOR ENDOWMENT-LIKE INVESTMENT

Endowment funds typically use multiple asset classes "while appropriately managing overall risk."[8] These assets may include stocks and bonds, BDCs, real estate or REITS, absolute returns, venture capital, and other forms of private equity.[9] Each of these asset classes serves a different purpose within a portfolio, offering different levels of risk, return, and liquidity. The reason endowments add alternative assets to the traditional stocks, bonds, and cash portfolio is correlation. "By adding more asset classes beyond stocks and bonds, the modified strategy's aim is to decrease correlation with stocks while maintaining strong portfolio performance."[10] In other words, endowments will search for assets that decrease correlation with stocks; since those investments/assets are not traded on a stock/bond market (they are typically illiquid), they do not participate in stock/bond market volatility.

Lending directly to a company or institution, often through BDCs, can be consideration for additional portfolio diversification. These loans are usually backed by collateral from the borrower. Depending on the interest rate, the returns may be substantial over time. With any investment there are pros and cons. While BDCs have the potential for favorable returns, BDCs are speculative and involve a high degree of risk, including the risk of a substantial loss of investment. Due to the illiquid nature of BDCs, you will be unable to reduce your exposure should there be a downturn in the BDCs portfolio of investments/loans. That is why it is important for you to be educated about your investments.

Real estate investment trusts (REITs) can offer the potential for reasonable returns over time. Real estate investment can generally be public—traded on an exchange like stocks—or private—arranged directly with the owner of the property. However, the barrier for entry for publicly traded REITs can be quite low,[11] making them a viable option for individual investors.

Absolute returns offer a way to take advantage of, or circumnavigate, the volatility of the stock market. By using different tactics, investors in absolute-return funds can potentially earn returns even when the market is falling or already in a slump. This can make them an ideal form of uncorrelated asset, depending on your or your advisor's ability to make use of the various strategic actions needed to make absolute returns work. This kind of fund may have higher fees, since it is usually a more actively traded fund and there is no assurance the fund will achieve its goal.

Private equity can be very lucrative but can also be risky. Think of private equity investment like house flipping for businesses: A private equity firm will buy a business, with a goal of quickly making it better (or at least more valuable), and then sell it off at a profit.[12] By investing directly in a company, investors can directly profit from the success of the business, but they also risk losing their investment if the business fails or can't be sold.

Venture capital is a particularly risky form of private equity, but it can also be particularly profitable.[13] Venture capitalists invest in start-ups and new businesses, often in technology or innovative products. These infant companies have a high rate of failure, which means a high risk of investment loss, but the returns from a successful start-up can be substantial.

No one of these asset classes can support a viable portfolio on its own; diversification is the key to creating durable income. Endowments use a variable mix of these different assets to balance each other. One asset may yield high returns but entail the risk of potential losses; another asset can offset that risk in exchange for less impressive return potential. I generally avoid using private equity and venture capital for my clients because of the considerable risk associated with them. An ideal combination of asset classes can help maximize returns while minimizing risk.

STRATEGIES FOR ENDOWMENT-LIKE INVESTMENT

The investment strategies used to allocate your portfolio form another three-legged stool that supports your retirement future. You'll recall that we separate asset classes into three broad strategic categories: passive, tactical, and alternative.

The REALM® Model
What are the Investment Options within REALM®?

Passive	Annuities, Structured Notes and CDs, Mutual Funds, Exchange Traded Funds (ETFs), and Separately Managed Accounts (SMA)
Tactical	Absolute Return Funds, Market Neutral and Short/Long Strategies
Alternative	Non-Traded REITs, Non-Traded Preferred Stock, Business Development Corporations, Interval Funds and Private Placements

The tripartite division of passive, tactical, and alternative strategies.

Passive investment is the old buy-and-hold model: You purchase some investment product, with the aim that over time it grows or matures into a return. Stocks and bonds are the standard examples of passive investment, but the approach also includes variable, fixed, and fixed indexed annuities; structured notes; and bank CDs.

Tactical investment requires hands-on management, ideally from a competent and trustworthy professional. The portfolio manager will need to actively analyze the investment options available at any given time and determine how they can best be used to work toward the

REDEFINING FINANCIAL LITERACY

investor's goals. The tactical strategy can incorporate absolute-return funds with short–long strategies, managed futures, and 200-day moving-average strategies.

Finally, the alternative investment strategy covers other asset classes, such as daily net asset value (NAV) funds, BDCs, nontraded REITs, private placements, and qualified opportunity-zone funds. Due to the complexity and the risks involved in this strategy, seeking an advisor to help you with this type of investing is prudent, and not all investors are suitable for these kinds of investments. These three strategies combined offer the necessary flexibility to potentially fuel sustained results that can support retirement withdrawals that are potentially higher than the 4% withdrawal rule of the 60/40 portfolio.[14]

LIQUIDITY

Liquidity is important if you need to move your money for some reason, to adjust your investment allocations, or to withdraw them for an emergency expense. Most investment instruments are available in a range of liquidity, meaning you could move or withdraw your funds daily, quarterly, annually, or only after a defined longer term, although you may be able to withdraw from certain assets earlier if you are willing to take a hefty financial penalty.

The passive approach involves both liquid and limited liquidity assets, the tactical approach has a high degree of liquidity, and the alternative approach utilizes both limited liquidity and illiquid assets. Passive assets such as mutual funds, index funds, and exchange-traded funds can be sold each day the exchanges are open, whereas structured products such as annuities offer limited liquidity. Tactical assets,

192

which include absolute-return funds and managed futures, can be sold each day the exchanges are open, whereas 200-day moving averages will offer limited liquidity. Alternative assets, such as publicly traded REITs, provide immediate liquidity, nontraded preferred stock and interval funds offer limited liquidity, and nontraded REITs and private placements are illiquid.

The power of diversification affords you the breathing room to pursue specific investments within each type of investment. You might choose very low-risk stocks and bonds and gradually increase the risk with alternatives. Conversely, you might take the opposite approach of selecting conservative alternative assets but increase risk with stocks. There is enough flexibility to construct a balanced portfolio in terms of how much liquidity you want, the diversification you need, and your growth goal to replenish your portfolio, which can support consistent withdrawals, which represent the income you need for the retirement you want.

SO WHAT DO YOU CALL THIS THING?

Although there are monumental economic challenges today, these are also exciting times for the individual investor. Many of the product offerings that were once the exclusive province of endowments and other large institutional investors are now available to the individual investor. These product offerings became popular because large investment firms follow the money, and now you can too.

Now, as I mentioned earlier, I don't recommend simply following the endowment model; instead, I help my clients pick and choose the appropriate aspects of the endowment model for their situation, adapted for individual retail investors like you. I call this approach the Retail Endowment Allocation Like Model, or REALM.

The three strategies of REALM are adapted from the endowment model: passive, tactical, and alternative. However, we focus on five asset classes (dropping those too-risky classes, private equity and venture capital), which work together in synergistic harmony to potentially offer managed risk for durable income in retirement.

The REALM® Model
What 5 Asset Classes Encompass REALM®?

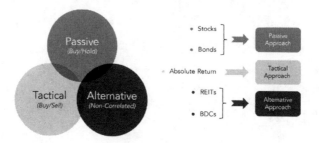

The REALM approach offers three strategies, with five asset classes.

What makes REALM a powerful model of investing are these two fundamental ideas: First, we apply a different strategy to classic assets like stocks and bonds. Second, we merge those newly available types of alternative assets to create *dynamic diversification.* REALM adapts the endowment model and adjusts the risk and time horizons appropriate to the individual investor. Just as endowments are managed by professional money managers, the individual investor can rely on an experienced financial advisor who, in turn, relies on professional money managers.

The five asset classes of REALM are stocks, bonds, absolute-return funds, real estate investment trusts, and business development companies. Stocks and bonds define the passive approach, absolute returns form the tactical approach, and REITS plus BDCs are the alternative approach.

The passive, tactical, and alternative strategies must be integrated in such a way as to form dynamic diversification. Keep in mind each pillar has multiple structures, and you should see a qualified financial planner to help you select and customize a structure that is in line with your specific goals.

REALM also addresses certain important factors that may complicate investment returns. REALM is designed to potentially alleviate—or at least ameliorate—these problems:[15]

- Low interest rates

- High price-to-earnings ratios for equities

- Downturns in the stock market

- Increased and ongoing volatility in the markets

- The potentially ongoing, increased, and direct correlation of stocks and bonds that can undermine traditional diversification models

REALM is designed to maximize value from an array of investment options. It also offers potentially sustainable returns by constructing a portfolio containing a variety of assets with varied risk and time horizons. This creates synergistic balance from a more diversified portfolio. The power of REALM is derived from both the mix of assets and a rigorously applied strategy to manage those assets.

REALM ASSET ALLOCATION

The goal of REALM is not to replace modern portfolio theory; rather, the aim is to integrate and adapt it for the modern world. Although stocks and bonds are typically the foundation of any meaningful portfolio, the focus of REALM is to offer different proportions of stocks and bonds and by using a hands-on approach as well as an automated target-date strategy. Let's begin that reallocation with the general example of how to set up a portfolio within REALM. This is not meant to be a one-size-fits-all solution for every retiree's life goals, but it is a good starting point.

The first step of adapting REALM to a retirement plan is to reduce the traditional 60% investment in the stock market to 20%. This takes that huge proportion of risk (more than half of your total portfolio!) and reduces it to a portion that, although it is still significant, wouldn't devastate your portfolio if there were a sharp downturn just as you enter retirement and begin withdrawals. This 20% stock investment is typically in low-cost funds and will be held indefinitely for growth potential. By reducing equity from 60% to 20%, you open up your portfolio to incorporate other asset classes, which can potentially offer avenues for more durable income and less risk.

We'll also reduce the percentage you have invested in bonds to 20%. These are also generally in low-cost funds, with the expectation of cycling in potentially higher-paying bond funds as they become available. This change from the traditional approach, like the shift in stocks, opens up your portfolio for more diversification. It also allows you to reclaim the protection that bonds historically offered as a balance to the stock market; it allows potentially more effective risk management for your entire portfolio.

For the remaining 60% of your portfolio, you'll need to assess your need for liquidity and choose tactical assets accordingly. You'll also want to choose alternative assets that are not directly or heavily correlated to the stock and bond markets. I generally start with a recommendation of 20% each in BDCs, public real estate (REITs), and absolute-return funds.

This general case of even allocation among our five key asset classes provides a more diversified portfolio than the old 60/40 model. This approach may be enough—depending on your personal goals, starting investment, age, and many other factors—to provide managed risk for durable income. But this is just the beginning of REALM's potential.

Be advised that alternative investments are speculative by nature and have various risks, including possible lack of liquidity, lack of control, changes in business conditions and devaluation based on the investment, the economy, and or regulatory changes. As a result, the values of alternative investments do fluctuate, resulting in the value at sale being more or less than the original price paid if a liquid market for the securities is found. There is no assurance that any strategy will achieve its objectives.

DYNAMIC REALLOCATION

REALM's true power lies in its being flexible and customizable. REALM includes options for all three investment strategies, for any level of liquidity, and for different levels of risk that can interact to support a portfolio designed for durable income. A more effective approach is to have a financial planner help you tailor your options to suit your individual needs.

Although you now know to pad your stocks and bonds with uncorrelated assets, every investment is subject to volatility. Ideally, the volatility is lower than that of the stock market, but you may need to reallocate over time, changing your portfolio's makeup and strategy. This is called *dynamic reallocation*. The goal of dynamic reallocation is to simultaneously expand the asset classes in your portfolio while potentially reducing your exposure from any existing allocations, such as stocks and bonds.

The importance of asset allocation[16] cannot be overstated. In fact, research has shown that "over 90% of long-term investment volatility came from decisions about one's asset allocation."[17] However, it is important to keep in mind that asset allocation must not be static. Think of it this way: You don't want any of your asset classes exposed to unnecessary risk. With dynamic reallocation, you or your portfolio manager actively change both the number of assets and the amount of exposure of those assets based on several factors, including your risk tolerance, the market conditions, market indicators, and so on.

Luckily, you have many options to customize—and dynamically reallocate—your portfolio within each of our three investment strategies.

PASSIVE INVESTMENT OPTIONS

The passive category, like all aspects of a personalized portfolio, must be synchronized with your investment cycle and milestones.

Passive strategies include both correlated and uncorrelated asset classes, such as these:

- Annuities
- Structured notes

- Certificates of deposit (CDs)

- Mutual funds

- Exchange-traded funds (ETFs)

- Index funds

- Separately managed accounts (SMAs)

TACTICAL INVESTMENT OPTIONS

The tactical strategy includes short-term liquid assets that are designed to protect gains in your accounts and that you can tap into as needed. Tactical investments are designed to take advantage of short-term market fluctuations but always with diversification to help minimize your losses.

Tactical assets offer liquidity that balances the illiquidity and limited liquidity of BDC and nontraded REITs or interval funds. These proactive tactics are designed to zig when the market zags, in order to help diversify your assets while seeking opportunistic growth in short bursts. I believe that tactical assets are critical for helping reduce risk and volatility, and creating a dynamic strategy for investors. Tactical allocations are actively adjusted, which means that you could potentially sidestep a market crash that could undermine your financial goals.

Your tactical product offerings include these options:

- Absolute-return funds

- Market-neutral funds

- Managed futures

ALTERNATIVE INVESTMENT OPTIONS

Alternative assets are often illiquid and take time to strive for the potential for greater returns than stocks and bonds. Nontraditional asset classes like interval funds add time as an active investment factor. These investments require a commitment of months or even years and are designed to potentially deliver equity-like results.

The key alternative structures that diversify a portfolio include:

- Daily NAV funds

- BDCs

- Traded and nontraded REITs

- Private placements (Regulation A or D)

- Qualified opportunity-zone funds

- Interval funds

- Nontraded preferred stocks

Alternative investments involve substantial risks that may be greater than those associated with traditional investments and may be offered only to clients who meet specific suitability requirements, including minimum net worth tests. These risks include but are not limited to: limited or no liquidity, tax considerations, incentive fee structures, speculative investment strategies, and different regulatory and reporting requirements. There is no assurance that any investment will meet its investment objectives or that substantial losses will be avoided.

REALM IN ACTION
UNCONVENTIONAL SUCCESS

In 2017 I read David Swensen's groundbreaking *Unconventional Success: A Fundamental Approach to Personal Investment*, and I was shocked by what I read. Swensen's ideas about asset allocation, diversification, and alternative asset classes were dramatically similar to what I had developed into REALM after years of working with clients and sifting through the options to try to find the best path for retail investors. By the time I finished reading the book, in one sitting, I felt a powerful sense of vindication. I had created an investment strategy for the individual investor that turned out to be similar to the endowment model used by Yale University and by numerous other colleges. I wanted to address the long-term retirement needs of the individual investor, and once certain asset classes were made available to the general public, my approach paralleled these endowments—but for regular people like you and me.

One of the strengths of REALM is the ability to address that number-one fear of many older Americans—that we'll outlive our retirement income. It's a fundamental truth that we are living longer today than ever before, and I believe that the traditional 60/40 portfolio can no longer meet our retirement needs. For decades "advisors have leaned on the 60/40 portfolio to deliver a less-volatile but still relatively reliable return for balanced investors due to their lack of tolerance for the volatility and draw-downs of a pure equity allocation."[18] The individual investor simply accepted the idea that the old binary structure was the only way to realize durable income while maintaining low volatility. Now you know better.

REALM potentially provides you the following benefits:

- Potentially better results with five core investments rather than with two asset classes
- Potentially reduced sequence-of-return risk due to less volatility
- Potentially higher durable income sources
- Potential equity-like returns with bond-like volatility
- Potential protection from things you can't control
- Managed risk

REALM goes beyond the 60/40 model by using a sophisticated set of strategies and diversifying into five core asset classes instead of only two, which allows it to potentially deliver better outcomes throughout our longer retirement years. The benefits include potentially durable income sources, diversification during bear markets, competitive fee structure, and potentially low volatility. My hope is that this helps reduce the fear of running out of money in retirement for my clients.

Given that REALM is a complex multi-asset model with many moving parts and customization options, you will need to seek the advice of a knowledgeable and experienced advisor to help you construct a customized portfolio. The customization and the potentially more reliable income, with managed risk, offered by REALM can be arranged to help offset the associated fees.

Now that you understand REALM, how it works, and why I developed it, you need to ask yourself a fundamental question: Do you want to stay with the potentially outdated 60/40 investment strategy, or do you want to open yourself up to another approach to help protect yourself from inevitable market swings?

If you are a baby boomer, you are either in retirement or retirement is around the corner for you. You should have a sense of urgency for your future. For the millennials, and other generations reading this book, you have the luxury of time, but you can start now—first by increasing your financial literacy and then by getting your portfolio started so you have decades to accumulate returns. The knowledge you gain today can help you live a much more fulfilling life tomorrow.

Because REALM combines growth opportunity with diversification, it can help shield you against the inevitable nature of economic cycles. During your 20s, 30s, and 40s, you are more likely to accumulate savings and invest by relying on the limited menu of options offered by your company's retirement plan. During the accumulation stage, REALM can potentially help you capture better results.

The title of this book is *Redefining Financial Literacy*. I have argued that we need to broaden our definition of what it means to be financially literate. For example, I've argued that we need to understand the hidden historical, political, and economic forces that influence and impact our investment strategy. Another aspect of broadening our financial awareness is to understand how incredibly challenging it has been for women to improve their financial literacy and the urgent need to address this issue.

Chapter 8

TO DARE GREATLY

"How wrong it is for a woman to expect the man to
build the world she wants, rather than to create it herself."

–ANAÏS NIN

———

The title of this chapter anticipates my next book, which will be devoted to women. For too long, I feel that women have been passive spectators to a financial world that largely ignored them. The unique vulnerabilities that women experience have at times been directed back at them and amplified in such a way as to validate why we live in a male-dominated financial culture. Vulnerability, however, is an asset that demonstrates strength in the face of uncertainty. Brené Brown argued in *Daring Greatly* that "vulnerability is the birthplace of innovation, creativity, and change."[1] For Brown, "vulnerability is not weakness, and the uncertainty, risk and emotional exposure we face every day are not optional. Our only choice is a question of engagement. Our willingness to own and engage with our vulnerability determines the depth of our courage and the clarity of our purpose; the level to which we protect ourselves from being vulnerable is a measure of our fear and disconnection."[2]

Women have been vulnerable for centuries. We have been ignored, looked down upon, rendered irrelevant, harassed, boxed up, and smiled upon with condescension. The good news today is that vulnerability, the wounds we carry with us, will be our strength. You see, the challenges and setbacks we've experienced in the past have been transmitted to us by those women who paved the way for us to become engaged and to push forward. Progress for women—and for men who want to reclaim their financial independence—can only come about through active engagement. The moment is now, and I believe that things are about to change dramatically.

Women are on the verge of historic change, both broadly and in the financial world. Today, we need a rallying cry for women to stop complaining from the sidelines and to be engaged. The statistics overwhelmingly support that women will soon become the face of the financial world. According to a white paper from the Family Wealth Advisors Council, "95% of women will be their family's primary financial decision maker at some point in their lives." Women now control more than half (51% or $22 trillion[3]) of the personal wealth in America, and that amount is expected to jump by 30% over the next 40 years.[4]

Although women have forged ahead as today's dominant consumers, many still continue to lack the financial literacy necessary to navigate the complex world of investment. Consider the following facts,[5] which are both relevant and alarming:

- Women earn less over a lifetime; in 2020, women earned 81 cents for every dollar earned by men.[6]

- Women spend approximately 11–13 years out of work, mostly raising their children and taking care of family matters, which leads women to accumulate fewer assets over a lifetime.

- For women who attempt to stay in the workplace, the high cost of child care forces many women to leave, which affects retirement, savings, investing, and, in most cases, reclaiming their position upon return to work.

- Women carry a similar debt balance as men, but the ratio of debt to income is higher due to their lower income.

- 50% of marriages end in divorce, and most women keep the mortgage and the house for the children's sake instead of contributing to a pension or retirement income.

- Women live between five and seven years longer than men.

- Due to their lower income, women end up with little, if any, nest egg.

- 15% of senior women end up in poverty.

And although the lack of financial literacy has created a problem for all Americans, there is a "persistent gender gap in both financial and investment understanding."[7] The Financial Industry Regulatory Authority's (FINRA) National Financial Capability Study revealed some disturbing truths, including the fact that women are more likely to respond "I don't know" to basic financial literacy questions.[8] To exacerbate matters, a 2017 survey by the Retirement Income Literacy

Report, administered by the American College of Financial Services, revealed that retirement-age women were significantly behind their male counterparts when it came to financial literacy. The survey found that "only 18 percent of female respondents between the age of 60 and 75 could pass the retirement income focused literacy quiz, while roughly 35 percent of male respondents could pass the quiz."[9] Although it's troubling that only 35 percent of men passed the literacy quiz, the fact that only 18 percent of retirement-age women passed is alarming. The same study found a direct link among financial literacy, retirement planning, and financial behavior.

Despite their general lack of financial knowledge, many women today have amassed more wealth than at any other time in history. It is this density of wealth that must be managed and leveraged, in order to produce generational wealth for women. Once you create generational wealth, future generations of women can collectively gain financial literacy to match or exceed the knowledge and power of men. The profound irony here is that, regardless of the level of professional success women are beginning to enjoy, "they [aren't] in control."[10] The fact that women are beginning to amass wealth is a step in the right direction, but women will not become equal players until they are proportionally represented in the very structure of financial decision making.

According to the 2019 Allianz Women, Money, and Power Study, 90% of the women surveyed "say they are taking more responsibility for managing household long-term savings and finances (90% in 2019 versus 86% in 2016)."[11] The vast majority of women want to improve their financial literacy, in order to be more involved in their own financial planning.

To bridge the seemingly oceanic gap between men and women in the financial world, I believe that women need to do two things: become financially literate and seek out the services of female advisors. In fact, if we merge these two conditions, women will have a very powerful partner to help them work toward their financial goals while learning about the financial markets.

Sallie Krawcheck is the cofounder and CEO of Ellevest, a digital financial platform created for women. Krawcheck believes that for change to happen, women should be empowered. We cannot wait for power to be given to us; in fact, "we shouldn't count on anyone else doing this for us."[12] We must take this power and shape it by affirming our right to financial self-determination. Krawcheck also offers gender-based investing that focuses on women's needs and that takes into account "women's generally lower incomes, different lifetime earnings curve, and longer lifespan into portfolio construction."[13]

Krawcheck is not an isolated case. Today, there is a growing demand for female financial advisors. While my own company, Cinergy Financial, caters to both men and women, I make every effort to accommodate women. Our focus is a gender-conscious approach to investing. Our mission statement is two pronged: to offer clients potentially strong returns while managing risk and to promote financial literacy. In fact, one of the things we started doing at Cinergy Financial was to offer monthly informational seminars, podcasts, webinars, and radio broadcasts, so that clients could better understand the forces that impact their investments. Many of the topics I cover are designed to help people change their mindset about money and investing. The knowledge I offer is informational, and that information is actionable. Remember, financial literacy gives you knowledge, and knowledge gives you power.

Despite the dizzying pace of change, the profound and disturbing irony, of course, is that when it comes to financial literacy, women continue to be at a disadvantage in both investing their money and becoming financial experts. In many ways, the history of women is the history of structural inequality, which created a binary reality. On one hand, men continue to dominate the financial world, while women watch in silence, as greed, corruption, and ignorance contribute to the deterioration of our capitalist system. On the other hand, women continue to exist outside the corridors of financial power, always knocking on the door, ready and willing to contribute something of value to our understanding of investing, risk, and uncertainty, as well as the virtues of honesty, integrity, and fairness.

We have already seen that men dominate the financial-planning sector. Women who work in the industry, as well as those who seek financial help, "believe their gender is a key factor in the disrespect and condescension they have often experienced and the poor financial advice they have received."[14] What we have today is a disconnect between a promising future where women will be the financial decision makers and the skewed reality of women being intimidated by male financial advisors.

According to a national survey conducted by Tiller, LLC, women felt an oceanic separation between what they wanted and what is available to them in the financial-services market. The numbers are striking, to say the least: 91% of women felt that financial companies were more interested in selling them something, as opposed to educating them; 84% believed they are or expect to be responsible for managing their own finances; 63% of women felt that investing is confusing; and 75% lamented that it is difficult to stay informed about the near-infinite supply of financial information available today. Finally, 71% believed that Wall Street is not in touch with women's financial needs.[15]

Once women accept their new role as financial decision makers, they will start to gravitate toward female advisors. If you are a woman reading this book, you want to be able to trust an advisor "with your dreams, your fears, the money hang-ups many of us are so uncomfortable tackling—in other words: with some of the most intimate aspects of your life. It's only logical, that the same way you might feel most comfortable with a female doctor or female therapist, some people are going to gravitate to female advisors."[16] We are already beginning to see change. For example, the *Wall Street Journal* "cites some concrete evidence that the field may be poised to improve, if slowly. For instance, UBS, a global financial services company, says women now account for 21% of financial advisors, up from 19% in 2011, while Merrill Lynch Wealth Management says a record one-third of the roughly 3,500 employees in its U.S. advisor training program this year (2019) are women."[17] To continue this change toward greater financial freedom, women need to stop being spectators and become educated about the financial world.

Chapter 9

COVID-19 AND PORTFOLIO RECOVERY

"Every time you confront something painful, you are at a potentially important juncture in your life—you have the opportunity to choose healthy and painful truth or unhealthy but comfortable delusion."

–RAY DALIO

———

As the COVID-19 pandemic swept through the globe, the equities (stock) markets plummeted and volatility skyrocketed. Levels of market volatility in the United States "rival or surpass those seen in October 1987 and December 2008 and, before that, in late 1929 and the early 1930s."[1] What is even more remarkable is that since 1900, there is "not a single instance in which contemporary newspaper accounts attributed a large daily market move to pandemic-related developments. That includes the Spanish Flu of 1918–1920, which killed an estimated 2.0 percent of the world's population."[2] In addition to the equities market, oil prices crashed, at one point dropping to negative $37.63 per barrel, which means traders would have to pay someone to take their oil. The US Treasury bond yield is currently at 0.621% (as of April 22, 2020), and the number of investors "scurrying for low-risk government securities has led some to start preparing for the possibility that the U.S. debt yields could turn negative."[3] The COVID-19 pandemic revealed the inherent weakness of the 60/40 portfolio.

The dramatic market downturn we've witnessed has highlighted the potential risks of a portfolio with a high exposure (60%) to stocks. As a result of the high volatility from the pandemic, "a traditional 60/40 portfolio of stocks and bonds suffered steep losses as many asset classes moved in the same direction—causing diversification benefits to evaporate."[4] Throughout this book I've attempted to warn the reader of the potentially broken 60/40 investment portfolio, and now the pandemic has revealed the risks of having a high exposure to the stock market.

I developed the REALM model in order to offer my clients potentially better returns, while managing risk. A multi-asset-class strategy generally offers "a much wider range of assets to choose from when investing, something that in theory is meant to allow them to weather a downturn."[5] Despite the fact that central banks injected trillions of dollars into the global economy, volatility remains high. According to Clive Emery of Asset Portfolio Strategist, one of the strengths of a multi-asset strategy is that portfolio managers are "looking for new opportunities that the current market dislocation has thrown up."[6] I developed the REALM model, in part, to anticipate and withstand sudden market corrections. I have argued that greater diversification helps manage risk, which is why I was recently encouraged to see a path toward more diversification in 401(k) plans.

On June 3, 2020, the US Department of Labor (DOL) issued a new guidance to 401(k) investment committees "that want to include private equity as a component of a target date fund or other diversified investment fund offered within a 401(k) plan."[7] This marks the first time the DOL has addressed the use of private equity in defined contribution plans. It is important to remember that for decades, large institutional investors, like endowments and pensions, have invested in private equity, but 401(k) plans have been reluctant to diversify without clear guidelines from the DOL. I believe it is a move in the right direction for the government to support greater diversification in 401(k) plans.

When I started writing this book in 2018, I could not have imagined that a pandemic would bring the global economy to its knees. Based on history, I anticipated that a market correction was coming, which is one of the reasons I wrote the book. The other reason was to redefine our understanding of financial literacy. What is happening in the world today perfectly illustrates the argument I made in the preface. We need to broaden our understanding of financial literacy to include basic knowledge of the hidden forces that can impact your bottom line. It is imperative, now more than ever before, to understand how past market corrections impacted investment strategies, the role of the Federal Reserve in responding to the global crises, and the role of governments in addressing sustained bear markets.

There will be many people who will potentially lose much of their retirement savings. It is important that you speak to your financial advisor about your investment strategy and the steps you need to take to help protect yourself. You and your advisor need to address what I call the portfolio recovery of your investment. You might be asking what is portfolio recovery? There are millions of people whose current portfolio may not be offering them the returns they deserve. Portfolio recovery is the process of evaluating your current investment strategy to determine your suitability for a multi-asset-class model that could potentially offer you better returns while managing risk. As a practitioner of portfolio construction, I have helped hundreds of individuals prepare for their retirement.

What makes these "practitioners" different from other financial advisors is the hands-on application of rigorous knowledge and empirical evidence. There are financial advisors such as Suze Orman and Dave Ramsey who do a brilliant job of educating us through books, radio, and television shows. I applaud these individuals for what they do, but if you need portfolio recovery and construction, you must seek the help of a qualified and experienced practitioner who can guide you through the complex process of building a custom portfolio.

THE NEXT TEN YEARS

In 2006 an obscure professor of economics at New York University stood before an audience of economists at the New York headquarters of the International Monetary Fund (IMF). Nouriel Roubini warned the assembled group that the housing market was in a bubble and would soon collapse under its own artificially inflated prices. This one statement alone would have secured Roubini's status as an economic prophet. However, that was not all he had to say. Roubini informed the experts at the IMF that once the housing bubble burst, it could bring the global financial system to its knees. He connected the dots for them by explaining that "once those [home] prices came back to earth, millions of underwater homeowners would default on their mortgages, trillions of dollars worth of mortgage-backed securities would unravel, and hedge funds, investment banks, and lenders like Fannie Mae and Freddie Mac could sink into insolvency."[8] The assembled group, of course, rejected Roubini's alarmist remarks and questioned his "psychological well-being."[9]

By 2008 the housing bubble did burst, triggering a global financial meltdown, with trillions of dollars lost, and the obscure professor from NYU became a Wall Street celebrity. Today Roubini is predicting a possible depression in the wake of the COVID-19 pandemic. As a contrarian, Roubini is rejecting the popular idea of a V-shaped recovery and predicts an L-shaped recovery in the long run. To better understand what he's saying, let's unpack the technical language. As the name implies, a V-shaped recovery involves a sharp economic decline followed by a sharp rise to the previous high. An L-shaped recovery, on the other hand, is a steep economic decline followed by a persistent flat recovery.

The "V" Shaped Recovery

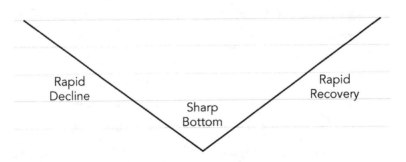

V-Shaped Recovery

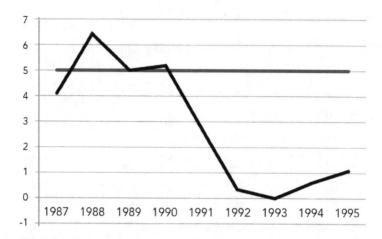

L-Shaped Recovery

In the immediate aftermath of the pandemic, Roubini predicts a slow economic rebound followed by a "collapse beneath the weight of the global economy's accumulated debt."[10] His argument, which I believe we should listen to, rests on the idea that the combined accrued debt from the 2008 global financial meltdown, coupled with the COVID-19 debt, will depress consumption and weaken what will be a short-lived recovery.

Roubini predicts that inflation will go from 1% to 4%; the 10-year Treasury bonds, which are currently offering interest rates close to zero, will go to 5%. Remember, as interest rates rise, bond prices fall. This is where the hidden forces I've been talking about could have a direct impact on your financial future. Let's suppose your money is invested in a 60/40 portfolio. Bond prices are not offering the same interest rates they once did. If Roubini's prediction holds up, your portfolio may no longer generate the kind of return you expected. Here is an actionable step you can take today. Consult with a qualified financial advisor who has experience with multi-asset-class portfolios and request an evaluation of your portfolio.

Roubini, of course, is not the only one who is predicting difficult days ahead. Billionaire investor Ray Dalio, of Bridgewater Associates, is predicting that the current economic downturn in response to the COVID-19 pandemic will resemble the Great Depression. Dalio, who runs the world's largest hedge fund, suggests we are already in a depression: "I think you could look at this like a tsunami that's hit—the virus itself and the social distancing—and then what are the consequences in terms of the wreckage."[11] What Dalio means by the "wreckage" is the long-term impact on the economy. Dalio was sounding the alarm on a protracted economic decline long before the pandemic rattled global markets. In January 2019 he identified red flags that he believed were similar to the Great Depression. These red flags include "the country's large debts, large wealth and political gaps, and U.S. conflict with China as a rising power, to name a few."[12] We are today living through uncertain times, and you need to protect yourself. Our debt is larger than ever before and the wealth gap continues to widen.

As the founder and CEO of Cinergy Financial, I've spent the better part of 2020 rebalancing my clients' portfolios, as well as fielding phone calls from dozens of people who wanted me to evaluate their existing portfolio, and possibly adapt it to a multi-asset-class strategy. I worked 16-hour days to help ensure my clients' portfolios had a level of diversification, while simultaneously evaluating the suitability of new clients for the REALM model. There was a time when I thought I couldn't keep up with the demand for portfolio recovery.

Another important thing I do as a practitioner of portfolio construction is forecasting. This is a critical part of my job, where I use empirical evidence to create forward-looking and historically aware forecasts. I carefully examine five-year asset-class outlooks from multiple sources in order to make intelligent decisions about asset allocations. Keep in mind, however, that these forecasts are not exact and are not guaranteed. But for example, according to Northern Trust, one of the oldest investment banks in the United States, the five-year outlook for equities is a 5.7% annual return.[13] While this seems to be a respectable return, when you factor in inflation, the result will be significantly less. According to Knoema, a global data firm, "over the longer-term up to 2024, CPI (consumer price index) inflation in the US is expected to be around 2.3 percent."[14] After factoring inflation, stocks are expected to return 3.4% annually.

Let's compare that with the global real estate forecast, which is 6.3%. The numbers get better with alternative assets such as private investments, and hedge funds are expected to return 7.7% annually.[15] Bonds likely may not offer much in terms of protection. According to Morningstar Investment Management, which is one of the largest global financial services firms, US aggregate bonds will return just 2.1%.[16] Given these lackluster forecasts for stocks and bonds, I believe it is critical that you explore the potential benefits of a multi-asset-class model.

Throughout this book, I've built the case that the 60/40 portfolio is potentially broken. Baby boomers are living longer than ever before, which is why 45% of investors feel they will outlive their savings.[17] You can't necessarily rely upon pensions and Social Security to protect you completely. I've also argued that hidden forces both directly and indirectly impact your money, which is why you need to be aware of them. Finally, I've stressed the importance of broadening our definition of financial literacy to include a basic understanding of the political, economic, and historical forces that shape your financial future.

The point I'm trying to make is this: Don't let history repeat itself. I've connected the dots for you every step of the way. During times of uncertainty and market corrections, average Americans like you lost their hard-earned money. I dedicated myself to building a flexible and customizable multi-asset investment model to potentially protect the average investor from the unpredictable swings of the market. I am someone who believes in the ethical impulse to help others. I'm someone who is committed to my clients and my community. We are living through extraordinary times, but we will triumph over this sinister virus. The American people will once again thrive, but you need to take action today, not tomorrow. We, the city on a hill, are the epitome of resourcefulness and ingenuity.

THE FUTURE OF CAPITALISM

Pandemics have a stubborn habit of leaving a path of death and destruction. The cost in terms of lives and livelihood is both staggering and unimaginable. In addition to the global recession brought about by COVID-19, our current capitalist system may never be the same again. According to billionaire investor Leon Cooperman, what we're experiencing today "has very lasting implications for the long term. No. 1: Capitalism as we know it will likely be changed forever."[18] Cooperman's argument is that "when the government is called upon to protect you on the downside, they have every right to regulate you on the upside."[19] He pointed out that consistently low interest rates are symptomatic of a troubled economy and the fact the country is shifting to the left regardless of who wins the 2020 presidential election.[20] Another reason capitalism will change is that America was fundamentally unprepared for a recession.[21]

One of the glaring red flags, which is both dramatic and disturbing, was a Federal Reserve report in 2019 that warned that nearly 40 percent of Americans couldn't come up with $400. This report would have gone unnoticed if a pandemic hadn't exposed the cracks in the way our current capitalist system is constructed. As a result of COVID-19, "millions of people are lining up at food banks, pleading for help on social media and going to work in the midst of a pandemic because they need the money."[22] If this is not enough, Columbia University's Center on Poverty and Social Policy warns that it is only a matter of time before tens of millions fall out of the middle class and into poverty.[23] As I've stated earlier, pandemics have a habit of changing us.

From a broader historical perspective, major crises like pandemics, wars, and economic collapses tend to do two things. They both expose the failures of economic systems and change the status quo. The Black Death of the 14th century helped bring about the end of feudalism. The stock market crash of 1929 exposed the failures of free-market capitalism and led to the New Deal. The end of World War II helped give rise to the middle class. We are today living through the unfolding of a pandemic none of us have experienced in our lifetime. The full extent of the economic damage, both here and abroad, has yet to be understood, but if history is any guide, our current capitalist system will change.

The pandemic is exposing just how precarious life is for many Americans. In addition to the glaring inequality that existed prior to COVID-19, the pandemic revealed the disturbing facts that workers don't have protection in terms of nationwide sick leave and minimal labor union membership. It took a pandemic to force change. For example, Congress has given some workers paid sick leave. Companies started to offer paid leave, subsidized child care, and flexible work schedules. Millions are now working from home, which could change the workplace even when things return to normal—whatever that normal is going to be. In many ways, the pandemic is widening the inequality gap, and how we as a society respond will determine what kind of capitalism we will have. Let's not forget that the pandemic is a global phenomenon.

If we take a comparative approach and look at other developed nations, we find the economic impact of the pandemic has not been as severe. For example, according Harry Kretchmer, writing for the World Economic Forum, "the US Congressional Budget Office predicts 15% of people could be unemployed by the third quarter of this year—up from less than 4% in the first quarter."[24] In contrast, the unemployment rate in Germany has risen to 5.8%. In Japan, the unemployment rate, as of March 2020, was 2.5%. It is important to understand that unemployment is an important indicator of an economy's health. Given the magnitude of unemployment in the United States, a speedy recovery, in my opinion, is unlikely. The reason I say this is that of the millions of temporary layoffs, "many could turn into permanent job losses as the shutdowns drag on."[25] We are today living through one of those defining moments in history. The capitalism of old must give way to a more inclusive system.

Millions of Americans lost their jobs, along with their health insurance and other benefits. Congress, which for a brief time addressed the grave economic issues facing Americans, has reverted to partisan bickering. The cultural shock of this pandemic might be what is needed to create a more equitable and distributive brand of capitalism, a capitalism that is ethical and inclusive. It was Milton Friedman who argued that the sole responsibility of business is to make money. This philosophy rings hollow when millions of people are struggling to survive. The purpose of business must change from making profits at any cost to creating equity and value so that maybe, just maybe, the American Dream is something we all can embrace.

Let me close this book with a quote from F. Scott Fitzgerald about the wealthy elite: "Let me tell you about the very rich. They are different from you and me. They possess and enjoy early, and it does something to them, makes them soft where we are hard, and cynical where we are trustful, in a way that, unless you were born rich, it is very difficult to understand. They think, deep in their hearts, that they are better than we are because we had to discover the compensations and refuges of life for ourselves. Even when they enter deep into our world or sink below us, they still think that they are better than we."[26] The problem with the wealthy elites of today is they are not only different from the rest of us, they are also different from the wealthy few of past generations. I believe that today's wealthy elites are divorced from the realities and actualities of the world around them.

What is demanded today, more than at any other time in history, is the Herculean task of bridging the gap between the rich and poor. One step toward this lofty and noble goal is for people to have an awakening about the financial world around them. We need a revolution in consciousness raising. Part of this revolution will begin with financial literacy, which is the fundamental purpose of this book. The

more we understand how the financial world operates, the less tolerant we will be of its excesses. We cannot acquiesce to the inevitable
notion that our lot in life is immutable. The American Dream was
conceived as a participatory experiment; a virtuous longing to better
ourselves and be on an equal footing with everyone else.

What is needed today is a fundamental redefinition of financial
literacy to include those hidden forces that always impact our financial future. We need to unlock the hidden forces, bring them to light,
analyze them, anticipate them, and counteract them. In addition to
revealing the hidden forces, I've also offered you potentially powerful
solutions. You see, to unlock something is itself an act of finding a solution. In a broader sense, this book is about how to focus knowledge and
make it accessible, practical, and relevant. We need knowledge, logic,
and actionable information that will change our mindset about money.
We need to calmly, and without emotion, become forward looking by
anticipating and preparing for what is to come. We should consider the
results of endowment experts who have perfected the multi-asset model
for institutional investing. We need to bravely acknowledge that baby
boomers hurt millennials, and other generations, with their overcon-
sumption and mounting debt.

I need to say a few words about millennials. As a group, millennials are often looked upon as lazy and uninterested in work. They are
unfairly labeled as the social media generation. Here is the truth: Millennials inherited an economic mess. They are saddled with a mountain
of student-loan debt, home ownership is out of reach, and the American
Dream is a distant memory of a time long gone. I wrote this book with
millennials in mind. I wrote this book to inspire them and to let them
know that I understand their frustration.

Millennials need to know that they must be the agents of change. Change will not be handed to them. This is why financial literacy is critically important. Although there is time to plan and prepare for retirement, millennials must take action now. Millennials will soon be our political leaders, and it will be up to them to address the structural inequalities that have come to define our current form of capitalism. Rather than capitalism becoming equitable, ethical, and distributive, it has managed to concentrate wealth in the hands of a powerful minority.

What has ended up happening is that a select few managed to figure out a way to manipulate the rules in order to favor themselves at the expense of countless millions. We need to bring back an ethical impulse toward others. We need to bring back our moral compass to caution us against the disease of greed. Knowledge, coupled with an ethical framework to help us navigate the constantly evolving complexity of the economic world around us, can serve as a counterweight to the injustice we see all around us. Individual investors who want to protect their hard-earned money and have something for retirement have choices today. I developed the REALM model out of a powerful sense of helping others. From a philosophical perspective, I am someone whose action in the world is guided by a divine spark toward others.

Appendix A

SEQUENCE-OF-RETURN RISK

So far in this book, we've only discussed the first part of investing for retirement: the *accumulation phase.* As you can probably guess, this phase is when you're accumulating wealth through work and investments. Your goal, as you know well by this point, is to maximize your returns while minimizing losses through risk mitigation. The accumulation phase is what people generally think of or mean by the term *investment.* However, it's only half the picture.

The work of financial planning doesn't end with a fat portfolio and a bright future of golf, sandy beaches, and finally time to crisscross the country in a new RV. It's not a simple matter of withdrawing whatever you need now that you've earned it—at least not if you want your retirement to last the 30 years or so you'll probably need it to. After your retirement, you enter into the *distribution phase* of investment—when you actually begin to use all of the wealth you've accumulated to support yourself and your family. It's typically no longer the necessary goal at this stage to maximize investments and earn returns; instead, you'll want to maximize the longevity of your accounts and minimize your tax burden. Your focus must change from accumulation to risk management and capital preservation.

One of the often misunderstood challenges of portfolio management is the sequence-of-return risk. This type of risk comes from the order in which you receive returns from your investments and "affects you when you are periodically adding or withdrawing money from your investments."[1] In effect, the market conditions of withdrawing money from your portfolio, particularly during bear markets, may cause lasting damage to the amount of income the portfolio generates. If you make withdrawals during a period of reduced or negative returns, the value of your portfolio may become depleted.

Let's suppose that investor A and investor B each started with a $1 million investment portfolio at age 60. Both investors will earn an average of 6% annual return, which will grow at the same rate over the next 25 years. The difference between investor A and investor B is that they will experience their annual returns in an inverse order: Investor A will experience returns during an "up" (bull) market, while investor B will experience returns during a "down" (bear) market. Regardless of the type of market our two investors find themselves in, by the end of the 25 years, they have earned the same amount.

Table 6.1. Sequence of Returns Accumulation.

Age	Investor A (Up Market)		Investor B (Down Market)	
	Annual Return (%)	Year End Value	Annual Return (%)	Year End Value
60	-	$1,000,000	-	$1,000,000
61	5	$1,050,000	-25	$750,000
62	28	$1,344,000	-14	$645,000
63	22	$1,639,680	-10	$580,500
64	-5	$1,557,696	16	$673,380
65	20	$1,869,235	21	$814,790
66	19	$2,224,390	5	$855,529
67	23	$2,736,000	-16	$718,645
68	9	$2,982,240	8	$776,136
69	16	$3,459,398	14	$884,795
70	23	$4,255,059	24	$1,097,146
71	22	$5,191,172	14	$1,250,747
72	26	$3,841,468	5	$1,313,284
73	-15	$3,265,247	-15	$1,116,291
74	5	$3,428,510	-26	$826,056
75	14	$3,908,501	22	$1,007,788
76	24	$4,846,541	23	$1,239,579
77	14	$5,525,057	16	$1,437,912
78	8	$5,967,062	9	$1,567,324
79	-16	$5,012,332	23	$1,927,808
80	5	$5,262,949	19	$2,294,092
81	21	$6,363,168	20	$2,752,910
82	16	$7,387,075	-5	$2,615,264
83	-10	$6,648,367	22	$3,190,623
84	14	$5,717,596	23	$4,083,997
85	-25	**$4,288,197**	5	**$4,288,197**[2]

Example shown for illustrative purposes only and does not represent any specific investment. It does not reflect taxes or investment fees, which would reduce the figures shown here.

Although the two investors had different sequences of return—meaning one earned when the other lost—they eventually accumulated the same amount in their respective portfolios ($4,288,197). This example, of course, assumes that neither investor A nor investor B withdrew any amount from their initial investment. The sequence of returns, whether the investor's returns began during a growing market or during a downturn, did not affect the end result of the portfolios because the losses were offset by the gains. Despite the inherent volatility of market rises and falls, the average trend over a long period was up, so both portfolios grew.

However, the sequence of returns affects these two investors very differently when you distribute the funds. Let's assume that both investors A and B make 5% annual withdrawals from the initial investment outlay; after 25 years of withdrawals, the difference is dramatic.

Investor A withdrew 5% of their initial investment each year, and their portfolio fluctuated with the market, the ups and downs causing the portfolio to grow when the market was up and fall when the market was down. However, because the withdrawals were mostly taken during upswings of the market, the growth offset the withdrawals.

Investor B also withdrew 5% of the initial investment on an annual basis, but this scenario takes place during a down market. In this case, the withdrawals outpace the portfolio's ability to recover when the market picks up again. Two mathematical factors work against investor B: First, the negative returns lower the value of the portfolio. Coupled with that yearly $50,000 withdrawal, it becomes impossible for the portfolio to bounce back, even when positive returns come in later years. Eventually, investor B runs out of money.

Table 6.2 Sequence of Returns Distribution.

Age	Investor A (Up Market)			Investor B (Down Market)		
	5% Annual Withdrawals	Annual Return (%)	Year End Value	5% Annual Withdrawals	Annual Return (%)	Year End Value
60	-	-	$1,000,000	-	-	$1,000,000
61	$50,000	5	$1,000,000	$50,000	-25	$700,00
62	$50,000	28	$1,230,000	$50,000	-14	$552,000
63	$50,000	22	$1,450,600	$50,000	-10	$446,800
64	$50,000	-5	$1,328,070	$50,000	16	$468,288
65	$50,000	20	$1,543,684	$50,000	21	$516,628
66	$50,000	19	$1,786,984	$50,000	5	$492,460
67	$50,000	23	$2,147,990	$50,000	-16	$363,666
68	$50,000	9	$2,291,309	$50,000	8	$342,760
69	$50,000	16	$2,607,919	$50,000	14	$340,746
70	$50,000	23	$3,157,740	$50,000	24	$372,525
71	$50,000	22	$3,802,443	$50,000	14	$374,679
72	$50,000	-26	$2,763,808	$50,000	5	$343,412
73	$50,000	-15	$2,299,237	$50,000	-15	$241,901
74	$50,000	5	$2,364,199	$50,000	-26	$129,006
75	$50,000	14	$2,645,186	$50,000	22	$107,388
76	$50,000	24	$3,230,031	$50,000	23	$82,087
77	$50,000	14	$3,632,235	$50,000	16	$45,221
78	$50,000	8	$3,872,814	$45,221	9	$0
79	$50,000	-16	$3,203,164	$0	23	$0
80	$50,000	5	$3,313,322	$0	19	$0
81	$50,000	21	$3,959,120	$0	20	$0
82	$50,000	16	$4,542,579	$0	-5	$0
83	$50,000	-10	$4,038,321	$0	22	$0
84	$50,000	-14	$3,422,956	$0	28	$0
85	$50,000	-25	$2,517,217	$0	5	$0[1]

Example shown for illustrative purposes only and does not represent any specific investment. It does not reflect taxes or investment fees, which would reduce the figures shown here.

The timing of your withdrawals can be more important than the withdrawals themselves. Withdrawals during a troubled market end up being more expensive than withdrawals of the same amount during a market upswing. Of course, you can't control the market, and you're going to have to start withdrawing money when you retire; that's your new annual income. But there are several strategies designed to mitigate against sequence-of-return risk.

First, you need to develop a comprehensive financial plan that accounts for all your spending needs and the projected income from your investments. "A comprehensive plan gives you a baseline from which to make adjustments to account for market downturns, unexpected expenses and other changes in your financial situation."[3] Another tactic is to create a bucket strategy, which means you keep some money for short-term expenses in bonds or cash. This will better enable you to cover your liabilities in the near term without worrying about market downturns. This will also give your other assets time to hopefully rebound from a downturn. In other words, you need to have some cash saved in order to anticipate market downturns.

NOTES

PREFACE

1. Robin Sherwood, "Record Number of Women Become CFP® Professionals," htgadvisors.com, June 4, 2020.
2. Amanda Barroso, "Key Takeaways on Americans' Views on Gender Equality a Century After U.S. Women Gained the Right to Vote," Pew Research Center, August 13, 2020, https://www.pewresearch.org/fact-tank/2020/08/13/key-takeaways-on-americans-views-on-gender-equality-a-century-after-u-s-women-gained-the-right-to-vote/.
3. Joris Luyendijk, "Women in Finance: The Past 50 Years," *The Guardian,* August 20, 2012, https://www.theguardian.com/lifeandstyle/2012/aug/20/women-in-finance-50-years.
4. "Bonds May No Longer Provide a Hedge Against Stocks, Warns Jim Bianco," Seekingalpha, October 12, 2018, https://seekingalpha.com/article/4211241-bonds-may-no-longer-provide-hedge-against-stocks-warns-jim-bianco.
5. Mebane T. Faber and Eric W. Richardson, *The Ivy Portfolio: How to Invest Like the Top Endowments and Avoid Bear Markets* (Hoboken, NJ: Wiley, April 1, 2009), pp. 1–240.
6. Casey Bond, "Here's What It Actually Takes to Change Your Money Habits," Huffpost, May 9, 2019, https://www.huffpost.com/entry/get-better-with-money-habits_l_5cd30aa9e4b0a7dffcd0416d.
7. Julie Beck, "This Article Won't Change Your Mind," *The Atlantic,* March 13, 2017, https://www.theatlantic.com/science/archive/2017/03/this-article-wont-change-your-mind/519093/.
8. Mike Moffatt, "What Is Microeconomics," ThoughtCo., March 3, 2019, https://www.thoughtco.com/overview-of-microeconomics-1146353.

9. Scott Wolla, "Financial Literacy: Benefits for the 'Micro' and the 'Macro,'" Council for Economic Education, April 18, 2013, https://www.councilforeconed.org/2013/04/18/financial-literacy-benefits-for-the-micro-and-the-macro/.

10. David F. Swensen, *Pioneering Portfolio Management: An Unconventional Approach to Institutional Investment, Fully Revised and Updated* (New York: Free Press, January 6, 2009), p. 1.

11. Geraldine Fabrikant, "Keep It Simple, Says Yale's Top Investor," *New York Times,* February 17, 2008, https://www.nytimes.com/2008/02/17/business/17swensen.html.

12. Kate Rooney and Ari Levy, "The Most Influential Endowment Manager Just Jumped into Crypto with Bets on Two Silicon Valley Funds," CNBC, October 5, 2018, https://www.cnbc.com/2018/10/05/yale-investment-chief-david-swensen-jumps-into-crypto-with-bets-on-two-silicon-valley-funds.html.

13. Marie Huillet, "94% of Surveyed Endowment Funds Are Allocating to Crypto Investments: Study," Cointelegraph.com, April 15, 2019, https://cointelegraph.com/news/94-of-surveyed-endowment-funds-are-allocating-to-crypto-investments-study.

14. Michael Aloi, "5 Reasons You Need a Financial Advisor," Fool.com, updated April 26, 2019, https://www.fool.com/investing/2019/02/16/5-reasons-you-need-a-financial-advisor.aspx.

INTRODUCTION

1. *New York Times*, "What Is a Stock Market Correction?" *New York Times*, February 27, 2020, https://www.nytimes.com/2020/02/27/business/what-is-a-stock-market-correction.html.

2. Peter Nesvold, "The Financial Devastation of COVID-19: Here's How to Help (and Find Help)," Forbes, August 16, 2020, https://www.forbes.com/sites/peternesvold/2020/08/18/the-financial-devastation-of-covid-19-heres-how-to-help-and-find-help/#35efdbec4f73.

3. Ibid.

4. Douglas P. McCormick, "Financial Literacy—The Big Problem No One Is Talking About," Huffpost.com, June 3, 2017, https://www.huffpost.com/entry/financial-literacythe-big_b_10264622.

5. "What Is the Financial Literacy Rates Around the World?" Howmuch.net, retrieved October 4, 2018, https://howmuch.net/articles/financial-literacy-around-the-world.

6. Ibid.

7. PYMNTS, "Study: Americans Overestimate Their Financial Literacy," PYMNTS.com, June 15, 2018, https://www.pymnts.com/consumer-finance/2018/study-americans-financial-literacy-personal-finance-knowledge/.

8. James R. Penner and Joshua D. Spizman, "An Investigation of Personal Financial Literacy Education," Digital Commons at Loyola Marymount University and Loyola Law School, May 10, 2019, https://digitalcommons.lmu.edu/cgi/viewcontent.cgi?article=1280&context=honors-thesis.

9. National Financial Educators Council, "National Financial Literacy Results," financialeducatorscouncil.org, copyright 2019, retrieved September 9, 2020, https://www.financialeducatorscouncil.org/national-financial-literacy-test/.

10. National Financial Educators Council, "Survey: Americans Agree Schools Should Teach High School Students Financial Literacy Coursework," financialeducatorscouncil.org, retrieved September 9, 2020, https://www.financialeducatorscouncil.org/financial-literacy-subject-survey/.

11. Greg Iacurci, "Financial Literacy: An Epic Fai in America," investmentnews.com, March 2, 2019, https://www.investmentnews.com/financial-literacy-an-epic-fail-in-america-78385.

12. Ibid.

13. Jessica Dickler, "75 Percent of Americans Are Winging It When It Comes to Their Financial Future," CNBC.com, updated April 9, 2019, https://www.cnbc.com/2019/04/01/when-it-comes-to-their-financial-future-most-americans-are-winging-it.html.

14. James McWhinney, "The Demise of the Defined-Benefit Plan," Investopedia.com, February 18, 2020, https://www.investopedia.com/articles/retirement/06/demiseofdbplan.asp.

15. Crain-api, "Advisers Can—and Must—Help Improve Financial Literacy in America," Investmentnews.com, March 9, 2019, https://www.investmentnews.com/advisers-can-and-must-help-improve-financial-literacy-in-america-78519.

16. Rebecca Lake, "The 60/40 Portfolio Is Dead for Retirement Planning," *US News,* April 23, 2019, https://money.usnews.com/investing/investing-101/articles/why-the-60-40-portfolio-is-dead-for-retirement-planning.

17. Ibid.

18. Ibid.

19. Ibid.

20. Jonathan Brock, "United States Public Sector Employment," Springerlink.com, retrieved June 6, 2019, https://link.springer.com/chapter/10.1057/9781403920171_5.

21. Stephen Miller, "Corporate Pension Plans Hit Hard in 2018," SHRM. org, January 8, 2019, https://www.shrm.org/resourcesandtools/hr-topics/benefits/pages/corporate-pension-plans-hit-hard.aspx.

22. Fola Akinnibi, "Public Pensions Face Reckoning from Equity Rout, Tax Losses," Bloombergtax.com, April 15, 2020, https://news.bloombergtax.com/daily-tax-report/public-pensions-face-reckoning-from-equity-rout-and-tax-losses?utm_source=rss&utm_medium=DTNW&utm_campaign=00000171-7f27-d2ab-a5f1-7f7785de0000.

23. Michael Edesess, "The Reason Underfunded Pensions Are a Disaster Waiting to Happen," MarketWatch, April 5, 2017, https://www.marketwatch.com/story/the-reason-underfunded-pensions-are-a-disaster-waiting-to-happen-2017-04-03.

24. John Mauldin, "The Coming Pension Crisis Is So Big That It's a Problem for Everyone," *Forbes*, May 20, 2019, https://www.forbes.com/sites/johnmauldin/2019/05/20/the-coming-pension-crisis-is-so-big-that-its-a-problem-for-everyone/#1a69d13237fc.

25. Ibid.

26. Eric Hines, *A Conservative Treatise on American Government: A Brief Discussion of What a Government, Subordinate to the Sovereign People, Must Do* (Bloomington, IN: Xlibris, June 28, 2012), p. 211.

27. Sean Williams, "Social Security Will Burn Through $3 Trillion in Asset Reserves by 2034—Here's Why," Fool.com, February 3, 2018, https://www.fool.com/retirement/2018/02/03/social-security-will-burn-through-3-trillion-in-as.aspx.

28. Sean Williams, "Could Social Security Actually Run Out of Money?" Fool.com, May 19, 2018, https://www.fool.com/retirement/2018/05/19/could-social-security-actually-run-out-of-money.aspx.

29. Ester Bloom, "Here's How Many Americans Have Nothing at All Saved for Retirement," CNBC.com, June 13, 2017, https://www.cnbc.com/2017/06/13/heres-how-many-americans-have-nothing-at-all-saved-for-retirement.html.

30. Jean Folger, "Can You Have a Pension and a 401(k)?" Investopedia, July 2, 2020, https://www.investopedia.com/can-you-have-a-pension-and-a-401-k-4770883.

31. Ibid.

32. Lorie Konish, "These Pension Plans Are at Risk of Going Broke. Now Lawmakers Need to Agree on a Fix," CNBC.com, July 12, 2019, https://www.cnbc.com/2019/07/12/these-pension-plans-are-at-risk-of-going-broke-lawmakers-need-a-fix.html.

33. Chris Hogan, "Don't Count on Social Security: Here's Why," Chrishogan360.com, retrieved August 21, 2019, https://www.chrishogan360.com/retirement/dont-count-on-social-security.

34. Ibid.

35. John Mauldin, "Yet Another Debt Crisis Is Brewing," *Forbes,* July 13, 2018, https://www.forbes.com/sites/johnmauldin/2018/06/13/yet-another-debt-crisis-is-brewing/#5fc1a0b1ff57.

36. Ibid.

37. Ibid.

38. Investopedia staff, "Will Corporate Debt Drag Your Stock Down?" Investopedia, March 23, 2020, https://www.investopedia.com/articles/basics/03/091903.asp.

39. Joy Wiltermuth, "Junk Bonds Are Getting Worse, and Investors Are Starting to Take Notice," MarketWatch, August 16, 2019, https://www.marketwatch.com/story/junk-bonds-are-getting-worse-and-investors-are-starting-to-take-notice-2019-08-15.

40. Maria LaMagna, "A Growing Number of Americans Have More Credit-Card Debt than Savings," MarketWatch, February 13, 2019, https://www.marketwatch.com/story/a-growing-number-of-americans-have-more-credit-card-debt-than-savings-2019-02-13.

41. Kimberly Amadeo, "Asset Bubbles: Causes and Trends," The Balance, April 1, 2020, https://www.thebalance.com/asset-bubble-causes-examples-and-how-to-protect-yourself-3305908.

42. Ben Reynolds, "New Bubbles, Mounting Debt: Preparing for the Coming Crisis," Resilience.org, November 7, 2019, https://www.resilience.org/stories/2019-11-07/new-bubbles-mounting-debt-preparing-for-the-coming-crisis/.

43. Annamaria Lusardi and Olivia S. Mitchell, "The Economic Importance of Financial Literacy: Theory and Evidence," *Journal of Economic Literature*, vol. 52, no.1 (2014): 5–44, https://www.ncbi.nlm.nih.gov/pmc/articles/PMC5450829/.

44. Shelly Eickholt, "Why You Should Care About Your Child's Financial Literacy," Central Insurance Companies, March 26, 2020, https://blog.central-insurance.com/2020/03/26/why-you-should-care-about-your-childs-financial-literacy/.

45. Ibid.

46. David R. Harper, "The Equity Risk Premium: More Risk for Higher Returns," Investopedia, March 17, 2020, https://www.investopedia.com/articles/04/012104.asp.

47. David Wildermuth, "Is the Endowment Model Relevant for Individual Investors?" InvestmentNews, October 22, 2018, https://www.investmentnews.com/is-the-endowment-model-relevant-for-individual-investors-76607.

48. Nicholas Vardy, "Why You Should (Still) Invest Like Yale," Stockinvestor. com, December 19, 2017, https://www.stockinvestor.com/31663/still-invest-like-yale/.

CHAPTER 1

1. Will Kenton, "Financial Literacy," Investopedia, April 19, 2020, https://www.investopedia.com/terms/f/financial-literacy.asp.
2. Chris Blank, "How Economic Factors Affect the Pay of Employees," Chron, retrieved January 24, 2020, https://smallbusiness.chron.com/economic-factors-affect-pay-employees-26017.html.
3. Nathan Bomey, "'It's Really Over': Corporate Pensions Head for Extinction as Nature of Retirement Plans Changes," *USA Today,* December 10, 2019, https://www.usatoday.com/story/money/2019/12/10/corporate-pensions-defined-benefit-mercer-report/2618501001/.
4. Jackie Freyman, "Looking at the Past to Create a Map to the Future," Forbes, April 27, 2020, https://www.forbes.com/sites/forbescommunicationscouncil/2020/04/27/looking-at-the-past-to-create-a-map-to-the-future/#7a3b37f865ce.
5. Karen Demasters, "Women Hold Majority of Personal Wealth, But Still Minorities in Advisory Field," Financial Advisor Magazine, March 25, 2020, https://www.fa-mag.com/news/women-need-to-lead-in-finances--consultant-says-54850.html.
6. "Overview of the Gilded Age," digitalhistory.com, retrieved September 16, 2019, https://www.digitalhistory.uh.edu/era.cfm?eraid=9.
7. Alan Axelrod, *The Gilded Age: 1876–1912: Overture to the American Century* (New York: Sterling, November 14, 2017), pp. 2–3.
8. "America's Gilded Age: Robber Barons and Captains of Industry," Maryville University, retrieved October 4, 2019, https://online.maryville.edu/business-degrees/americas-gilded-age/.
9. Ibid.
10. "Politics in the Gilded Age: The Age of Political Machines," Sageamericanhistory.com, retrieved October 5, 2019, http://sageamericanhistory.net/gildedage/topics/gildedagepolitics.html.
11. Lily Rothman, "How American Inequality in the Gilded Age Compares to Today," *Time*, February 5, 2018, https://time.com/5122375/american-inequality-gilded-age/.
12. Julie Marks, "What Caused the Stock Market Crash of 1929?" History.com, April 13, 2018, https://www.history.com/news/what-caused-the-stock-market-crash-of-1929.

13. Kimberly Amadeo, "President Herbert Hoover's Economic Policies," T
    Balance, January 31, 2020, https://www.thebalance.com/president-hoo
    economic-policies-4583019.
14. Kimberly Amadeo, "The Great Depression, What Happened, What Cause
    It, How It Ended," The Balance, updated May 27, 2020, https://www.
    thebalance.com/the-great-depression-of-1929-3306033.
15. "Her Life: The Woman Behind the New Deal," Frances Perkins Center,
    retrieved September 23, 2019, https://francesperkinscenter.org/life-new/.
16. Kimberly Amadeo, "Glass-Steagall Act of 1933, Its Purpose and Repeal," The
    Balance, April 14, 2020, https://www.thebalance.com/glass-steagall-act-
    definition-purpose-and-repeal-3305850.
17. Nicola Pizzolato, *The Making and Unmaking of Fordism* (London:
    Palgrave Macmillan, 2013), p. 19, https://link.springer.com/
    chapter/10.1057/9781137311702_2.
18. Jim Chappelow, "Laissez-Faire," Investopedia, July 25, 2019, https://www.
    investopedia.com/terms/l/laissezfaire.asp.
19. Rick Paulas, "The Case Against Milton Friedman's Capitalism," *Pacific
    Standard*, March 16, 2018, https://psmag.com/economics/the-case-against-
    milton-friedmans-capitalism.
20. Moyers & Company, "The Powell Memo: A Call-to-Arms for Corporations,"
    Billmoyers.com, September 14, 2012, https://billmoyers.com/content/the-
    powell-memo-a-call-to-arms-for-corporations/.
21. Paul Lewis, "Nixon's Economic Policies Return to Haunt G.O.P.," *New York
    Times*, August 15, 1976, https://www.nytimes.com/1976/08/15/archives/
    nixons-economic-policies-return-to-haunt-the-gop-nixons-economic.html.
22. Nicholas Clairmont, "'Those Who do Not Learn History Are Doomed to
    Repeat It.' Really?" Bigthink.com, July 31, 2013, https://bigthink.com/
    the-proverbial-skeptic/those-who-do-not-learn-history-doomed-to-repeat-it-
    really.
23. John Russell, "Did the Bretton Woods Agreements Succeed?" The Balance,
    February 23, 2019, https://www.thebalance.com/bretton-woods-1345012.
24. Mike Moffatt, "Understanding the Bretton Woods System: Tying World
    Currency to the Dollar," thoughtco.com, January 27, 2020, https://www.
    thoughtco.com/the-bretton-woods-system-overview-1147446.
25. Ibid.
26. Ibid.
27. Carol M. Kopp, "Globalization," Investopedia, April 30, 2020, https://www.
    investopedia.com/terms/g/globalization.asp.
28. Chad Borgman, "Re-Capturing the American Dream: How to Restore
    Middle Class America," *Harvard Political Review,* March 28, 2017, https://

nited-states/re-capturing-the-american-dream-how-to-
nerica/.

he Top 10 Percent Own 70 Percent of U.S. Wealth,"
14, 2019, https://www.statista.com/chart/19635/
-percentiles-in-the-us/.

ʋotcom Bubble," Investopedia, June 25, 2019, https://www.
.com/terms/d/dotcom-bubble.asp.

ar 2002: Stock Market Crash," Myvoleo.com, July 28, 2016,
/www.myvoleo.com/blog/year-2002-stock-market-crash.

nberly Amadeo, "The Stock Market Crash of 2008," The Balance,
updated April 20, 2020, https://www.thebalance.com/stock-market-crash-
of-2008-3305535.

33. Jim Chappelow, "Stagflation," Investopedia, June 30, 2020, https://www.
investopedia.com/terms/s/stagflation.asp.

34. James Chen, "Money Market," Investopedia, May 31, 2020, https://www.
investopedia.com/terms/m/moneymarket.asp.

35. Will Kenton, "Savings and Loan Crisis—S&L Crisis," Investopedia, May 16,
2019, https://www.investopedia.com/terms/s/sl-crisis.asp.

36. Kimberly Amadeo, "Savings and Loan Crisis Explained," The Balance,
January 13, 2020, https://www.thebalance.com/savings-and-loans-crisis-
causes-cost-3306035.

37. Ibid.

38. Craig Harris, Dennis Wagner, et al., "Charles H. Keating Jr. Dies at Age
90," azcentral.com, April 1, 2014, https://www.azcentral.com/story/news/
politics/2014/04/01/charles-keating-jr-dies-saving-loans/7182675/.

39. Richard Vague, *A Brief History of Doom* (Philadelphia: University of
Pennsylvania Press, March 25, 2019), pp. 63-64.

40. Rob Wells, "Rob Wells: Keating Anniversary Should Have Us Rethinking
Journalism," *Charleston Gazette-Mail*, October 30, 2019, https://www.
wvgazettemail.com/opinion/columnists/rob-wells-keating-anniversary-
should-have-us-rethinking-journalism/article_1b11d540-c9ff-5f03-a3b1-
04851be913cd.html.

41. Kimberly Amadeo, "Savings and Loan Crisis Explained," The Balance,
January 13, 2020, https://www.thebalance.com/savings-and-loans-crisis-
causes-cost-3306035.

42. Will Kenton, "Savings and Loan Crisis—S&L Crisis," Investopedia, May 16,
2019, https://www.investopedia.com/terms/s/sl-crisis.asp.

43. Brian McCullough, "A Revealing Look at the Dot-Com Bubble of 2000 and
How It Shapes our Lives Today," ideas.ted.com, December 4, 2018, https://
ideas.ted.com/an-eye-opening-look-at-the-dot-com-bubble-of-2000-and-
how-it-shapes-our-lives-today/.

44. Ibid.

45. Ibid.

46. James Chen, "Enron," Investopedia, October 6, 2019, https://www. investopedia.com/terms/e/enron.asp.

47. Troy Segal, "Enron Scandal: The Fall of a Wall Street Darling," Investopedia, May 4, 2020, https://www.investopedia.com/updates/enron-scandal-summary/.

48. Adam Hayes, "The Rise and Fall of WorldCom," Investopedia, May 5, 2020, https://www.investopedia.com/terms/w/worldcom.asp.

49. Mano Sabani, *Mano Sabani's Money Secrets: Cruise Your Way to Financial Freedom* (Singapore: Marshall Cavendish Publishing, Reprint Edition September 23, 2019), p. 8.

50. Kimberly Amadeo, "Causes of the 2008 Global Financial Crisis," Investopedia, May 29, 2020, https://www.thebalance.com/what-caused-2008-global-financial-crisis-3306176.

51. Nick Lioudis, "The Collapse of Lehman Brothers: A Case Study," Investopedia, November 26, 2019, https://www.investopedia.com/articles/economics/09/lehman-brothers-collapse.asp.

52. Renee Merle, "A Guide to the Financial Crisis—10 Years Later," *Washington Post*, September 10, 2018, https://www.washingtonpost.com/business/economy/a-guide-to-the-financial-crisis--10-years-later/2018/09/10/114b76ba-af10-11e8-a20b-5f4f84429666_story.html.

53. Rick Hampson, "America's Second Gilded Age: More Class Envy Than Class Conflict," *USA Today,* May 17, 2018, https://www.usatoday.com/story/news/2018/05/17/americas-gilded-ages-then-and-now-and-how-they-differ/615185002/.

54. Ibid.

55. Ibid.

56. Grace Guarnier, "Trump Tells Rich Mar-a-Lago Friends 'You All Just Got a Lot Richer' After Tax Bill," *Newsweek,* December 24, 2017, https://www.newsweek.com/president-donald-trump-rich-friends-lot-richer-tax-bill-758234.

57. "Trump: 'I Just Don't Want a Poor Person' Running the Economy," CNBC. com, June 22, 2017, https://www.cnbc.com/2017/06/22/trump-i-just-dont-want-a-poor-person-running-the-economy.html.

58. Kimberly Amadeo, "Late Stage Capitalism, Its Characteristics, and Why the Term Is Trending," The Balance, June 17, 2020, https://www.thebalance.com/late-stage-capitalism-definition-why-it-s-trending-4172369.

m Worth Saving?" Vox.com, February 26, 2019,
!019/1/2/18130630/american-capitalism-
arlstein.

ı—What Comes Next?" Thought Economics,
.tps://thoughteconomics.com/capitalism-what-

₹

.o, "What Is the American Dream Today? Has It Drifted
.n of Our Founding Fathers?" The Balance, April 14, 2020,
w.thebalance.com/what-is-the-american-dream-today-3306027.

.rnard Shaw, *The Intelligent Woman's Guide: To Socialism, Capitalism,
Sovietism, and Fascism* (London: Alma Books, April 1, 2013), p. 214.

CHAPTER 2

1. Ken Little, "Understanding Investing Risk," The Balance, September 16, 2019, https://www.thebalance.com/understanding-risk-3141268.
2. Ibid.
3. Akhilesh Ganti, "Asset Class," Investopedia, March 5, 2020, https://www.investopedia.com/terms/a/assetclasses.asp.
4. James Chen, "Corporate Bond," Investopedia, August 31, 2020, https://www.investopedia.com/terms/c/corporatebond.asp.
5. James Chen, "Modern Portfolio Theory (MPT)," Investopedia, February 4, 2020, https://www.investopedia.com/terms/m/modernportfoliotheory.asp.
6. Rebecca Lake, "What Is the 60/40 Portfolio (And Should You Have One)?" Smartasset.com, September 19, 2019, https://smartasset.com/investing/60-40-portfolio.
7. Yun Li, "The Standard '60-40' Retirement Portfolio of Stocks and Bonds Just Went into the Green for the Year," cnbc.com, June 4, 2020, https://www.cnbc.com/2020/06/04/the-standard-60-40-retirement-portfolio-of-stocks-and-bonds-just-went-into-the-green-for-the-year.html.
8. Ibid.
9. Rob Isbitts, "Why the 60/40 Portfolios Are in a Slump," *Forbes*, June 25, 2019, https://www.forbes.com/sites/robisbitts2/2019/06/25/why-6040-portfolios-are-in-a-slump/#7491dc14aa0b.
10. Ibid.
11. Rebecca Lake, "The 60/40 Portfolio Is Dead for Retirement Planning," *U.S. News*, April 23, 2019, https://money.usnews.com/investing/investing-101/articles/why-the-60-40-portfolio-is-dead-for-retirement-planning.

12. Julia Kagan, "Four Percent Rule," Investopedia, May 1, 2020, https://www.investopedia.com/terms/f/four-percent-rule.asp.

13. Wade Pfau, "The 4% Rule and the Search for a Safe Withdrawal Rate," Retirementresearcher.com, retrieved August 18, 2019, https://retirementresearcher.com/the-4-rule-and-the-search-for-a-safe-withdrawal-rate/.

14. Allison Schrager, "The 60-40 Split Between Stocks and Bonds Was Once Solid Financial Advice—But No Longer," Yahoo!, November 29, 2019, https://finance.yahoo.com/news/60-40-split-between-stocks-120057862.html.

15. Ellen Chang, "Why the 60/40 Asset Allocation Rule Is Dead," Thestreet.com, November 9, 2017, https://www.thestreet.com/retirement/why-the-60-40-asset-allocation-rule-is-dead-14384738.

16. Ibid.

17. Thomas Franck, "Here's How Long Stock Market Corrections Last and How Bad They Can Get," cnbc.com, February 27, 2020, https://www.cnbc.com/2020/02/27/heres-how-long-stock-market-corrections-last-and-how-bad-they-can-get.html.

18. Sean Williams, "50 Years of Stock Market Corrections, and the 1 Figure That Stands Out," Yahoo!, March 27, 2018, https://finance.yahoo.com/news/50-years-stock-market-corrections-103600928.html.

19. Norm Alster, "How to Deal with Head-Spinning Market Swings," *New York Times*, October 11, 2019, https://www.nytimes.com/2019/10/11/business/stock-market-swings-volatility.html.

20. Ibid.

21. Sean Williams, "50 Years of Stock Market Corrections, and the 1 Figure That Stands Out," Yahoo!, March 27, 2018, https://finance.yahoo.com/news/50-years-stock-market-corrections-103600928.html.

CHAPTER 3

1. Elijah Baldwin, "The Problems with Modern Portfolio Theory," Medium.com, February 2, 2019, https://medium.com/@elidb/the-problems-with-modern-portfolio-theory-696bf4dd1f60.

2. Ibid.

3. Dana Anspach, "Why Average Investors Earn Below Average Market Returns," The Balance, January 28, 2019, https://www.thebalance.com/why-average-investors-earn-below-average-market-returns-2388519.

4. Ibid.

5. Ibid.

6. Ben Le Fort, "Why Our Brains Make Bad Investment Decisions," Medium.com, December 10, 2018, https://medium.com/makingofamillionaire/why-our-brains-make-bad-investment-decisions-8ae7bc63c7d9.

7. Ibid.

8. Ibid.

9. James Chen, "Prospect Theory," Investopedia, July 28, 2020, https://www.investopedia.com/terms/p/prospecttheory.asp.

10. Ibid.

11. Ibid.

12. Gordon Scott, "Confirmation Bias," Investopedia, August 2, 2019, https://www.investopedia.com/terms/c/confirmation-bias.asp.

13. Ibid.

14. Harry S. Dent, *Zero Hour: Turn the Greatest Political and Financial Upheaval in Modern History to Your Advantage* (Melbourne, Australia: Schwartz, January 29, 2018), p. 5.

15. Akash Peshin, "What Is the 'Google Effect?'" scienceabc.com, December 12, 2019, https://www.scienceabc.com/eyeopeners/what-is-the-google-effect.html.

16. Genevieve Roberts, "Google Effect: Is Technology Making Us Stupid?" Independent, July 15, 2015, https://www.independent.co.uk/life-style/gadgets-and-tech/features/google-effect-is-technology-making-us-stupid-10391564.html.

17. Ibid.

18. Maryanne Wolf, "Skim Reading Is the New Normal. The Effect on Society Is Profound," *The Guardian*, August 25, 2018, https://www.theguardian.com/commentisfree/2018/aug/25/skim-reading-new-normal-maryanne-wolf.

19. Ibid.

20. Nicholas Carr, "Is Google Making Us Stupid?" *The Atlantic*, July/August, 2008, https://www.theatlantic.com/magazine/archive/2008/07/is-google-making-us-stupid/306868/.

21. Nicholas Carr, *The Shallows: What the Internet Is Doing to Our Brains* (New York: W. W. Norton & Company, January 1, 2010), pp. 5–6.

22. Marguerita Cheng, "Financial Literacy Is the Greatest Gift of All," *Forbes*, June 18, 2018, https://www.forbes.com/sites/margueritacheng/2018/06/18/financial-literacy-is-the-greatest-gift-of-all/#303e7a8069c3.

23. Kendra Cherry, "The Dunning-Kruger Effect," Verywellmind.com, June 14, 2019, https://www.verywellmind.com/an-overview-of-the-dunning-kruger-effect-4160740.

24. Ibid.

25. Ibid.

26. Ibid.

27. Ibid.

28. Ibid.

29. Ben Carlson, "The Many Uncertainties Involved with Retirement Planning," Linkedin.com, January 30, 2017, https://www.linkedin.com/pulse/many-uncertainties-involved-retirement-planning-ben-carlson-cfa/.

30. Paul Scott Anderson, "Goldilocks Stars: Just Right for Habitable Planets," Earthsky.org, March 17, 2019, https://earthsky.org/space/k-stars-goldilocks-stars-ideal-for-habitable-planets.

31. Johannes Steffens, "The Trust Paradox: Implications of the 2020 Edelman Barometer," Historyfactory.com, February 19, 2020, https://www.historyfactory.com/insights/the-trust-paradox-implications-of-the-2020-edelman-trust-barometer/.

32. Ibid.

33. Rebecca Lake, "Trust: An Advisor's Most Important Asset," Investopedia, October 17, 2019, https://www.investopedia.com/financial-advisor/trust-advisors-most-important-asset/.

34. Ibid.

35. Rebecca Lake, "3 Reasons to Avoid Robo Advisors," *U.S. News,* April 26, 2019, https://money.usnews.com/investing/investing-101/articles/3-reasons-to-avoid-robo-advisors.

36. Ibid.

37. Ibid.

38. Ibid.

39. Budd, Melone & Company, "Mirror, Mirror on the Wall...Who's the Fairest Investor of Them All?" buddmelone.com, © 2020, retrieved October 3, 2020, https://www.buddmelone.com/mirrormirroronthewall.

40. Dana Anspach, "Why Average Investors Earn Below Average Market Returns," The Balance, January 28, 2019, https://www.thebalance.com/why-average-investors-earn-below-average-market-returns-2388519.

41. Ibid.

CHAPTER 4

1. Chris Isidore, "JP Morgan Exec Warns Stock Market Could Fall by 40%," CNN Business, March 8, 2018, https://money.cnn.com/2018/03/08/investing/jpmorgan-market-correction/index.html.

2. Valeriy Zakamulin, "Graham Vs. Shiller: Is the U.S. Stock Market Overvalued?" Seekingalpha.com, March 5, 2018, https://seekingalpha.com/article/4153186-graham-vs-shiller-is-u-s-stock-market-overvalued.

3. Nicholas Vardy, "Why You Should (Still) Invest Like Yale," Stockinvestor. com, December 19, 2017, https://www.stockinvestor.com/31663/still-invest-like-yale/.

4. Ibid.

5. David F. Swensen, *Unconventional Success: A Fundamental Approach to Personal Investment* (New York: Free Press, August 9, 2005), p. 12.

6. Robert McIlhatton, "Unconventional Success Analysis: Asset Allocation after the Financial Crisis," Berkeley.edu, December 8, 2017, https://www.stat. berkeley.edu/~aldous/157/Old_Projects/Robert_McIlhatton.pdf.

7. Stephen G. Dimmock, Neng Wang, et al., "The Endowment Model and Modern Portfolio Theory," National Bureau of Economic Research, April, 23, 2018, https://www.nber.org/2018LTAM/yang.pdf.

8. Lecture 6, "Lecture 6: Guest Speaker: David Swensen," bookdown.org, Google Cache, September 21, 2020, https://bookdown.org/Albert/finance-shiller/guest-speaker-david-swensen.html.

9. Degree Query, "The 20 Largest College Endowments (1990–2020)," degreequery.com, copyright 2020, retrieved September 9, 2020, https://www. degreequery.com/largest-college-endowments/.

10. Financial Samurai staff, "How Do the Rich Invest? A Look Inside Yale Endowment's Asset Allocation," Financialsamurai.com, retrieved July 8, 2019, https://www.financialsamurai.com/a-look-inside-investment-asset-allocation-of-massive-university-endowments/.

11. Bloomberg Editorial Board, "Where Have All the Public Companies Gone?" Bloomberg.com, April 9, 2018, https://www.bloomberg.com/opinion/ articles/2018-04-09/where-have-all-the-u-s-public-companies-gone.

12. Ibid.

13. Jeff Sommer, "The Stock Market Is Shrinking. That's a Problem for Everyone," *New York Times,* August 4, 2018, https://www.nytimes.com/2018/08/04/ business/shrinking-stock-market.html.

14. Stephen G. Dimmock, Neng Wang, et al., "The Endowment Model and Modern Portfolio Theory," National Bureau of Economic Research, April 23, 2018, https://www.nber.org/2018LTAM/yang.pdf.

15. Ibid.

16. First 30 Days, "Mathew Tuttle on Retirement Planning," first30days.com, Google Cache, August 22, 2020, https://www.first30days.com/planning-for-retirement/articles/matthew-tuttle-on-retirement-planning.html.

17. Lisa Mahapatra, "8 Brilliant Lessons from the Investor That Taught Warren Buffett Everything He Knows," Businessinsider.com, February 6, 2013, https://www.businessinsider.com/eight-lessons-from-benjamin-graham-2013-2.

18. David Kaufman, "Revisiting Benjamin Graham, the Father of Alternative Investing," Financialpost.com, April 26, 2013, https://financialpost.com/investing/benjamin-graham-revisited.

19. Lex Zaharoff, "What Is an Alternative Investment?" HTG Investment Advisors, October 12, 2017, https://www.htgadvisors.com/what-is-an-alternative-investment/.

20. James Chen, "Venture Capital," Investopedia, February 25, 2020, https://www.investopedia.com/terms/v/venturecapital.asp.

21. World Economic Forum, "Alternative Investments 2020: Regulatory Reforms and Alternative Investments," World Economic Forum, October 2015, http://www3.weforum.org/docs/WEF_Alternative_Investments_2020_Regulatory_Reform.pdf.

22. Elizabeth Bauer, "Understanding the Central States Pension Plan's Tale of Woe," Forbes, December 3, 2018, https://www.forbes.com/sites/ebauer/2018/12/03/understanding-the-central-states-pension-plans-tale-of-woe/#fa9f7436c10b.

23. Pension Benefit Guaranty Corporation, "History of PBGC," pbgc.gov, last updated August 17, 2020, https://www.pbgc.gov/about/who-we-are/pg/history-of-pbgc.

24. Austin Wehrwein, "Hoffa Convicted on Use of Funds: Faces 20 Years," *New York Times,* July 27, 1964, https://www.nytimes.com/1964/07/27/archives/hoffa-convicted-on-use-of-funds-faces-20-years-he-and-6-others-are.html.

25. Department of Labor, "Employee Retirement Income Security Act (ERISA)," US Department of Labor, retrieved March 3, 2020, https://www.dol.gov/general/topic/retirement/erisa.

26. J. Waggoner, "More Advisors Use Alts, But Few Understand Them," Investmentnews.com, April 28, 2018, https://www.investmentnews.com/more-advisers-use-alts-but-few-understand-them-74114.

27. "Global Alternative AUM Hits $10 Trillion," February 6, 2020, https://www.pionline.com/alternatives/preqin-global-alternative-aum-hits-10-trillion#:~:text=trillion%20by%202023.-,Global%20alternative%20assets%20under%20management%20topped%20%2410%20trillion%20as%20of,%2C%20%22Alternatives%20in%202020.%2.2.

28. Knowledge at Wharton, "The Time Bomb Inside Public Pension Plans," University of Pennsylvania, August 23, 2018, https://knowledge.wharton.upenn.edu/article/the-time-bomb-inside-public-pension-plans/.

29. Ibid.

30. Mainstar Trust, "Building Retirement Wealth Through Alternative Investing," Mainstartrust.com, March 28, 2018, https://www.mainstartrust.com/blog-building-retirement-wealth-through-alternative-investing.

31. Blackrock, "What Are Alternative Investments?" Blackrock.com, retrieved February 8, 2020, https://www.blackrock.com/ch/individual/en/themes/alternative-investments.

32. Realty Mogul, "What Investors Should Know about the Jobs Act," Realtymogul.com, retrieved January 24, 2020, https://www.realtymogul.com/knowledge-center/article/what-investors-should-know-about-jobs-act.

33. "Investment Return of 5.7% Brings Yale Endowment Value to $30.3 Billion," September 27, 2019, https://news.yale.edu/2019/09/27/investment-return-57-brings-yale-endowment-value-303-billion.

34. Mainstar Trust, "Building Retirement Wealth Through Alternative Investing," Mainstartrust.com, March 28, 2018, https://www.mainstartrust.com/blog-building-retirement-wealth-through-alternative-investing.

35. Bloomberg Editorial Board, "Where Have All the Public Companies Gone?" Bloomberg.com, April 9, 2018, https://www.bloomberg.com/opinion/articles/2018-04-09/where-have-all-the-u-s-public-companies-gone.

36. Alpha Investing, "Why Does Commercial Real Estate Belong in Your Portfolio?" Alphai.com, retrieved March 16, 2020, https://www.alphai.com/articles/why-does-commercial-real-estate-belong-in-your-portfolio/.

37. Jim Berry, "COVID-19 Implications for Commercial Real Estate: Preparing for the 'Next Normal,'" Deloitte, May 1, 2020, https://www2.deloitte.com/us/en/insights/economy/covid-19/covid-19-implications-for-commercial-real-estate-cre.html.

38. Ron Derven, "Experts Speak: COVID-19's Impact on Commercial Real Estate," naiop.org, Summer 2020, https://www.naiop.org/en/Research-and-Publications/Magazine/2020/Summer-2020/Business-Trends/Experts-Speak-on-COVID19s-Impact-on-Commercial-Real-Estate.

39. Ibid.

40. Griffin Capital, "Commercial Real Estate: Six Potential Benefits," griffincapital.com, retrieved March 4, 2020, https://www.griffincapital.com/investor-education/commercial-real-estate-six-potential-benefits.

41. Ibid.

42. Ibid.

43. Ibid.

44. Ibid.

45. Ibid.

46. CFA Institute, "Introduction to Alternative Investments," cfainstitute.com, retrieved February 4, 2020, https://www.cfainstitute.org/en/membership/professional-development/refresher-readings/2020/introduction-alternative-investments.

47. Nareit Real Estate, "History of REITs & Real Estate Investing," reit.com, retrieved January 20, 2020, https://www.reit.com/what-reit/history-reits.

48. Matthew DiLallo, "Buying a Non-Traded REIT: What You Need to Know," Fool.com, December 21, 2019, https://www.fool.com/millionacres/real-estate-investing/reits/buying-non-traded-reit-what-you-need-know/.

49. The Real Deal Staff, "Non-Traded REITs Limit Withdrawals Amid Investor Rush to Retrieve Cash," therealdeal.com, April 15, 2020, https://therealdeal.com/2020/04/15/non-traded-reits-limit-withdrawals-amid-investor-rush-to-retrieve-cash/.

50. Ibid.

51. Ibid.

52. Thomas Parker, "Non-Traded REITs Offer Certain Buffers Against Stock Market Volatility," Upsideavenue.com, September 26, 2019, https://upsideavenue.com/invest-non-traded-reit/.

53. The DI Wire staff, "Stanger and IPA Launch Non-Traded REIT Performance Indexes," Thediwire.com, February 6, 2019, https://thediwire.com/stanger-ipa-launch-non-traded-reit-performance-indexes/.

54. Ibid.

55. Ibid.

56. Ibid.

57. Will Ashworth, "10 BDCs to Buy for Big-Time Income," Kiplinger.com, August 26, 2019, https://www.kiplinger.com/slideshow/investing/t018-s001-10-bdcs-to-buy-for-big-time-income/index.html.

58. Jussi Askola, "The Dark Side of BDC Investments," Seekingalpha.com, December 5, 2019, https://seekingalpha.com/article/4309284-dark-side-of-bdc-investments.

59. Will Kenton, "Sarbanes-Oxley (SOX) Act of 2002," Investopedia, February 4, 2020, https://www.investopedia.com/terms/s/sarbanesoxleyact.asp.

60. Eversheds Sutherland, "Should BDCs Be Part of the 'Main Street Lending Program'?" Eversheds Sutherland, April 13, 2020, https://us.eversheds-sutherland.com/mobile/NewsCommentary/Legal-Alerts/231128/Should-BDCs-be-part-of-the-Main-Street-Lending-Program.

61. Ibid.

62. Brett Owens, "BDCs: Where 9% Yields Are the Norm," Forbes, February 24, 2020, https://www.forbes.com/sites/brettowens/2020/02/24/bdcs-where-9-yields-are-the-norm/#22410b0d2ec2.

63. Cliffwater LLC, "2020 Q2 Report on U.S. Direct Lending," cliffwater.com, retrieved October 3, 2020, https://www.cliffwater.com/reader/viewer.html?file=https%3A//storage.googleapis.com/cdli/Cliffwater2020Q2ReportOnUSDirectLending.pdf.

64. Macrotrends, "S&P 500 Historical Annual Returns," macrotrends.net, retrieved October 3, 2020, https://www.macrotrends.net/2526/sp-500-historical-annual-returns.

65. Matthew Fox, "5 Companies Now Make up 20% of the S&P 500. Here's Why Goldman Sachs Says That's a Bad Signal for Future Returns (MSFT, AAPL, AMZN, GOOGL, FB)," *Business Insider,* April 27, 2020, https://markets.businessinsider.com/news/stocks/sp500-concentration-large-cap-bad-sign-future-returns-effect-market-2020-4-1029133505.

66. James Chen, "Business Development Company (BDC)," Investopedia, March 16, 2020, https://www.investopedia.com/terms/b/bdc.asp.

67. Ibid.

68. Securities Exchange Commission, "What Is a Business Development Company?" Sec.gov, retrieved April 2, 2020, https://www.sec.gov/Archives/edgar/data/1422183/000119312511139456/d497ad.htm.

69. Cliffwater, "CWBDC," bdcs.com, retrieved March 4, 2020, http://bdcs.com/.

70. James Chen, "Interval Fund," Investopedia, June 11, 2018, https://www.investopedia.com/terms/i/intervalscheme.asp.

71. PIMCO, "Understanding Interval Funds," Pimco.com, May 18, 2020, https://www.pimco.com/en-us/resources/education/understanding-interval-funds.

72. Angel Oak Capital, "Interval Funds: the Future of Alternatives," angeloakcapital.com, November 29, 2017, https://angeloakcapital.com/interval-funds-future-alternatives/.

73. Jim Probasco, "What Is an Interval Fund?" Investopedia, June 25, 2019, https://www.investopedia.com/articles/investing/120516/what-interval-fund.asp.

74. Barbara Friedberg, "The Difference in Strategic vs. Tactical Asset Allocation," *U.S. News,* July 25, 2018, https://money.usnews.com/investing/investing-101/articles/2018-07-25/whats-the-difference-between-strategic-and-tactical-asset-allocation.

75. Manoj, Singh, "How to Invest Like an Endowment," Investopedia, August 5, 2019, https://www.investopedia.com/articles/financial-theory/09/ivy-league-endowments-money-management.asp.

76. Capital Management Group, "Relative Returns vs. Absolute Returns," Cmgwealth.com, retrieved January 12, 2020, https://www.cmgwealth.com/wp-content/uploads/2012/10/RelativeReturnsvsAbsoluteReturns-CMG.pdf.

77. Putnam Investments, "Absolute Return Funds," Putnam.com, retrieved March 9, 2020, https://www.putnam.com/individual/mutual-funds/absolute-return-funds/?mkey=1003201186&msrc=277656989434&gclid=Cj0KCQj

w6ar4BRDnARIsAITGzlACH85WfZBZYQfTVjn9JhTeGbSWWhoUNxJ
rYjqTDG5Z0I_AQ3fe-M0aAiLhEALw_wcB.

78. James Chen, "Absolute Return," Investopedia, April 24, 2020, https://www.
    investopedia.com/terms/a/absolutereturn.asp.

79. Katrina Lamb, "An Introduction to Structured Products," Investopedia,
    January 12, 2020, https://www.investopedia.com/articles/
    optioninvestor/07/structured_products.asp.

80. Structured Products Association, "U.S. Issuance Hits $50 Billion in 2005,
    Yet Structured Products Continue to Remain 'Wall Street's Best Kept
    Secret,'" press release, retrieved April 14, 2020, https://www.prweb.com/
    releases/2006/02/prweb343330.htm.

81. Katrina Lamb, "An Introduction to Structured Products," Investopedia,
    January 12, 2020, https://www.investopedia.com/articles/
    optioninvestor/07/structured_products.asp.

82. Ibid.

83. Jason Whitby, "Why Structured Notes Might Not be Right for You,"
    Investopedia, March 31, 2020, https://www.investopedia.com/articles/
    bonds/10/structured-notes.asp.

84. Craig Rickman, "How Risky Are Structured Products?" FT Advisor, October
    31, 2019, exhibits volatility that is substantially lower than stocks and closer
    to bonds, which may help reduce portfolio volatility.

85. Lara Rhame, "Market Volatility Is Dead: Long Live Volatility!"
    Fsinvestments.com, July 28, 2017, https://www.fsinvestments.com/
    perspectives/articles/market-volatility-is-dead-long-live-volatility.

CHAPTER 5

1. Merriam-Webster, "Reallocate," Merriam-webster.com, retrieved September
   22, 2019, https://www.merriam-webster.com/dictionary/reallocate.

2. Rob Isbitts, "Bank of America Says 60-40 Portfolios Are Dead, They're
   Right," Forbes, October 18, 2019, https://www.forbes.com/sites/
   robisbitts2/2019/10/18/bank-of-america-says-60-40-portfolios-are-dead-
   theyre-right/#470461cc3991.

3. Allison Schrager, "The 60-40 Split Between Stocks and Bonds Was Once
   Solid Financial Advice—But No Longer," Yahoo!, November 29, 2019,
   https://finance.yahoo.com/news/60-40-split-between-stocks-120057862.
   html.

4. Mark Kolakowski, "Why Morgan Stanley Says the 60/40 Portfolio Is
   Doomed," Investopedia, November 6, 2019, https://www.investopedia.com/
   why-morgan-stanley-says-the-60-40-portfolio-is-doomed-4775352.

5. Dhara Singh, "Suze Orman: 'The 60-40 Portfolio Is Dead,'" Yahoo!, February 26, 2020, https://money.yahoo.com/you-should-have-a-threeyear-emergency-fund-172846902.html?guccounter=1&guce_referrer=aHR0cHM6Ly93d3cuZ29vZ2xlLmNvbS88&guce_referrer_sig=AQAAAJySMFF-t31HZVP7U9gZ2iLWCWSnB6He-en01HChVrMRa3BvQmMzx5nUmPQLf_u_pHZd-ir0yIK_hH1suXmIMwUwlgoX4BCXxyel-39iij4V6UQovkmHdOFiJUH0lDd2--lcFMCvay5hSj_AdJIx-Hvq-nH1Z2es-ZS3bkTKckIR.

6. David F. Swensen, *Pioneering Portfolio Management: An Unconventional Approach to Institutional Investment, Fully Revised and Updated* (New York: Free Press, January 6, 2009), p. 1.

7. Kate Rooney and Ari Levy, "The Most Influential Endowment Manager Just Jumped into Crypto with Bets on Two Silicon Valley Funds," CNBC.com, October 5, 2018, https://www.cnbc.com/2018/10/05/yale-investment-chief-david-swensen-jumps-into-crypto-with-bets-on-two-silicon-valley-funds.html.

8. James Chen, "Passive Investing," Investopedia, June 12, 2019, https://www.investopedia.com/terms/p/passiveinvesting.asp.

9. Ibid.

10. Stephanie Landsman, "Passive Investing Is a 'Chaotic System' That Could Be Dangerous, Warns Robert Shiller," CNBC.com, November 14, 2017, https://www.cnbc.com/2017/11/14/robert-shiller-passive-investing-is-a-dangerous-chaotic-system.html.

11. Ibid.

12. Ibid.

13. Dennis Hartman, "What Determines Whether the Price of a Mutual Fund Goes Up?" finance.zacks.com, retrieved October 3, 2020, https://finance.zacks.com/determines-whether-price-mutual-fund-goes-up-1370.html.

14. Adam Hayes, "Mutual Fund," Investopedia, February 24, 2020, https://www.investopedia.com/terms/m/mutualfund.asp.

15. US Securities and Exchange Commission, "Mutual Funds," Investor.gov, retrieved April 5, 2020, https://www.investor.gov/introduction-investing/investing-basics/investment-products/mutual-funds-and-exchange-traded-1.

16. Ibid.

17. Ibid.

18. US Securities and Exchange Commission, "Exchange-Traded Funds (ETFs)," Investor.gov, retrieved April 5, 2020, https://www.investor.gov/introduction-investing/investing-basics/investment-products/mutual-funds-and-exchange-traded-2.

19. Ibid.

20. James Chen, "What Is an Index Fund?" Investopedia, May 23, 2020, https://www.investopedia.com/terms/i/indexfund.asp.

21. Wikipedia, "S&P 500 Index," Wikipedia.com, retrieved April 6, 2020, https://en.wikipedia.org/wiki/S%26P_500_Index.

22. US Securities and Exchange Commission, "Index Funds," Investor.gov, retrieved April 12, 2020, https://www.investor.gov/introduction-investing/investing-basics/investment-products/mutual-funds-and-exchange-traded-4.

23. James Chen, "Structured Note," Investopedia, May 3, 2020, https://www.investopedia.com/terms/s/structurednote.asp.

24. Bruce Kelly, "Demand Grows for Structured Notes," Investmentnews.com, June 6, 2018, https://www.investmentnews.com/demand-grows-for-structured-notes-74475.

25. Eric Reed, "What Are Structured Notes and How Do They Work?" smartasset.com, August 15, 2019, https://smartasset.com/investing/structured-notes.

26. Kempton Asset, "Structured Products," kemptonasset.com, retrieved April 21, 2020, https://www.kemptonasset.com/wp-content/uploads/2018/05/why-structured-notes.pdf.

27. James Chen, "Structured Note," Investopedia, May 3, 2020, https://www.investopedia.com/terms/s/structurednote.asp.

28. Katrina Lamb, "An Introduction to Structured Products," Investopedia, January 12, 2020, https://www.investopedia.com/articles/optioninvestor/07/structured_products.asp.

29. New Retirement, "Lifetime Annuity Calculator," Newretirement.com, retrieved January 26, 2020, https://www.newretirement.com/services/annuity_calculator.aspx.

30. Annuity Digest, "Sequence of Returns Risk Report," Annuitydigest.com, retrieved March 9, 2020, http://www.annuitydigest.com/sequence-returns-risk-report.

31. Retirebyforty, "Should Annuities Be a Part of Your Retirement Plan?" Retirebyforty.org, March 12, 2020, https://retireby40.org/annuities-part-of-retirement-plan/.

32. Pam Krueger, "Active vs. Passive Investing: What's the Difference?" Investopedia, April 15, 2019, https://www.investopedia.com/news/active-vs-passive-investing/.

33. Ibid.

34. US Securities and Exchange Commission, "Alternative Mutual Fund (Alt Fund)," Investor.gov, April 15, 2020, https://www.investor.gov/introduction-investing/investing-basics/glossary/alternative-mutual-fund-alt-fund.

35. James Chen, "Absolute Return," Investopedia.com, April 24, 2020, https://www.investopedia.com/terms/a/absolutereturn.asp.

36. Ibid.

37. US Securities and Exchange Commission, "Futures Contract," Investor.gov, retrieved April 18, 2020, https://www.investor.gov/introduction-investing/investing-basics/glossary/futures-contract.

38. TIAA Portfolio, "Managed Income Strategies," Tiaa.org, retrieved May 4, 2020, https://www.tiaa.org/public/pdf/pafactsheet_MIS_13.pdf.

39. James Chen, "Managed Futures," Investopedia, January 8, 2020, https://www.investopedia.com/terms/m/managed-futures.asp.

40. Ibid.

41. Catalyst Funds, "Adding Alternatives: Top Managed Futures Research of 2018," Catalystmf.com, November 2018, https://catalystmf.com/adding-alternatives-top-managed-futures-research-of-2018/.

42. Ibid.

43. Mutual Funds, "Market Neutral Funds," Mutualfunds.com, retrieved October 16, 2019, https://mutualfunds.com/categories/all-funds/strategy-funds/market-neutral-funds/#tm=1-fund-category&r=Channel%23403&only=meta%2Cdata&selected_symbols=.

44. J. B. Maverick, "What Is the 200-Day Simple Moving Average?" Investopedia, March 29, 2020, https://www.investopedia.com/ask/answers/013015/why-200-simple-moving-average-sma-so-common-traders-and-analysts.asp.

45. TSP Folio, "Managing Risk with a Simple Moving Average (SMA)," Tspfolio.com, retrieved November 6, 2019, http://www.tspfolio.com/blog/21/Managing_risk_with_a_Simple_Moving_Average__SMA_.

46. TradingSim, "Best Strategies to Use with the 200-Day Simple Moving Average," Tradingsim.com, retrieved November 2, 2019, https://tradingsim.com/blog/200-day-simple-moving-average/.

47. Virginia B. Morris, *Guide to Alternative Investments* (New York: Lightbulb Press, 2015), p. 2.

48. Ibid., pp. 12–13.

49. Lee Ann Obringer, "How REITs Work," Howstuffworks.com, retrieved December 21, 2019, https://home.howstuffworks.com/real-estate/buying-home/reit3.htm.

50. Christine Giordano, "Senior Secured Debt Can Be Lucrative for Investors," *U.S. News,* June 13, 2016, https://money.usnews.com/investing/articles/2016-06-13/senior-secured-debt-can-be-lucrative-for-investors.

51. Ibid.

52. Ibid.

53. Coin Investments, "Private Credit in the Modern Portfolio," Coininvestments.com, retrieved April 24, 2020, https://www.coininvestments.com/insights/private-credit-in-portfolio/.

54. Financial Poise Editors, "90 Second Lesson: What Are BDCs? A Look at the Business Development Company Model," financialpoise.com, August 21, 2020, https://www.financialpoise.com/what-are-bdcs/.

55. Ibid.

56. US Securities and Exchange Commission, "In Response to Self-Executing Congressional Mandates, SEC Adopts Offering Reforms for Business Development Companies and Registered Closed-End Funds," press release, April 8, 2020, https://www.sec.gov/news/press-release/2020-83.

57. Ibid.

58. Jim Probasco, "What Is an Interval Fund?" Investopedia, June 25, 2019, https://www.investopedia.com/articles/investing/120516/what-interval-fund.asp.

59. FINRA, "Interval Funds—6 Things to Know Before You Invest," Finra.org, retrieved February 16, 2020, https://www.finra.org/investors/insights/interval-funds.

60. Jim Probasco, "What Is an Interval Fund?" Investopedia, June 25, 2019, https://www.investopedia.com/articles/investing/120516/what-interval-fund.asp.

61. James Chen, "Cumulative Preferred Stock," Investopedia, April 9, 2019, https://www.investopedia.com/terms/c/cumulative_preferred_stock.asp.

62. Eleanor Laise, "How Retirees Can Earn Income from Preferred Stock," Kiplinger.com, September 15, 2016, https://www.kiplinger.com/article/retirement/t052-c000-s004-preferred-stocks-offer-advantages.html.

63. Ibid.

64. Akhilesh Ganti, "Private Placement," Investopedia, March 4, 2020, https://www.investopedia.com/terms/p/privateplacement.asp.

65. Will Kenton, "SEC Regulation D (Reg D)," Investopedia, February 28, 2020, https://www.investopedia.com/terms/r/regulationd.asp.

66. Will Kenton, "Regulation A," Investopedia, May 6, 2020, https://www.investopedia.com/terms/r/regulationa.asp.

67. Investing Answers, "Standard Deviation," Investinganswers.com, October 1, 2019, https://investinganswers.com/dictionary/s/standard-deviation.

68. Caroline Banton, "Alpha vs. Beta: What's the Difference?" Investopedia, March 14, 2020, https://www.investopedia.com/ask/answers/102714/whats-difference-between-alpha-and-beta.asp.

69. Ibid.

70. Kahler Financial Group, "Non-Traded REITs Not All Equal," Kahlerfinancial. com, November 6, 2017, https://kahlerfinancial.com/financial-awakenings/ weekly-column/non-traded-reits-not-all-equal.

71. Matthew DiLallo, "Buying a Non-Traded REIT: What You Need to Know," Fool.com, December 21, 2019, https://www.fool.com/millionacres/real- estate-investing/reits/buying-non-traded-reit-what-you-need-know/.

72. Goldman Sachs, "Goldman Sachs Standard Deviation," macroaxis. com, retrieved February 12, 2020, https://www.macroaxis.com/invest/ technicalIndicator/GSBD--Standard-Deviation.

73. Samuel Taube, "How to Invest in Business Development Companies (BDCs)," Wealth Dailey, August 9, 2020. From 2008 to 2016 BDCs had an average annual return of 13.5%, compared to the 10.4% average annual return of the S&P 500 .

74. Michael Kitces, "Capturing an Excess Return Premium for Illiquidity Is a Privilege Not a Right!" Kitces.com, December 9, 2015, https://www.kitces. com/blog/capturing-an-excess-return-premium-for-illiquidity-is-a-privilege- not-a-right/.

75. Ibid.

76. Ibid.

CHAPTER 6

1. Darla Mercado, "Working Past 65? Don't Overlook These 3 Key Facts about Your Employee Benefits," CNBC.com, November 5, 2019, https://www. cnbc.com/2019/11/05/working-past-65-dont-overlook-these-3-facts-about- your-work-benefits.html.

2. Maurie Backman, "49% of Americans Worry about Outliving Their Savings. Here's How to Ease that Fear," fool.com, May 22, 2020, https://www.fool. com/retirement/2020/05/22/49-of-americans-worry-about-outliving-their- saving.aspx.

3. Brandon Buckingham, "Managing the Seven Risks to Retirement Income," Prudential.com, retrieved October 21, 2019, https://www.prudential.com/ advisors/insights/retirement-readiness/managing-risks-to-retirement.

4. Alex Veiga, "A Look at What Happens When Stocks Enter a Bear Market," apnews.com, March 12, 2020, https://apnews. com/84ee301c404539d8731da34128330752.

5. Ibid.

6. Brandon Buckingham, "Managing the Seven Risks to Retirement Income," Prudential.com, retrieved October 21, 2019, https://www.prudential.com/ advisors/insights/retirement-readiness/managing-risks-to-retirement.

7. Social Security Administration, "Retirement Benefits: If You Were Born in 1955 Your Full Retirement Age Is 66 and 2 Months," Ssa.gov, retrieved March 18, 2020, https://www.ssa.gov/benefits/retirement/planner/1955.html.

8. Social Security Administration, "Retirement Benefits: If You Were Born in 1960 Your Full Retirement Age Is 67," Ssa.gov, retrieved March 18, 2020, https://www.ssa.gov/benefits/retirement/planner/1960.html.

9. Social Security, "Retirement Benefits," ssa.gov, retrieved October 3, 2020, https://www.ssa.gov/benefits/retirement/planner/1943-delay.html.

10. Darla Mercado, "Working Past 65? Don't Overlook These 3 Key Facts about Your Employee Benefits," CNBC.com, November 5, 2019, https://www.cnbc.com/2019/11/05/working-past-65-dont-overlook-these-3-facts-about-your-work-benefits.html.

11. Philip Moeller, "What to Ask about Your Employer Health Coverage after Age 65," Pbs.org, August 15, 2018, https://www.pbs.org/newshour/economy/making-sense/what-to-ask-about-your-employer-health-coverage-after-age-65.

12. Darla Mercado, "Working Past 65? Don't Overlook These 3 Key Facts about Your Employee Benefits," CNBC.com, November 5, 2019, https://www.cnbc.com/2019/11/05/working-past-65-dont-overlook-these-3-facts-about-your-work-benefits.html.

13. Ibid.

14. IRS, "Retirement Plan and IRA Required Minimum Distributions FAQs," IRS.gov, retrieved January 23, 2020, https://www.irs.gov/retirement-plans/retirement-plans-faqs-regarding-required-minimum-distributions.

15. William Perez, "Withholding Requirements for Retirement Plan Distributions," The Balance, July 28, 2019, https://www.thebalance.com/withholding-on-retirement-plan-distributions-3192942.

16. FINRA, "Senior Investors," Finra.org, retrieved November 17, 2019, https://www.finra.org/rules-guidance/key-topics/senior-investors.

17. Cory Mitchell, "Drawdown Definition and Example," Investopedia, June 25, 2019, https://www.investopedia.com/terms/d/drawdown.asp.

18. Leslie Kramer, "Portfolio Withdrawal Strategies for Down Markets," Investopedia, April 24, 2015, https://www.investopedia.com/articles/financial-advisors/042415/portfolio-withdrawal-strategies-down-markets.asp.

19. Patrick B. Healey, "How a Multi-Asset Portfolio Investing Strategy Can Mitigate Risk," Kiplinger.com, February 27, 2020, https://www.kiplinger.com/article/investing/t047-c032-s014-a-multi-asset-investing-strategy-can-mitigate-risk.html.

20. Ibid.

21. Mary Beth Franklin, "How to Battle Sequence-of-Returns Risk," Investmentnews.com, May 25, 2019, https://www.investmentnews.com/how-to-battle-sequence-of-returns-risk-79685.

CHAPTER 7

1. Brad Thomas, "A Peek Inside the Durable Income Portfolio," Forbes, March 6, 2017, https://www.forbes.com/sites/bradthomas/2017/03/06/a-peak-inside-the-durable-income-portfolio/#3b5c1d363e53.
2. Ibid.
3. Stephen G. Dimmock, Neng Wang, et al., "The Endowment Model and Modern Portfolio Theory," National Bureau of Economic Research, April 23, 2018, https://www.nber.org/2018LTAM/yang.pdf.
4. Gary Ran, "The Power of Non-Correlating Assets: With So Much Uncertainty in the Markets, Having a Well-Diversified Investment Portfolio Is Especially Important," Kiplinger.com, February 3, 2017, https://www.kiplinger.com/article/investing/t023-c032-s014-the-power-of-non-correlating-assets.html.
5. World Economic Forum, "Alternative Investments 2020: An Introduction to Alternative Investments," World Economic Forum, July 2015, http://www3.weforum.org/docs/WEF_Alternative_Investments_2020_An_Introduction_to_AI.pdf.
6. Barclay Palmer, "5 Tips for Diversifying Your Portfolio," Investopedia, March 24, 2020, https://www.investopedia.com/articles/03/072303.asp.
7. Ibid.
8. Northwestern Investment Office, "Asset Allocation," Northwestern.edu, retrieved March 14, 2020, https://www.northwestern.edu/investment/asset-allocation-and-objective.html.
9. Ibid.
10. Daniel Wildermuth, "Is the Endowment Model Relevant for Individual Investors?" Investmentnews.com, October 22, 2018, https://www.investmentnews.com/is-the-endowment-model-relevant-for-individual-investors-76607.
11. Investopedia Staff, "REIT vs. Real Estate Fund: What's the Difference?" Investopedia, April 14, 2020, https://www.investopedia.com/ask/answers/012015/what-difference-between-reit-and-real-estate-fund.asp.
12. Sophia Kunthara, "Risky Business: The Difference Between Private Equity and Venture Capital," Crunchbase.com, October 18, 2019, https://news.crunchbase.com/news/risky-business-the-difference-between-private-equity-and-venture-capital/.

13. Ibid.

14. Ibid.

15. Ibid.

16. Asset allocation cannot ensure a profit or guarantee against losses.

17. Robert Farrington, "The Only Thing That Matters in Investing: Asset Allocation," The College Investor, October 17, 2019, https://thecollegeinvestor.com/19023/investing-asset-allocation/.

18. Jon Robinson and Brandon Langley, "The 60/40 Problem: Examining the Traditional 60/40 Portfolio in an Uncertain Rate Environment," Ssrn.com, April 27, 2017, https://papers.ssrn.com/sol3/papers.cfm?abstract_id=2959015.

CHAPTER 8

1. Dana Staves, "The Best Brené Brown Quotes on Vulnerability, Love, and Belonging," Bookriot.com, April 16, 2018, https://bookriot.com/brene-brown-quotes/.

2. Brené Brown, *Daring Greatly: How the Courage to Be Vulnerable Transforms the Way We Live, Love, Parent, and Lead* (New York: Avery Publishing, April 7, 2015), p. 2.

3. Consuelo Mack, "51% of Personal Wealth in the U.S. is Controlled by Women," wealthtrack.com, June 28, 2019, https://wealthtrack.com/51-percent-of-personal-wealth-in-the-u-s-is-controlled-by-women/.

4. Ibid.

5. Penn State, "Chapter 1. Financial Challenges Specific to Women," Instructure.com, retrieved November 22, 2019, https://psu.instructure.com/courses/1806581/pages/chapter-1-financial-challenges-specific-to-women/.

6. Kathleen Elkins, "Here's How Much Men and Women Earn at Every Age," Cnbc.com, July 18, 2020. From 2008 to 2016 BDCs had an average annual return of 13.5%, compared to the 10.4% average annual return of the S&P 500.

7. Dawn Doebler, "12 Reasons Women Need to Close the Financial Literacy Gap," Wtop.com, September 5, 2018, https://wtop.com/business-finance/2018/09/12-reasons-women-need-to-close-the-financial-literacy-gap/.

8. Ibid.

9. Jamie Hopkins, "Abysmal Financial Literacy Rates for Women Are Hurting Retirement Security," *Forbes,* July 26, 2017, https://www.forbes.com/sites/jamiehopkins/2017/07/26/abysmal-financial-literacy-rates-for-women-are-hurting-their-retirement-security/#577b5357719a.

10. Suze Orman, "Women & Money: Are You Truly Financially Empowered?" Suzeorman.com, September 6, 2018, https://www.suzeorman.com/blog/Women-Money-Are-You-Truly-Financially-Empowered.

11. Insurance news net, "Allianz Study: Women Report Steady Decline in Financial Confidence," insurancenewsnet.com, June 24, 2019. From 2008 to 2016 BDCs had an average annual return of 13.5%, compared to the 10.4% average annual return of the S&P 500.

12. Sallie Krawcheck, *Own It: The Power of Women at Work* (New South Wales, Australia: Currency Publishing, January 17, 2017), p. 2.

13. Arielle O'Shea, "Ellevest Review 2020: Pros, Cons and How It Compares," Nerdwallet.com, July 10, 2020, https://www.nerdwallet.com/reviews/investing/advisors/ellevest.

14. Ibid.

15. Vanessa McGrady, "Survey: Women Feel Disconnected from Financial Services Companies," *Forbes,* March 17, 2016, https://www.forbes.com/sites/vanessamcgrady/2016/03/17/worthfm/#2515faaf1942.

16. Kristen Bellstrom and Emma Hinchliffe, "Why More Clients Want Female Financial Advisors: The Broadsheet," *Fortune,* August 27, 2019, https://fortune.com/2019/08/27/female-financial-advisers/.

17. Ibid.

CHAPTER 9

1. Scott R. Baker, Nicholas Bloom, et al., "The Unprecedented Stock-Market Reaction to COVID-19," KellogInsight, April 1, 2020, https://insight.kellogg.northwestern.edu/article/what-explains-the-unprecedented-stock-market-reaction-to-covid-19.

2. Ibid.

3. Karen Brettell, "Once Unthinkable, Negative Treasury Yields Enter the Realm of Possibility," Yahoo.com, March 6, 2020, https://finance.yahoo.com/news/once-unthinkable-negative-treasury-yields-025723619.html.

4. Melissa R. Brown, "Defensive Strategies That Shine in Volatile Times," Stoxx.com, April 9, 2020, https://www.stoxx.com/pulse-details?articleId=1766551117.

5. Simon Jessop, "How Multi-Strategy Funds Are Faring as Coronavirus Slashes Returns," Reuters.com, March 27, 2020, https://www.reuters.com/article/us-health-coronavirus-absolute-return-gr/how-multi-strategy-funds-are-faring-as-coronavirus-slashes-returns-idUSKBN21E1EN.

6. Ibid.

7. Groom Law Group, "Department of Labor Issues Groundbreaking 401(k) Guidance to Groom," press release, June 3, 2020, https://www.prnewswire.com/news-releases/department-of-labor-issues-groundbreaking-401k-guidance-to-groom-301070163.html.

8. Eric Levitz, "Why Our Economy May Be Headed for a Decade of Depression," *New York Magazine,* May 22, 2020, https://nymag.com/intelligencer/2020/05/why-the-economy-is-headed-for-a-post-coronavirus-depression-nouriel-roubini.html.

9. Ibid.

10. Ibid.

11. Tom Huddleston Jr., "Ray Dalio Predicts a Coronavirus Depression: 'This Is Bigger Than What Happened in 2008,'" CNBC.com, April 9, 2020, https://www.cnbc.com/2020/04/09/ray-dalio-predicts-coronavirus-depression-this-is-bigger-than-2008.html.

12. Ibid.

13. Northern Trust Asset Management, "Capital Market Assumptions: Five-Year Outlook," Capitalmarketassumptions.com, retrieved February 19, 2020.

14. Knoema, "US Inflation Forecast: 2020, 2021 and Long Term to 2060/Data and Charts," Knoema.com, retrieved April 11, 2020, https://knoema.com/kyaewad/us-inflation-forecast-2020-2021-and-long-term-to-2060-data-and-charts.

15. Ibid.

16. Christine Benz, "Experts Forecast Long-Term Stock and Bond Returns: 2020 Edition," Morningstar.com, January 16, 2020, https://www.morningstar.com/articles/962169/experts-forecast-long-term-stock-and-bond-returns-2020-edition.

17. Emmie Mortin, "Here's How Much Americans Have Saved for Retirement," cnbc.com, June 26, 2019, https://www.cnbc.com/2019/06/26/how-much-americans-have-saved-for-retirement.html.

18. Graham Rapier, "'Capitalism as We Know It Will Likely Be Changed Forever,' Billionaire Investor Leon Cooperman Says," Businessinsider.com, April 23, 2020, https://www.businessinsider.com/capitalism-will-be-changed-forever-by-coronavirus-leon-cooperman-prediction-2020-4.

19. Jesse Pound, "Leon Cooperman Says the Coronavirus Crisis Will Change Capitalism Forever and Taxes Have to Go Up," CNBC.com, April 23, 2020, https://www.cnbc.com/2020/04/23/leon-cooperman-says-the-coronavirus-crisis-will-change-capitalism-forever-and-taxes-have-to-go-up.html.

20. Ibid.

21. Heather Long, "Coronavirus Economy Shows How Easy It Is to Fall from the Middle Class into Poverty," *Washington Post,* May 8, 2020, https://www.washingtonpost.com/business/2020/05/08/layoffs-poverty-coronavirus/.
22. Ibid.
23. Ibid.
24. Harry Kretchmer, "How Coronavirus Has Hit Employment in G7 Economies," Weforum.com, May 13, 2020, https://www.weforum.org/agenda/2020/05/coronavirus-unemployment-jobs-work-impact-g7-pandemic/.
25. Ben Casselman, "Unemployment Numbers Will Be Terrible. Here's How to Interpret Them," *New York Times,* May 6, 2020, https://www.nytimes.com/2020/05/06/business/economy/coronavirus-unemployment-jobs-report.html.
26. F. Scott Fitzgerald, "The Rich Boy," *Red Book*, Project Guttenberg, January and February 1926, http://gutenberg.net.au/fsf/THE-RICH-BOY.html.

APPENDIX A

1. Dana Anspach, "Sequence Risk's Impact on Your Retirement Money," The Balance, February 8, 2019, https://www.thebalance.com/how-sequence-risk-affects-your-retirement-money-2388672.
2. Baird, "Sequence of Return Risk," Bairdfinancialadvisor.com, retrieved October 16, 2019, http://www.bairdfinancialadvisor.com/chris.trumble/mediahandler/media/118612/Sequence%20of%20Returns%20Risk.pdf.
3. Ibid.
4. Kate Stalter, "How to Avoid Sequence-of-Returns Risk," *U.S. News,* April 30, 2019, https://money.usnews.com/money/blogs/the-smarter-mutual-fund-investor/articles/how-to-avoid-sequence-of-returns-risk.

ABOUT THE AUTHOR

CINDY COUYOUMJIAN is the founder of Cinergy Financial. She is a certified financial planner with 34 years of experience in the financial industry. She holds numerous securities licenses, including her FINRA Series 63, 6, 65, 7, 22, 24, 26, and 31. In addition, Cindy holds the California Insurance License (License # 0719038).

Cindy is also the architect behind the REALM investment portfolio, which is an innovative, multi-asset-class portfolio that is both flexible and customizable to each individual investor. Beyond the numerous financial services Cindy offers, she is also an educator and motivational speaker. When she is not meeting with clients, you may find her giving her monthly lectures and seminars on such groundbreaking topics as the Google Mind, the Gilded Age, and the Moral Imperative of Financial Literacy. Cindy is also the host of two weekly radio shows on financial literacy. You can listen every Saturday from 8:30 a.m. to 9:00 a.m. on AM870 KRLA, as well as 790AM KABC every Sunday from 6:30 a.m. to 7:00 a.m. and 11:00 a.m. to 11:30 a.m.

Cindy is currently working on her next book, a powerful and unique exploration of the historically marginalized status of women from the perspective of hope and reconciliation. Women are today on the verge of defining their own narrative, and financial freedom will give them the courage to embrace their destiny as powerful agents of change.

If you are interested in attending one of Cindy's lectures or you have a question or comment, please email her at cindy@cinergyfinancial. com. You may also visit her website, www.CinergyFinancial.com, to obtain information and updates on her latest projects.